LUK THUNG

LUK THUNG

The Culture and Politics of Thailand's Most Popular Music

James Leonard Mitchell

ISBN: 978-616-215-106-4
© 2015 Silkworm Books
All rights reserved

No part of this publication may be reproduced, stored in a retrieval system,
or transmitted, in any form or by any means, electronic, mechanical, photocopying,
recording or otherwise, without the prior permission in writing of the publisher.

First published in 2015 by
Silkworm Books
6 Sukkasem Road, T. Suthep
Chiang Mai 50200 Thailand
info@silkwormbooks.com
www.silkwormbooks.com

Typeset in Minion Pro 10 pt. by Silk Type

Contents

Introduction
1

ONE
Luk Thung: A Thai Story, an Isan Story
7

TWO
A Musical Analysis of *Luk Thung*'s Form and Development
45

THREE
Soraphet Phinyo, Isan Songwriter
77

FOUR
Fans, Isan Identity, and the Contemporary *Luk Thung* Scene
107

FIVE
Luk Thung and Political Expression
133

Coda
175

Appendix I: Who's Who
179

Appendix II: Important Dates
187

Notes
191

References
199

Index
205

Introduction

On a coolish Sunday night on January 16, 2011, I accompanied my friend Peter Garrity to a funeral concert at a temple in suburban Bangkok. We did not know the person who had died, but we approved of his taste in music. He and his family had decided that his life would be celebrated by a *luk thung*, or Thai country song, concert performed by the highly professional Nopporn Silver Gold troupe. Peter was personally informed about the concert by Nopporn Silver Gold's main drawcard, Mangpor (Dragonfly) Chonticha. In her late twenties, Mangpor is among the most exciting and experienced performers on the Bangkok circuit, having performed since she was thirteen years old.

Arriving early at 7:30 p.m. we sit down with other Mangpor fan club members on woven mats laid in front of the huge stage. Peter introduces me to Lung (Uncle) Kaeo, who like Peter spends practically all his free time attending *luk thung* concerts. Kaeo tells me he has seen Mangpor perform over thirty times, but he still seems genuinely excited. We don't have long to converse before the band announces that the first singer is ready—a very young girl wearing high heels and a shimmering black and white dress who eases into a slow, heartbreaking song about being left to fend for herself in the ricefields. Her singing is highly ornamented with a wavering tone that never quite goes out of tune. She is accompanied by eight female dancers wearing flowing ankle-length gold dresses, black gloves, and chokers and moving in a dramatic ballet style. During an instrumental section the diminutive singer comes to the front of the stage to take a one hundred-baht note from an older woman dressed elegantly in funereal black.

When the song draws to a close the crowd applauds, and the girl's place is taken by a young man who jokes briefly in the language of Isan, or northeastern Thailand, before launching into a fast and risqué *molam*-style number. The extremely loud music is provided by a large string combo band featuring a full brass section. Nopphon's second dance troupe, wearing very short, fully gathered skirts, then performs an energetic dance routine reminiscent of Brazilian samba. The singer covers the whole stage and poses with a silly face when he sees me about to take a photo. I assume that he is one of the main singers, but after two songs he is replaced by a gorgeous young woman in a very brief sky blue dress that reveals bare shoulders and thighs, though both she and the dancers are wearing shorts underneath their costumes so that male fans near the stage don't see more than they should. The woman in blue sings a fast *luk thung* song with a cha-cha rhythm, followed by a slow song which calms the atmosphere. For the first time, male dancers appear, dressed in leather pants and glittering red sleeveless shirts.

There is then a five-minute break before the band strikes up a *ramwong*-style song in a kind of funk rhythm known as *soeng*. Both dance troupes enter with the twenty female dancers wearing silver shorts, shirts, and gloves along with enormous feathered headdresses and trains, and the four males in silver and pink long pants and waistcoats. They dance in the style of a Las Vegas revue for several minutes before the *phitthikon* (emcees) appear. Nong Sai and Phi Nok compere the Nopporn Silver Gold television show *Chum thang siang thong* (*Community of Golden Voices*) and are well known to the crowd, who for the first time cheer unreservedly.

FIGURE A. Dancer in Las Vegas–style costume. (Peter Garrity)

After the emcees sing a comic duet and work the crowd ("whoever's single, make some noise" and "if you're good looking, make some noise"), there are shorts sets from four different singers, with predominantly fast songs. The two dance troupes alternate, changing costumes between sets. Dancing fans—mostly drunk men and a few older women—fill the area in front of the stage. Other fans approach to give paper garlands and roses to the singers, who adeptly accept the gifts without losing their place in the song.

Then it is time for comedy—the emcees reappear accompanied by Obah, the resident *Chum thang siang thong* comedian, and three of his friends, all dressed in pure white suits. Their jokes, however, are far from pure, and as a conspicuous foreigner close to the stage, I soon become the target of ribald humor involving me pretending to eat an ice cream. Fortunately the comedy is curtailed by an announcement that it is time for the funeral fireworks. The crowd looks to the sky as the starbursts explode, and then the deceased's name is spelled out in flames behind the crowd. The emcees thank the man's family and present them with a flower arrangement.

FIGURE B. Nopporn MCs and comedians. Obah is on the far right. (James Mitchell)

After these formalities it is time to celebrate, and following sets by emerging artists Phimyada and Sally Khanitta, Mangpor, the main attraction, makes her appearance. Mangpor is famous for her up-tempo dance numbers, and hits such as "Nancy," about a transsexual, and "Tam ha Somchai" (Looking for Somchai) soon have the crowd on their feet. Despite the constant movement, her voice is obviously cleaner and clearer than the supporting vocalists. During instrumental sections and between songs, a constant stream of fans approach the stage to present roses, money, and flower garlands. Mangpor accepts the gifts and holds them until there is an opportunity to pass them to an assistant.

When the concert draws to a close, Peter and other members of the Mangpor fan club shepherd me to the side of the stage and we pass through to the rear without being questioned. Mangpor appears genuinely pleased to see Peter, and she seems to know each of her fans by name. She poses for photos and distributes fan club t-shirts and signs them. As we are leaving she tells Lung Kaeo and Peter that she will see them at the next concert in three days time.

About a year later, Peter and his wife arranged for me to interview Mangpor. We met at a Starbucks on the outskirts of Bangkok and conversed for over two hours. I learned that she was born in Khon Kaen, my wife's hometown in northeastern Thailand, but that she grew up in Chon Buri, southeast of Bangkok. She was ethnically Lao but thought of herself as Thai, and most of her fans came from Bangkok and the South. Perhaps the most surprising thing she said was that she had never been paid any dividends from her fifteen years of recording. Her record company took forty percent of her booking fees for concerts and all income from her numerous sound and video recordings. Mangpor had experienced the best and worst of the Thai music industry but had succeeded in forging a career far removed from her birth place and station.

My interview with Mangpor occurred just after I had submitted my PhD thesis. During the previous five years I had learned about the history of Thai music and how constant experimentation had resulted in a working-class genre that seemed old-fashioned but was the most popular music in Thailand. I had attended *luk thung* and *molam* concerts in Khon Kaen and Bangkok and observed the surprising closeness that existed between stars and their fans. And I had met a famous *luk thung* songwriter, Soraphet Phinyo, translated his songs, and been confronted by their stories of hardship and loss but also impressed by the joys of rural living they communicated. Living in Khon Kaen I watched the daily *luk thung* competition and promotional shows on television and saw how *luk thung* was enjoyed throughout Thai society. Then, as Thailand's hard-won political stability began to unravel I was able to document how music, and especially *luk thung*, was used by the so-called red shirts and yellow shirts for protest and propaganda.

INTRODUCTION

Every night in Thailand, concerts attract large crowds to temple fairs, funerals, product promotions, and night clubs. Within Thailand *luk thung* holds a far more significant position than *enka* does in Japan, or perhaps even *dangdut* in Indonesia, but both of those genres have already attracted major studies.[1] Furthermore, the symbiotic relationship between *luk thung* and the Isan people from the Northeast of Thailand has been mentioned in a few scholarly articles, but the extent of the relationship and the impact it has had on Thai politics, both now and in the past, has rarely been discussed, and never with any depth. Although it has traditionally been working-class music, it now permeates every level of Thai society. In the color-coded political unrest that plagued Thailand starting in 2005, *luk thung* was at the forefront of the red-shirt movement and also present in the yellow shirts' activities. How did a genre that for so long appeared to avoid political commentary became so highly politicized?

Red-shirt protests *were* in fact *luk thung* concerts—complete with charismatic lead singers, dancing troupes wearing ornate costumes, emcees, and comedians. The protest leaders would sing their own adaptations of *luk thung* hits, and protesters could sing along because everyone knew the words. *Luk thung* was integral to the political struggle because the songs spoke about inequality, different standards for rich and poor, separation, and sorrow. But the protests were also celebrations, and like in most parties in Thailand, *luk thung* played an important role.

Any discussion of *luk thung* must make reference to Isan, the northeastern region of Thailand, and its inhabitants (about one third of the country's population), most of whom are ethnically Lao. In this book *luk thung* is considered within the context of the wider issues of Isan culture and the emergence of Isan political strength. This is not to suggest that the involvement of Isan people in the *luk thung* industry is the only reason for the Isan cultural and political revival or that *luk thung* is an Isan genre in the same way as the Isan folk-music genre *molam*. However, *luk thung* has provided a path for Isan people to enter the mainstream of Thai society, and through *luk thung* they have found their political voice.

Luk Thung: A Thai Story, an Isan Story

Isan natives are like people of African descent. We're both discriminated against over race and color, but what we have in common is a love of music and the ability to work hard.

—TV presenter and comedian Thongchai Prasongsanti (Kreangsak 2005, 3)

We're hard working for sure. In the past, people may have looked down on us. Today, when riding on a bus in Bangkok I can speak with my Isan accent and hold my head up high. Luk Isan (Northeasterners), whether artists or Olympic athletes have proven themselves with many success stories to be proud of.

—Singer and comedian Sompong "Eed" Kunaprathom, leader of Ponglang Sa-on (Kanokporn 2008)

The history of *luk thung* is entwined with the development of the modern Thai state and of Thai democracy. A significant element within each of these concepts has been Isan cultural identity. Almost fifty years ago Charles Keyes (1971, vii, 58–62) used the phrase "the northeastern problem" to refer to the threat posed to Thai national integration by the ethnic and regional identity of the large Lao-Isan minority. He concluded that the Thai Northeast did not develop a distinct geopolitical identity until the beginning of the twentieth century but that much of the population shared a common historical and cultural heritage different from that of central Thailand.

It is impossible to tell the full story of *luk thung* in one chapter, but by concentrating on one aspect—the Isan involvement within the *luk thung* industry—a useful beginning can be made. Instead of focusing on the few most well-known songwriters such as Phaibun Butkhan (1918–72) and performers such as Suraphon Sombatjaroen and Phumphuang Duangjan, who all hail from central Thailand, space is created for the contributions of Isan artists—contributions which have not always received official recognition.

The Development of *Phleng Thai Sakon*

Thai historians usually date the origin of *luk thung* from the first *phleng Thai sakon* with a rural subject, Hem Wechakon's "Chao sao chao rai" (The Vegetable Farmer's Bride), which was sung by Khamron Sambunnanon in 1938. However, this is problematic because throughout the 1930s, *phleng Thai sakon*, a genre of Western-style homophonic songs with Thai melodies and lyrics, was still developing, and *ramwong* and *phleng chiwit*, the key antecedents of *luk thung*, were yet to appear. *Luk thung* first became a separate genre during the 1950s when electrified ramwong was combined with Latin beats and elements of central Thai folk music, and lyrics became narratives of rural life. *Luk thung* has continued to evolve, and the sound of today's *luk thung* is very different to that of the 1950s and 1960s. Understanding the development of Thai popular music is therefore essential.

During the reign of King Mongkut (1851–68) Siam was under constant pressure from Britain and France to modernize, and this spurred a period of synthesizing Western culture and Thai civilization. The beginning of the process that led to the development of *luk thung* can perhaps be traced back to King Mongkut's decision to allow the royal *lakhon* (drama) to be performed outside the palaces by private troupes. When foreign military advisors, such as the American Jacob Feit (whose son Peter, granted the name Phra Chen Duriyang, was a key figure in the history of modern Thai music), introduced brass bands, the scene was set for the mixing of *lakhon* and Western marches and dance music. This process of mixing, absorbing, and experimenting in order to create something new is typical of the Thai approach to outside influences; in this case, the eventual result was the development of *phleng Thai sakon*.

During the latter part of the nineteenth century, *samniang phasa*, whereby rhythmic and melodic elements from the music of neighboring countries and the West were adopted and adapted within the Thai system, had been introduced into central Thai classical music (see Myers-Moro 1993, 73-81). There is a large body of classical songs based on these *samniang phasa*, and many of these melodies are now also heard in *luk thung* songs (see chapter two). Also during this period (approximately 1900) the royal anthem "Phleng sansoen phra barami" (Song in Praise of the Royal Majesty) was produced, which was the first Thai song using homophonic texture to be widely performed throughout the country; it was recorded when the Gramophone Company's recording engineer Fred Gaisberg toured through Southeast Asia in 1903.

The sung dance-drama genre *lakhon rong* (also known as *lakhon Pridalai* after the theater in which it was performed), appeared in the latter part of the reign of King Chulalongkorn (c. 1908) and continued to develop in the reign of King Vajiravudh (1910–25). This form originated when King Chulalongkorn's brother Prince Narathip incorporated some elements of Western and Malay opera into Thai classical *lakhon* by simplifying the dancing, using modern costumes and composing modern songs. He used modern storylines rather than the traditional stories. For example, he adapted the plot of *Madame Butterfly* into *Sao khruea fa* (*Miss Khruea Fa*), about a Siamese soldier who falls in love with a girl from Chiang Mai. In Narathip's *lakhon rong*, there was a greater emphasis on being able to understand the lyrics; thus the use of *uean* (melisma or using one syllable to sing over many notes), so typical of Thai classical singing, was greatly reduced. *Lakhon rong* spread throughout Thailand during King Vajiravudh's reign through the popularization of love songs written for these dramas, but it lost popularity with the rise of film in the 1920s.

Nevertheless, in the 1920s and 1930s there were a number of varieties of *lakhon*. According to Phaibun Thanwarachon, the grandson of Sino-Thai recording pioneer T. Ngekchuan, *lakhon rong* were usually sad love stories whereas *lakhon yoi* and *nathadontri* were comedies. In *lakhon rong*, women acted the roles of both hero and heroine, and did not dance. *Lakhon lam* had singing and also included dancing. *Lakhon yoi* and *nathadontri* later developed into *like*. During the Second World War it became difficult to show films and the outdated genre of *lakhon rong* was reworked into *lakhon rueang*, which took place on a stage.

Western music became popular in Thailand through film, which was introduced into Thailand at the beginning of the twentieth century. During the silent-film era, movies were accompanied by brass bands playing Western songs and *lakhon rong* songs using Western harmony, such as "Waltz Pluemjit" (written by King Chulalongkorn's son Prince Paribatra in 1903), "March Boriphat," and "Blackeagle." Western string orchestras were introduced by King Vajiravudh, and string ensembles soon became more popular than brass bands for the accompaniment of films. Jazz and ballroom dance music were introduced during the 1920s, and the latter especially became a key element in *phleng Thai sakon*.

The opening of a royal music school in 1917, called Rongrian Phran Luang, included the establishment of an ensemble known as Wong Khrueangsai Farang Luang (Large Western String Ensemble). Under the tutelage of the American Phra Chen Duriyang, this band produced songwriters such as Narot Thaworabut and Uea Sunthonsanan, who would go on to mold the development of *phleng Thai sakon*. After the absolute monarchy was overthrown in 1932, the Wong Khrueangsai Farang Luang was disbanded and its musicians were forced to enter the emerging popular music scene.

Around 1928–29 a non-royal known as Phranbun (Juangjan Jankhana) began writing songs in a new style called *nuea rong tem* (one note per word, without *uean*) or *nuea chapho* (only lyrics) within the genre of *lakhon rong*. Along with Mae Kaeo (Prawat Khojarik) and the famous *lakhon rong* troupe leader Phetcharat (Somprasong Ratanathasani), Phranbun pioneered the reworking of classical Thai melodies into popular songs with new lyrics. This marked an important beginning for modern Thai popular music as distinct from court-influenced music, although *phleng Thai sakon* was at first only available to the Bangkok elite. This new style of *lakhon rong* reached its height of popularity with the radio broadcast of *Rosita* (1931), which featured songs written by Phranbun and Phetcharat, including a new adaptation of "Waltz Pluemjit." The songs from *Rosita* also became a highly profitable set of recordings for T. Ngekchuan's homegrown Kratai (Rabbit) brand, which would go on to compete successfully with international brands such as Odeon, Columbia, Philips, and HMV and pave the way for the emergence of the independent *luk thung* music industry.

Soon after, two significant events in the development of *luk thung* took place. First, the popularity of early American "talking pictures" such as *King Of Jazz* (1930), a musical revue featuring Paul Whiteman and his orchestra, ensured that the first Thai film with sound, *Long thang* (*Lost Way*), produced by the iconic Thai film company Srikrung in 1931, featured a number of specially written songs. Second, a group of musicians who feared the loss of traditional music led a revival of folk melodies and began to write lyrics with rural themes (Ware 2006, 122). In 1938, these two phenomena were combined in a film musical called *Luk thung* produced by Thai Film, although the songs were not what would now be considered *luk thung*.

The mixing of Thai and Western music was accelerated by the restrictions placed on the performance of Thai classical music following the overthrow of the Thai monarchy in 1932 (Morton 1976, 16). In 1936, Uea Sunthonsanan (1910–81) assembled a performance group which included a number of classical musicians who had lost their royal appointments. In 1939, this group became the official band for military strongman Plaek Phibunsongkhram's Public Relations Department, but when booked for private functions the band performed under the name of Suntharaphon, a term which later became synonymous with *luk krung*. Suntharaphon musicians such as Uea Sunthonsanan, Sompong Thipayakarin, and Thanit Ponprasert had backgrounds in Thai classical music and consequently many *Thai doem* melodies were set to ballroom dance rhythms during the late 1930s and 1940s. In 1942, during Phibun's first regime (1938–44), Wichit Wathakan's Department of Fine Arts placed heavy restrictions on *lakhon*, *like*, and the playing of Thai string instruments (Sujachaya 1982, 87). Even traditional folk singing in the villages had to conform to specific guidelines laid out by the government's Cultural Committee and was confined to special festivals and locations. This provided the impetus for traditional musicians and singers to move into the emerging *ramwong* and *phleng chiwit* genres.

Ramwong and the Change to *Luk Thung*

Ramwong, in which men and women dance in a circle, dates back to 1944 when Phibun's wartime government introduced a suite of official dance songs to compete with the popularity of Western dances such as the foxtrot or waltz. Waeng claims that Phibun and his wife La-iat observed performances of village *ramthon* (drum dance), when they traveled upcountry to inspect Phetchabun and the surrounding area with a view to building a new capital. La-iat wrote down texts and some melodies and had the Fine Arts Department produce ten *ramwong matrathan* (standard circle dances). Waeng believes that, because of the high number of Lao-Isan people in the Phetchabun area, some of the standard *ramwong* melodies had a strong Lao character (2002, 113–14). This suggests that there was early Isan input into one of the key ingredients of *luk thung*.

What is certain is that many Isan people benefited from Phibun's patronage of *ramwong* and *ramthon* as a new Thai art form and that there was significant Isan involvement in the *ramwong* music industry that flourished in Thailand between 1945 and approximately 1955. *Ramwong* was performed by both upper-class bands such as Suntharaphon and lower-class rural touring troupes traveling between temple fairs and local festivals; it was through the latter that many Isan musicians received their start in the Thai entertainment industry. Two of these early Isan performers became influential in the development of *luk thung*.

Tumthong Chokchana, otherwise known as Benjamin, was born in Ubon Ratchathani in 1921 and rose to become the acknowledged "King of *Ramwong*." Benjamin was the main figure responsible for transforming *ramwong* from folk song into popular song by writing new lyrics, expanding the number of verses, adding Western instruments, and emphasizing the rhythm (Waeng 2002, 164, 193). He also possibly ranks as Thailand's first independent popular music star because he forged a career and celebrity without relying on established bands such as Suntharaphon and T. Ngekchuan's Kratai ensemble. As a songwriter he was instrumental in launching the career of the sweet-voiced Thun Thongchai with songs such as "Nuea fan" (Beyond Dreams). He was also an important figure in the history of Thai film, for example, producing *Mai mi sawan samrap khun* (*No Heaven for You*), featuring Patravadi Mejudhon, and starring in films such as *Suphapburut suea Thai* (*Gentleman Soldier*) (1949) and *Phuean tai* (*Friend in Need*).

Chaloemchai Sriruecha, born in Roi Et in 1927, popularized *ramwong* songs in Lao-Isan style using just *khaen* (bamboo mouth organ) and *klong* (drum), with songs such as "Lao cham chai" (Broken-Hearted Lao) and "Sao rim Khong" (Girl on the Banks of the Mekong) in 1954. During this early period he also wrote "Huachai im rak" (Heart Full of Love) and "Chakrawan chai" (Huge Heart) for Latda Sriworanan, perhaps the first Muslim woman to enter the Thai entertainment industry. In the 1960s he wrote famous *luk thung* songs for Samson Na Mueangsri ("Chep chai ching"—Heart Really Hurts) and Sangthong Sisai ("Nong Neng"—Miss Neng) and made use of Khmer language in a number of songs such as "Khamen tam ram phan" (Lowland Khmer Laments) (Waeng 2002, 211).

During Phibun's second term as prime minister (1948–57), the earliest incarnations of *luk thung*, variously known as *phleng chiwit* (life songs) or *phleng talat* (market songs), were renowned for their biting social criticism and popularity among the working class. Songwriters such as Saengnapha Bunrasri, Saneh Komarachun, Chalor Traitrongson, and Phaibun Butkhan decried the exploitation of farmers and extolled the virtues of the common man. It was during the period of Phibun's decline and eventual loss of power in 1957 that *phleng talat* superseded *ramwong* and *phleng chiwit* as the favored commercial genre of the working class. With the introduction of mambo and cha-cha beats around 1957, and with its main proponent removed, traditional *ramwong* must have suddenly appeared quite out of step with the times. Furthermore, although the *phleng chiwit* songwriters had worked to bring down Phibun, the military regimes of Thanom and Sarit (1958–73) that followed were even more restrictive. Strict censorship combined with better economic conditions encouraged songwriters such as Phaibun to abandon social commentary and move into writing commercial and sometimes nationalistic *luk thung*. For example, the ongoing dispute over the Preah Vihear (Phra Wihan) temple and the International Court of Justice's decision to assign ownership to Cambodia in 1962 inspired a series of nationalistic songs such as Phaibun's "Khao Phra Wihan haeng khwam lang" (Preah Vihear in the Past), Phayong Mukda's "Khong khao mai ao khong rao mai hai" (We Don't Want What's Yours and We Won't Give What's Ours) sung by Chaichana Bunnachot, "Khao Phra Wihan thi rak" (Beloved Preah Vihear) by Chai Mueangsing, "Khao Phra Wihan" by Suraphon Sombatjaroen, P. Chuenprayot's "Khao Phra Wihan tong pen khong Thai" (Preah Vihear must be Thai) sung by Kan Kaeosuphan, and Suchat Thianthong's "Thorani kan saeng Khao Phra Wihan" (The Earth Mourns for Preah Vihear). The existence of these songs suggests that most established songwriters in the Thai popular music industry were willing to participate in and encourage the increased emphasis on cultural nationalism under Sarit's regime (1958–63).

Suraphon, Chaloemchai, and Benjamin

One Thai writer who has highlighted the influence of Isan people and culture in *luk thung* goes by the name of Waeng Phalangwan. A central part of Waeng's argument that Lao-Isan people have contributed significantly to the development of *luk thung* is a revision of the history of Suraphon Sombatjaroen. Suraphon (1930–68), still known as "the King of Thai Country Song," has become a legendary figure in Thailand, dominating all discussion of early *luk thung*. Thailand's popular media (television, film, and newspapers) regularly present the romantic image of Suraphon as an individual genius killed in his prime:

> Suraphol died on August 16, 1968 from gunshot wounds, leaving a rich repertoire of luk thung songs that embodied the spirit of the 1960s when Elvis Presley and the Beatles were rocking the world with their electrifying performances. But Suraphol, who came from a humble background in Suphan Buri, had his own special way of crooning the songs he composed by himself. His music was rich in style and his lyrics reflected the changes Thai society was undergoing at that time. (Thanong 2002, 1)

Here are all the key elements of the Suraphon story. The Thai equivalent of Elvis or the Beatles, Suraphon is credited with a unique performance style, and it is stressed that he wrote all of his own songs. His music is said to be the soundtrack for the 1960s in Thailand. Thanong's description is representative of a multitude of articles, theses, and books that emphasize Suraphon's creativity and his singularity.

Possibly the most sensational claim in Waeng's *Luk thung Isan* is that Suraphon Sombatjaroen did not compose all of the songs that bear his name. Waeng makes the point, confirmed by Surin Phaksiri (2002, 162), that Suraphon had no Lao ancestry, could not speak the Isan language, and when he sang Isan words (in an attempt to appeal to the large Isan *luk thung* audience) they were often mispronounced. For example, in his first published song, "Namta Lao Wiang" (Tears of a Vientiane Girl), Suraphon mispronounces the Isan word for "house" (*huean*, with a middle tone) by substituting a falling tone, which changes the meaning to a kind of skin disease or leprosy (Waeng 2002, 216). The Thai education system during the 1940s and 1950s so discouraged the speaking of Isan that the idea that Suraphon could have immediately written Isan lyrics without considerable assistance is doubtful. Waeng's hypothesis that Suraphon would not have been able to write Isan songs, or songs using Isan elements, without help is supported indirectly by *Molam*[1] Ratri Sriwilai, who told me that Isan people were able to borrow from central Thailand because they could speak central Thai, but the opposite was not true because most central Thais could not speak Isan language. Clewley (1994, 446) confirms that since Isan performers are "brought up bilingually," they can easily switch between *luk thung* and *molam*, but central Thai artists are restricted to *luk thung*.

On the other hand, new research shows that Suraphon would have been surrounded by early recordings of *molam* during his first assignment as a songwriter with T. Ngekchuan's famous Tra Kratai, or Rabbit Brand. Suraphon was associated with T. Ngekchuan for less than two years (1953–54) but throughout this period Kratai was recording and issuing original *molam* performances under the description of *phleng Isan*. Suraphon practiced his songwriting with T. Ngekchuan's younger brother, and it is quite conceivable that Kratai's *molam* catalog and the existence of a *molam* audience could have provided the background and inspiration behind the subject matter of early songs such as "Namta Lao Wiang" (Tears of a Vientiane Girl), "Lao chom dong" (Lao Visiting the Jungle), and "Lao chom pa" (Lao Visiting the Forest). Thus it is possible that Waeng's hypothesis is somewhat overreaching.

Suraphon and Chaloemchai Sriruecha met while performing in the Air Force Orchestra in the early 1950s. Waeng (2002, 217–20) believes that Suraphon was only able to produce Isan-style songs that used Lao words because of his friendship with Chaloemchai, who had extensive knowledge of *molam* and Isan *ramthon*. Thus, Chaloemchai's major contribution to the history of *luk thung* was in facilitating the rise of Suraphon and enabling him to write in styles that Benjamin had already popularized. Waeng (2002, 210) concludes that some of the early songs upon which Suraphon built his popularity with Isan fans, such as "Namta Lao Wiang" and later songs such as "Khong plom" (Fake Things), were probably written or cowritten by Chaloemchai. Waeng (2002, 214) also questions the originality of Suraphon's legendary stage movement, suggesting that he imitated Chaloemchai's habit of shaking the microphone stand. These accusations cannot be proven and they should not detract from Suraphon's eventual reputation, but they do perhaps explain why Suraphon was able to compete with Benjamin in a form (*ramwong*) he had completely made his own. Suraphon's life was tragically cut short when he was shot dead at a performance in Nakhon Pathom in 1968. After Suraphon's death Chaloemchai disintegrated into alcoholism and eventually committed suicide at the age of sixty by jumping out of the hospital where he was being treated.

It is indeed significant that Suraphon put so much effort into appealing to the Isan audience during the early part of his career. He began his career performing *ramwong*, possibly in imitation of Benjamin's songwriting and performance style. For example, the similarities between Suraphon's "Suai ching na nong" (You're Really Beautiful, Girl) and Benjamin's "Ram toei"[2] are remarkable. Both begin with a distinctive piano accordion introduction (played in the style of a *khaen*) before settling into a *ramwong* ostinato. Suraphon appears to have adapted the opening words of "Ram toei," "Suai ko ching na sao, khao ko ching na nong" into the line "Suai ko ching na nong," which he uses to begin each verse. That Benjamin himself had adapted the line from a singer's greeting usually found in *lam klon* underscores that Suraphon's intention was to appeal to Benjamin's Isan fans. Competition between the established master and the brash new star was fierce and specific—Suraphon's first hit "Chuchok song kuman" (Chuchok and the Two Children) appears to have sparked an answer in Benjamin's "Chuchok." (These songs are named for characters in the *Vessantara Jataka, the story of the Buddha's penultimate rebirth as a human.*) Benjamin's "Farang mueang Thai" (Caucasian in Thailand), which combined mambo with *ramwong*, was quickly followed by Suraphon's own pastiche, "Mot fai mambo" (Blackout Mambo). When Benjamin achieved success with songs using Korean melodies, Suraphon responded with his own Korean-flavored songs such as "Khlang Kaoli" (Korean Storehouse) and "Rak ring-ngo" (Love under the Cherry Blossom Tree).

It may be possible to trace the ascendency of Suraphon (and consequently *luk thung*) to Benjamin's decision to join the army. In 1956 fellow northeasterner Field Marshal Sarit Thanarat convinced Benjamin to take up a military appointment, presumably as a performer, and he volunteered for a six-month posting in Korea. His absence from Thailand coincided with a change in Suraphon's output from *ramwong* to the new *phleng talat* style that eschewed ostinato (see chapter two) in favor of homophonic texture and dance rhythms such as the mambo and cha-cha. When Benjamin returned from Korea he continued to perform with the Army band and does not appear to have immediately realized that the music industry was moving on from *ramwong*.

Phleng kae or Dueling Songs

Benjamin spent five years in the army before embarking on a determined attempt to regain his position at the top of the Thai music industry. Frustrated by Suraphon's popularity, Benjamin intervened in a dispute between Suraphon and Phongsri Woranut (b. 1939), which was played out in a series of songs produced during the first half of the 1960s. According to Siriphon (2004, 246, my translation), the concept of dueling songs (*phleng to* or *phleng kae*) was begun by Suraphon: "Before he sang dueling songs with Phongsri Woranut he sang them with Benjamin because Benjamin thought that Suraphon had copied his style of singing." This is a somewhat misleading summary, and the significance of these events deserves a full explanation, which I was able to uncover through personal communication with *luk thung* aficionado Khanueng Saengthong and with Phongsri Woranut herself, who decided recently that she wanted to have her version of events memorialized and has therefore given frequent interviews to various writers.

In 1957 Suraphon and his friend Samniang Muangthong had adapted a Phayong Mukda song and renamed it "Luem mai long" (Unforgettable), although it is now legally recognized as belonging to Samniang alone. The new song was not popular and would have disappeared into obscurity had Suraphon, less than two years later, not begun to perform with the vibrant Phongsri Woranut, who had only just turned twenty. Suraphon and Samniang decided to incorporate the folk tradition of male and female voices dueling with each other and wrote an answering song from a female point of view. As performed by Phongsri, *Nai wa mai luem* ("You Won't Forget?") became a huge hit throughout 1959 and 1960 accompanied by a reissue of "Luem mai long." Several pairs of *phleng kae* were quickly issued on Suraphon's Dornjedi label, such as "Hen hua jai phi laeo" (I Saw Your Heart) (sung by Phongsri) and "Nao ja tai yu laeo" (Freezing Cold), and "Luk kaeo mia khwan" (Beloved Child, Beloved Wife) and "Alai rak" ("Sorrowful Love") (sung by Phongsri). Suraphon and Phongsri looked to be the new golden couple of *luk thung*, but in 1961 they parted ways in acrimonious circumstances.

Phongsri recalls that Field Marshall Sarit had declared a 9:00 p.m. curfew for the armed forces in Bangkok, and Suraphon, whose band included multiple air-force members and used the air-force band equipment, was obliged to recess for a number of weeks. Needing to support her mother, Phongsri asked Suraphon if she could travel to Nakhon Sawan to sing with Phayong Mukda's Army band for a weeklong engagement. Suraphon was reluctant but one of his band's comedians, Somphot Selakun, who was older than Suraphon and had been performing since the late 1940s, convinced him to let her go. Phongsri says she was too busy to listen to radio broadcasts while in Nakhon Sawan, so she returned to Bangkok unaware that the curfew had been lifted. When she went to Suraphon's house to tell him she was back, his wife Srinuan welcomed her, but both women were shocked when Suraphon accused Phongsri of betraying him and ordered her to leave the house. The darling couple of *lukthing* did not speak to each other ever again.

This parting was not the blow to Phongsri's career that Suraphon assumed it would be, and she appears to have benefited from the sympathy of both the *luk thung* audience and industry, with other songwriters and patrons keen to help her. Angry at her success, but ever the businessman, Suraphon wrote the song "Kaeo luem dong" (Parrot Forgets the Forest) attacking Phongsri for leaving his band: "the parrot forgot the forest. . . . You cheated me and flew away. . . . Now that you can fly by yourself you can make big money." Apart from the ironic criticism of Phongsri wanting more money, the song also implied that she should have been satisfied with being a support singer even though her popularity already rivaled Suraphon's. Phongsri recalls that she felt devastated when she first heard this song on the radio but had no intention of replying. Suraphon's close friend, Samniang Muangthong, was aware of the injustice of this attack and saw an opportunity to even the score while still helping Suraphon's career. He secretly asked Somphot Selakun, who also knew the full story, to write and record a *phleng kae* for Phongsri. When "Sarika luem phrai" (Blackbird Forgets the Jungle) appeared Suraphon was furious because the lyrics were even harsher than what he had originally written—"If you're really so good, why would I have left you. . . . Your voice and skin color are the same as me." The songs sold so well that Jinda Sombatjaroen responded on behalf of his older brother by writing and singing "Kaeo Sarika" and "Sarika na mon"

(Beautiful Blackbird) and Phongsri answered again through "Sarika long rang" (Blackbird Mistakes the Nest).

It was in this context that Benjamin wrote the highly venomous "Ya thiang kan loei" (Don't Argue), denouncing Suraphon for attacking Phongsri and also for allegedly copying his singing style. Suraphon responded with "Sip niu kho khama" (Ten Fingers Ask For Forgiveness), telling Benjamin not to interfere in the affairs of young people and denying that he had copied Benjamin's voice.[3] Close analysis of the lyrics reveals how the singers inspired and played off each other. Benjamin begins by continuing the bird imagery employed by Suraphon and Phongsri:

> Father Blackbird blamed her—
> Forgot the partner and when they used to fly together.
> You forget the sky and fly down in the dirt;
> You forget everything, even the person who trained you.

Benjamin makes it obvious whom he is referring to by alluding to the names of the previous songs: "luem dong luem phrai . . ." ("forgot the forest, forgot the jungle"). His criticism becomes progressively harsher ("In your stomach how many coils are there? / Get your intestines out to give to the crows") before he insults Suraphon by warning him not to pick on a woman ("We are male; do not fight with a woman / This brings no credit upon you") and by accusing him of copying his style of singing ("Even my voice people want to copy / Get a reference to work with my voice"). He then asks Suraphon to consider the audience who buy their records: "Have pity on them when they buy them. . . . / They spend lots of money on the singers who are complaining / It's funny isn't it? (*laughing*)" In the final lines of the song Benjamin appeals to national pride: "The story of music is the honor of Thailand / If there is too much [arguing] it will not be good," implying that Suraphon is being "un-Thai."

Suraphon's response begins with the declaration that he does not want to sing *lae* (the style chosen by Benjamin) but has been forced to do so. That he does so fairly skilfully suggests false modesty, as do the lines "I am a junior singer you may know / Not like the teacher who is a skilled composer." Suraphon wishes to be considered the underdog by the audience and to show that he is not reaching above his station. He counters Benjamin's insults with "You can see the lice on other people's heads / But there are also lice hiding on your head" and the deliciously pointed barb, considering that Suraphon was only younger by nine years, "Don't speak everywhere my teacher / The children will get annoyed and will pull out your white hair." He questions Benjamin's right to interfere in his friendly argument with Phongsri: "If you want to blame the children you must do it the right way / If I love my cow I tie it up but if I love my child I teach him right . . . / Try hard to teach composing." This appears to be a reference to Suraphon's past request to become Benjamin's student. Benjamin rejected him and then looked on as Suraphon became famous. As for the accusation that he had copied Benjamin's voice, Suraphon declares that "if the children become famous, you should be proud / If the children sing like you, you should applaud" and sarcastically queries the idea that it is really possible to copy someone else, "Well the voice of a person / It is difficult to find the same / If they wish to copy, Thailand will have only artists." His final remark, "I still love my honor as an artist," is a defense against Benjamin's charge that he is disgracing Thailand.

In the end the big winners out of this argument were Suraphon and Phongsri, who continued to produce phleng kae with other singers in their bands. Benjamin was left disheartened—he could create trends but his rival was always able to produce songs that were more commercially appealing. In 1964 he formed a new band called Benjamin Lae Sahai (Benjamin and Friends), but within a year he transferred leadership to his only protégé, Kuson Kamonsing, and withdrew from the music industry.

Development of the *Phleng Talat/Luk Thung* Industry

Isan performers were heavily involved in the early development of the *luk thung* industry. During the 1960s the threat of low-level communist insurgency and the stationing of American soldiers in Isan compelled the state to begin the development of the Northeast. During the Vietnam War there were four large United States Air Force bases within the Northeast— at Nakhon Ratchasima, Udon Thani, Ubon Ratchathani, and Nakhon Phanom—which provided much-needed infrastructure and employment, as well as exposure to Western rock music for Isan musicians. However, throughout the 1950s and 1960s ever-increasing numbers of Isan people migrated to Bangkok to find work, and many *ramwong* and *molam* musicians found their way into the emerging *luk thung* music industry. As with any market-driven musical genre, *luk thung* developed through a series of fashions, and Isan musicians were adept at both creating and following these fashions. Several features still found in modern *luk thung*, such as the use of certain Isan words to create a rural persona, the Mekong as a site of rural nostalgia, a fascination with travel and the exotic, and the widespread use of certain Isan instruments, can all be traced back to the input of various Isan musicans.

Waeng (2002, 164) notes that the first songwriter to popularize the use of Isan words in *luk thung* songs was Pong Prida. Pong, born in Khon Kaen in 1930, worked in factories and as a boxer and bus conductor while waiting for his break in the music industry. He gained work playing the *khaen* and providing sound effects for other singers' recordings and when, in 1958, he was finally given the chance to record his own song ("Klap ban"—Go Back Home) it was banned for allegedly criticizing the government. The singer is attracted by the city lifestyle ("All the shops are beautiful like they said / Whoever enters will not want to leave") but is repulsed by the chauvinism he experiences ("I only hear what they say: 'Those Isan are very lazy.'"). He responds by protesting the injustice:

> We are Isan; we still care about our home and rice fields.
> We are coming to look for a job. Don't say we are lazy.
> When it's time to plant rice, all of the Isan people will go home.
> (Waeng 2002, 230–31, my translation)

Not only does this song use Isan pronouns such as *khoi* and *ai* (I) but the main lyrical elements of modern *luk thung* are evident: poverty, urban migration, the attraction and dangers of the big city, rural romanticism, and Isan ethnoregional pride. Pong's patron, bandleader Mongkon Amathayakun, was most unimpressed with the negative reaction to "Klap ban" and Pong would probably not have been given another opportunity to record except that Chaloemchai's hit song "Boeng Khong" (an Isan-language title meaning "See the Mekong") began a fashion for "Mekong songs." Pong immediately wrote "Sao fang Khong" (Girl by the Mekong) and followed up its success with "Thiao fang Khong" (Visit by the Mekong), "Khit thueng fang Khong" (Thinking of the Mekong) and "Long Khong duean phen" (Boating on the Mekong at Full Moon). That this fascination with the

Mekong extends to the present day is illustrated by the ongoing popularity of television dramas such as *Phleng rak rim fang Khong* (*Love Song by the Bank of the Mekong*) (see Mitchell 2009, 94–98). In central Thai culture, the idea of travel as a lyrical subject extends back to the ancient Siamese travel literature genre *nirat* (see chapter five) but for Isan people travel has long been a part of their cultural makeup. Migration is engrained in the Isan character. To illustrate this, Waeng (2002, 58–61, my translation) quotes an old saying: "Whoever is brave enough to travel will end up with another person's wife." He suggests that, due to the poverty of the region, travel was traditionally undertaken by Isan men as an economic necessity and as a rite of passage. More recently, Pattana Kitiarsa (2009b, 384) writes that the Isan "geo-ethnocultural region has intensively embraced the transnational labour migration," so much so that "the terms 'overseas employments' and 'overseas travels' had become part of rural villagers' vernacular language in [the] early 1980s." Furthermore, Pattana (2009b, 392) finds that *molam* and *luk thung* enable Isan labor migrants to maintain their cultural identity, and that northeastern popular song lyrics reflect how Isan regional identity has been reinforced by the cultures of transnational labor migration.

The practice of writing about travel and incorporating foreign elements in *luk thung* songs can perhaps be traced back to Benjamin's six-month posting in Korea with the Thai army in 1956. While there he gathered lyrical and musical material, producing songs such as "Kaoli haeng khwam lang" (Korea of the Past) and "Aridang" (the name of the Korean village where he was posted). He also borrowed from Western sources, using the tune of Hank Williams's "Jambalaya" for "Chamdai mai la" (Do You Remember?). Like Benjamin, Chaloemchai loved to write about traveling, and he wrote a number of songs that made use of Khmer language, such as "Khamen tam ram phan." Also in the late 1950s, another Isan songwriter, Sombat Bunsiri, specialized in Vietnamese travel songs such as "Nirat rak Vietnam," which followed Benjamin's example by using foreign words and musical style. Sombat never actually went to Vietnam but he asked a Vietnamese boy in his neighborhood how to say certain phrases. From the end of the 1960s, Surin Phaksiri, born in Ubon Ratchathani, became the most famous adapter of melodies from other cultures, most notably with the Indian film-song influence in the film *Mon rak luk thung* (*Magic of Luk Thung*) (see chapter two). Surin now calculates that he has written more than fifty songs using melodies from the West, Japan, India, Malaysia, Korea, Vietnam, Laos, and Cambodia.

A final example of *luk thung* fashions begun by Isan musicians is "Phuyai Li" (Village Head Li), the most popular song of the 1960s and the signature tune of Isan-born Saksri Sriakson.[4] "Phuyai Li" is the most discussed song in the English literature on *luk thung*,[5] yet its Isan links have never been mentioned. Phongsri Woranut and Phumphuang Duangjan are popularly acclaimed as the female superstars of *luk thung*, but Saksri, who was actually the first female luk thung superstar, has been largely forgotten despite her enormous success. She was born in 1937 in Ubon Ratchathani and is unusual in that she kept her own name throughout her career.[6] After she graduated from high school she won a beauty contest and trained as an Isan dancer. Wishing to pursue a career in entertainment, she responded to a magazine advertisement for a singer which mentioned Phaibun Butkhan and the famous bandleader Phiphat Boribun. However, when she auditioned both Phaibun and Phiphat thought that her voice was strange, and Phaibun said that all she was good for was to be a wife. Soon after that audition she became Phiphat's wife and, in 1957, he launched her career with "Nuea fa fang Khong" (Above the Sky by the Mekong) and "Sao fang Khong" and Phaibun Butkhan's "Krathin bon krathang" (Leucaena Tree in a Pot). She toured with the Phiphat Boribun Band, which, at the time, included Chaloemchai Sriruecha, Phongsri Woranut and her husband Rachen Rueangnet, and Samanmit Koetkamphaeng.

One night in 1959, Saksri and Phiphat went to watch a *molam* performance in Ubon about Phuyai Li, an archetype of local officials in Isan, who were not used to central Thai language and were easily confused by government edicts. Soon thereafter Phiphat wrote "Phuyai Li" under the pen name Ing Chao-isan. The band performed the song in concert for two years before it was recorded with vocals by Saksri. Thinking that the song would not be a hit, Phiphat had only a small run of three hundred 78 rpm records made, and he deposited them with a shop in Bangkok before embarking on a tour of northern Thailand. On the way home the band stopped over in Phetchabun, and Phiphat was amazed to hear a young girl tending buffalos singing the song. When they reached Bangkok they found that "Phuyai Li" was all the rage and Saksri had become the most famous female singer in Thailand.

For the next decade and beyond, "Phuyai Li" was an unparalleled phenomenon in Thai music. The Phiphat Boribun Band had to be renamed the Saksri Sriakson Band, and there were numerous spin-off songs such as "Mia luang Phuyai Li" (Major Wife of Phuyai Li) sung by Chaichana

Bunnachot, "Phuyai Li ti khong" (Phuyai Li Strikes a Gong) sung by Srisa-ang Trinet, "Phuyai Li taeng ngan" (Phuyai Li Gets Married) sung by Phongsri Woranut, and "Siang khruan jak Phuyai Li" (The Sweet Sound of Phuyai Li) sung by Yongyut Chiaochanchai. Saksri was booked to appear in Bangkok nightclubs for 12,000 baht (USD370) per month, an unheard of amount especially for *luk thung* singers, and in 1964 she appeared opposite Dokdin Kanyaman in the film *Luksao Phuyai Li* (*Phuyai Li's Daughter*). Throughout the 1960s, Phiphat created other versions of the song, including "Phuyai Li Wathusi," which capitalized on the 1962–63 Watusi dance craze. There were also numerous lawsuits and even cases of murder attributed to the misuse of the song by those wishing to insult individuals named Li (Waeng 2002, 538–41).

Both the *khaen* (Lao free-reed mouth organ) and *phin* (Lao three-stringed lute) are almost ubiquitous in modern *luk thung*. The present popularity of these instruments can be traced back respectively to Samai Onwong and Nophadon Duangphon. Samai, born in Phetchaburi but of Isan descent, formed a band called Samai Silapin in 1957 and began issuing recordings in 1966. His *luk thung* band was pioneering in that it used the *khaen* as a melodic and harmonic instrument in homophonic arrangements.[7] Nophadon Duangphon began a *molam* band in 1971 under the name Phin Prayuk but changed the name to Phet Phin Thong (*phet* means "diamond;" *thong* means "gold") following an audience with the king. Thongsai Thapthanon was the original *phin* player and is generally acknowledged to be the finest exponent of the instrument. The three bands (of Saksri, Samai, and Nophadon) are linked through another famous *phin* player and comedian, Lung Naep, or Narong Phongphap, who was a member of each in turn.

Isan Parochialism and Influence in the Early *Luk Thung* Music Industry

During the 1960s, Sino-Thai businessmen dominated the corporate side of the music industry, partly through the use of the Teochew dialect as a business language. Similar circumstances existed in the field of songwriting where Isan migrants congregated and supplied each other with work. This may have been in part a necessary defense mechanism. The 1940s and 1950s had been dominated by the Suntharaphon group of songwriters such as Uea

Sunthonsanan, Wet Sunthonjamon, and Kaeo Atchariyakun, who shared a central Thai mindset and an interest in preserving the status quo in Thai society. Another of their number, Luan Khwantham, hailed from the South and so would only take on *luksit* (protégés) who were also southerners. The largest group of Isan songwriters, consisting of the students of *Khru* (teacher) Kor Kaeoprasoet, was active during the late 1950s and throughout the 1960s, and included Loet Srichok, Sombat Bunsiri, Wichian Sitthisong, Samson Na Mueangsri, Samran Arom, Cho Kachai, and Surin Phaksiri. A measure of Kor Kaeoprasoet's influence is that he was close friends with Suraphon Sombatjaroen and produced the most authoritative biography of the assassinated star in 1969, titled *Chiwit kan tor su khong Suraphon* (*Suraphon's Life of Struggle*).

FIGURE 1.1. Soraphet Phinyo playing a *khaen*. (James Mitchell)

A second circle of Isan songwriters developed toward the end of the 1960s; this group included Phongsak Chantharukkha, Sanya Chulaphon, also known as San Silaprasit, Thinakon Thiphamat, Prasit Nakhonphanom, and Songkhro Samatthaphaphong and was unofficially led by Surin Phaksiri. Surin worked as the musical director on a series of famous Rangsi Thasanaphayak films, including *Mon rak luk thung* and *Mon rak Maenam Mun* (*Magic of the Mun River*) (1977), and from this position was able to distribute opportunities to other Isan songwriters. Singers who wanted to appeal to the dominant *luk thung* fandom sought out the services of Isan songwriters, but they usually had to have some kind of Lao background themselves in order to be accepted by the composer and audience.

A major problem for those wishing to classify *luk thung* as an exclusively central Thai art form is the significant Isan populations of Bangkok and some central Thai provinces. Waeng (2002, 167, 177) notes that many people in Suphan Buri and Chon Buri have Lao ancestry because of Rama III's conquest of Vientiane and forced relocation of the Lao people. This is supported by Kobkul (1985, 188), who writes that "most singers are northeasterners in origin or live in the provinces where there are Laotian or northeasterner concentrations such as Suphan Buri and Chon Buri." For example, Sombat Bunsiri was born in Prachin Buri (eastern Thailand) but always "introduced himself loudly as 'Lao Prachin' because of his Ubon Ratchathani ancestors" (Waeng 2002, 250, my translation). Waiphot Phetsuphan was welcome in Surin Phaksiri's group because he was born in the Bang Pla Ma district of Suphan Buri, a place which had so many people of Lao descent that it was nicknamed "Lao Suphan," and consequently he was able to sing Isan-style songs (Waeng 2002, 168). Likewise, Phloen Phromdaen was born in Prachin Buri in eastern Thailand but grew up in a Lao-speaking area. Later he married Sakuntala Phromsawang, a dancer from Nong Khai, and he formed a writing relationship with Songkhro Samatthaphaphong that enabled him to become the "King of *Phleng Phut*" (speaking songs). Phanom Nopphon, Banchop Charoenphon, and Cholathi Thanthong were all born in the central Thai province of Chon Buri but were of Lao descent.

The Naming of *Luk Thung* and the Movie Soundtrack Period (1968–73)

Possibly no other music genre in the world has been named after a television show. The term *phleng luk thung* was coined in 1964 by Jamnong Rangsikun, the music manager of Channel 4. The emerging genre had previously been known variously as *phleng chao ban* (village songs), *phleng chiwit*, and *phleng talat*. A program consisting of such rural-themed performances had been attempted in 1963 under the title *Phleng chao ban* but was unsuccessful.

One year later, however, the genre had increased in popularity sufficiently to allow a new program titled *Phleng luk thung* to gain an audience. The phrase spread quickly as urban radio DJs picked up on this *thansamai* (modern) term being used on television (Anake 1978, 63–64). It appears that the oppositional term *luk krung* then developed in response and became commonly used to refer to Westernized city music, including the elite *phleng phudi* of Suntharaphon and the emerging, highly Westernized pop genre of *string*. Siriphon (2004, 180) suggests that the concurrent use of the term *phleng luk thung* in the media of television, radio, and film resulted in the widespread acceptance of the new term. In 1965, the film *Your Cheatin' Heart* (1964), the story of Hank Williams, was successfully distributed throughout Thailand under the title *Phleng luk thung*. The wide distribution of the film through urban cinemas and rural *nang re* (mobile movie caravans) played an important role in connecting the urban audience of *luk thung* television shows to the rural audience listening to *luk thung* shows on the radio. The first royal Phaensiang Thongkham (Gold Record) competition held in 1964 did not include *luk thung*, but by the second, held in 1966, *luk thung* was one of the four categories.

The history of *luk thung* is inextricably linked to that of the Thai musical—both as film, radio, and television. The years following the murder of Suraphon Sombatjaroen in 1968 became the golden age of *luk thung* musicals, and singer Rom Srithamarat suggests that this was no coincidence: "After Khru Suraphon passed away there was a lot of money available for *luk thung*. People realized that it was special. Suraphon turned *luk thung* into something valuable" (quoted in Siriphon 2004, 283, my translation). Suraphon's life was quickly memorialized in films such as *Rueang siphok pi haeng khwam lang* (*The Story of* [the song] *"Sixteen Years in the Past"*) and *Suraphon luk pho* (*Suraphon, My Son*), directed by Rangsi Thasanaphayak, who also directed *Mon rak luk thung*.

Mon rak luk thung, starring Mitr Chaibancha and Phetchara Chaowarat, featured songs by Surin Phaksiri and Phaibun Butkhan and the singing talents of Buppha Saichon, Phongsri Woranut, Banchop Charoenphon, and Phraiwan Lukphet. Released on May 15, 1970, the film was extremely popular and played in Thai cinemas for six months, partly as a result of Mitr's tragic death when filming a stunt for another movie. *Mon rak luk thung* was followed by a series of *luk thung* musicals which romanticized rural life in central Thailand and Isan. Some of the biggest hits included

Mae Sriphrai (1971), *Thung setthi* (*Millionaire's Field*) (1971) featuring singer Rungphet Laemsing, and *Lan sao kot* (*Place to Hug a Girl*) (1972). One of the major stars of the 1970s was Sombat Methani, who was born in Ubon Ratchathani. In 1971, he appeared opposite Phetchara Chaowarat in *Ai thui* (Isan language for *Mr. Buffalo*).

This period also saw a proliferation of new bands and the fragmentation of older groups such as Jularat, Mukdapan, and Ruam Daokrajai. In 1969, Chai Mueangsing, Sriphrai Jaiphra, Buppha Saichon, Kosit Nophakhun, and Phanom Nopphon all left Jularat to form their own bands, and Waiphot Phetsuphan and Rungphet Laemsing left Ruam Daokrajai. Suraphon's band was continued by his wife Srinuan under the name Sit Suraphon (Protégés of Suraphon) but stars such as Kangwanphrai Lukphet left to form their own touring bands.

The Development of *Hang Khrueang* (Dancing Revue)

The increased competition after the death of Suraphon meant that bands had to work to differentiate themselves while keeping up-to-date on developing trends. Chai Mueangsing recalls that, in both Jularat and Suraphon's band, singers who were not performing would stand on stage and play percussion instruments. But when he left Jularat to form Wong Lang Khao Prayuk in 1969, he began to assign *ramwong*-style dance moves to the backup singers and then had the idea of having dancers dressed in hill tribe or farming costumes (Siriphon 2004, 285). As the leading female star, Phongsri Woranut seems to have introduced the idea of having male and female dancers together, and Srinuan Sombatjaroen introduced Hawaiian-style dancing along with filmed backdrops. Phloen Phromdaen was the first to have the now ubiquitous dancing revue with twenty dancers dressed in extravagant costumes (Siriphon 2004, 286). Siriphon reports that Phloen's wife, Sakuntala Phromsawang, was at first jealous of the dancers, but she must have overcome her reluctance because she is now remembered for creating the modern style of "Moulin Rouge de Siam," when, in 1975, she adapted the costumes of dancers at Les Folies Bergeres and Moulin Rouge in Paris (Kitchana 2010), as shown in figure 1.2.

FIGURE 1.2. Moulin Rouge style dancing costume. (Peter Garrity)

Luk Thung Isan

The mixed genre of *luk thung prayuk* (sometimes referred to as *luk thung Isan*, Isan *luk thung*, or *luk thung molam*) has usually been presented as a development of the 1980s (for example, see Clewley 1994, 446), but its origins actually date back to the early 1970s. Early Isan songwriters such as Benjamin, Pong Prida, and Kor Kaeoprasoet did introduce Isan cultural elements into their music, but overall they sought to succeed in the Thai music industry by writing within established central Thai formats. Toward the end of the 1960s, however, there appears to have been a concerted attempt by some songwriters and performers to create an Isan variant of *luk thung*. The key personalities in the birth of this new subgenre were Surin Phaksiri, Saksayam Phetchomphu, Thepphon Phetubon, and Dao Bandon.

Born in 1942, Chanon Phaksiri adopted the stage name Surin (an Isan province), even though he was born in Ubon Ratchathani. In 1967, Kor Kaeoprasoet recommended him to established singer Phraiwan Lukphet, but Phraiwan was only interested in cha-cha-style songs. Surin had no experience writing in cha-cha rhythm, but after a short period of practice he produced four songs, including "Khon khi ngon" (Quick-Tempered Person) for Phraiwan and "Lam kiao sao" (Courtship Dance), sung by Kabin

Mueangubon, which, according to the songwriter (Surin et al. 2004, 9), was the first *luk thung* song to include verses of *lam phloen* (discussed in chapter two). Soon he was writing for performers of the caliber of Saksri Sriakson, Waiphot Phetsuphan, Samai Onwong, and Dam Daensuphan. He launched the career of Banchop Charoenphon with the song "Ya doen show" (Don't Parade Yourself) and, in 1971, was awarded a Phaensiang Thongkham for "Ngan nakrong" (Singer's Work), sung by Phonphrai Phetdamnoen.

That year the *luk thung Isan* subgenre began with Surin's "Isan lam phloen," which was written for the film *Bua Lamphu* (1971) and performed by Isan-born actress and singer Angkanang Khunachai. The success of this song emboldened Surin and, with his friend Phongsak Chantharukkha, he began a radio program that featured *molam* by artists such as Ken Dalao, Bunpheng Faiphiuchai, and Khampun Fungsuk, and Isan-flavored *luk thung*. The program was so popular that the station was soon broadcasting Isan music twenty-four hours per day, and cassettes of the show were distributed to northeastern radio networks (Waeng 2002, 338). Surin deliberately incorporated Isan cultural material into his songs, including the traditional humorous *nithan kom* stories. Two such songs are "Pha khao ma," named after the traditional cloth that Isan men wear around their waist, and "Bong kancha," about a bamboo pipe for smoking marijuana. The latter song, originally sung by Kawao Siangthong, follows in the tradition of "Phu yai Li" in juxtaposing the fun-loving naivety of Isan villagers against the petty hawkishness of the local government officials:

> Be happy at the festival.
> There is plenty of alcohol to drink—
> The assistant village head's rice whiskey . . .
> Suddenly Uncle Sa brings the bong to join the group.
> He chops the marijuana up into small pieces . . .
> The constable is watching for a long time.
> When the time is ready he arrests them and tells them off—
> The bong is evidence;
> The rice whiskey is illegal.
> Old man Sa gets very angry:
> "It is a bamboo bong—why are you calling it a marijuana bong?"
> (Waeng 2002, 111, my translation)

Thus, the plot, in which Isan culture loses out in the confrontation with central Thai law, reflects the history of the region.

One of the new *luk thung Isan* performers promoted by Surin was Saksayam Phetchomphu. Saksayam was born Bunchuen Senarat in Maha Sarakham province in 1952 and only completed up to fourth grade at primary school. He received his big break in 1972 when Jira Jiraphan (born in Nakhon Ratchasima), the headline singer for one of the bands of promoter Thephabut Satirodchomphu, came late for a performance and threw a music stand near his boss. Thephabut sacked Jira and gave his next recording session to Bunchuen. In that session Bunchuen recorded six songs written by Thepphon Sirimokun (later Phetubon), including Jira Jiraphan's signature song "Setthi khai khi krabong" (Millionaire Selling Isan Torches) (Waeng 2002, 401–405). Saksayam became a star overnight, and "Tam Nong klap Sarakham" (Bring the Girl Back to Maha Sarakham) became a banner song for Isan people because it cataloged the names of the northeastern provinces so that "all Isan felt that this was their song" (Waeng 2002, 317, my translation).

At that time the most popular band was that led by Sayan Sanya, who had come out of the shadow of the legendary Phongsri Woranut. However, by 1973 Sayan's popularity was rivaled by Saksayam's *Luk thung Isan* band, the name of which was coined by Surin Phaksiri in the first recorded use of the term (Waeng 2002, 323). Sayan and Saksayam joined forces to become the top-grossing show at the Lumphini boxing stage. Surin promoted their show as *Luk thung Isan patha luk thung phak klang* (Competition between northeastern and central Thai country song), and Saksayam was thereafter known by the title *Khunphon phleng luk thung haeng khwaen daen Isan* (*Luk Thung* Genius of the Isan Region). Saksayam reached the height of his fame from 1974 to 1976, when his band was renowned for its lavish production, featuring multiple troupes of dancing girls, amplified instruments, and huge sound and lighting systems.

Among the secondary singers in the *Lukthung Isan* band were Thepphon Phetubon (born in Ubon Ratchathani), the songwriter who started Saksayam's career. Thepphon had an unexpected hit in 1971 when his song "Khit hot na doe" (Isan language for "Please Think of Me") became a national farewell anthem when radio DJs decided to play it as they resigned en masse in protest of severe censorship resulting from the self-coup of Thanom Kittikachorn. Further success eluded him until 1975, when "Isan ban hao" (Isan, Our Home) became an anthem for Isan people. Other major Isan performers from the 1970s included Dao Bandon (born in Yasothon), who also started in Saksayam's band, and Sonchai Mekwichian and Saengsuri Rungrot, both born in Nakhon Ratchasima. One factor in the sudden emergence of Isan singing stars at this time was the gradual withdrawal of American soldiers from Thailand from 1972–74. Many of the Isan musicians who had serviced the American bases were forced to return to the local music scene, and in doing so they mixed rock music with *molam*.

After several years of promoting Isan performers, Surin Phaksiri decided to form his own *luk thung* band, an idea inspired by working on Rangsi Thasanaphayak's 1976 film *Mon rak nakrop* (*Magic of Warriors*), in which the government supports Isan villagers in their efforts to start a performance group. Surin built on the fame of his radio personality, Thitso Sutsanaen, and named his group the Thitso Lam Phloen band, which became a kind of Isan all-stars group featuring Surin's disciples Santi Sammat, Phairin Phonphibun, Sonthaya Kalasin, and Rungnakhon Phonamnat, with Thinakon Thiphamat as an announcer, Sanya Chulaphon in the ticket room, and Phongsak Chantharukkha as manager. In 1977, the band performed for five days and five nights at the Phuttha Phisek fair, beating the previous record of Phloen Phromdaen. In 1984, the group disbanded, and with *luk thung* increasing in popularity after the post-insurgency *phleng phuea chiwit* (songs for life) craze (c. 1980–83) abated, Surin devoted himself to songwriting once again.

Commercial *Luk Thung* in the 1980s and 1990s

In the early 1980s, consolidation took place within the Thai entertainment industry and, with the newfound commercial popularity of *phleng phuea chiwit*, *luk thung* appears to have lost market share, although no official figures are available. New players such as R.S. Promotion (which changed its name to RS Public Company Limited in 2006), founded by Kriengkai Chetchotisak in 1976, and Phaibun Damrongchaitham's Grammy, founded in 1983, were at first far more interested in *string* (Thai pop) than in *luk thung*. By 1987, the biggest touring bands, of Sayan Sanya and Yodrak Salakchai, had to disband because the popularity of their music and performance style declined, leading to financial problems.

Phumphuang Duangjan (1961–92), born in Suphan Buri, was certainly the most influential performer of the 1980s (fig. 1.3). Phumphuang's cassette albums *Hang noi, thoi nit* (*Move a Little Closer*) released in 1984 and *Krasae* (*Come on Baby*) in 1985, both featuring the compositions of Wichian Khamcharoen (Lop Burirat), represent the beginning of a new period of *luk thung*. Ubonrat suggests that these albums mark the point when *luk thung* aligns itself with modern pop/rock and also returns to the sexual openness of folk songs (1998, 217). Phumphuang's tragic death at the age of thirty from a stroke caused by lupus further stimulated interest in *luk thung* and cemented the position of Suphan Buri as the spiritual home of the genre.

FIGURE 1.3. Phumphuang Duangjan on the cover of *Racha Siang Thong* magazine in June 1987. (James Mitchell)

Throughout the 1980s, increasing numbers of Isan performers entered the *luk thung* industry, including Nong Nut Duangchiwan and Soraphet Phinyo, who are discussed in chapter three. The career path of Yenjit Phonthewi is typical of this generation of Isan singers, most of whom came from farming and *molam* backgrounds. Born in Waeng Noi district, in Khon Kaen province, she completed only fourth grade at primary school. In 1976, she won a singing competition, and composer Sumthum Phairimbueng supplied her with the songs to launch a *molam* career, which culminated with the 1981 hit song "Lam phloen to lom nao" (*Lam Phloen* Fights the

Cold Wind). The following year (1982) she changed to *luk thung* in an album called *Khit thueng thung Lui Lai* (Thinking of the Field at Lui Lai), which enabled her to embark on national tours (Siriphon 2004, 305).

Yenjit was soon followed by such talented performers as Chaloemphon Malakham from Surin, Phimpha Phonsiri (discussed in chapter three) from Chaiyaphum, Thongmi Malai from Yasothon (whose most famous song, "Chomrom taxi," described the lifestyle of Isan taxi drivers in Bangkok), Khwanchai Phetroiet from Roi Et, Onuma Singsiri from Khon Kaen, and Hongthong Dao Udon from Udon Thani. This generation of Isan singers were often mentored by the older Isan songwriters such as Surin, Sunthum, and Doi Inthanon, who actually was from Surin but was of the minority Kui ethnicity. Doi Inthanon wrote major hits for Sayan Sanya ("Mae dok salete"—White Ginger Girl) and Phongsri Woranut ("Chan on," which received the Sao Akat Thongkham [Golden Antenna] award in 1977) before shaping the careers of Sonchai Mekwichian and Hongthong Dao Udon with songs that combined *molam* and *luk thung*. The success of these older songwriters encouraged more and more Isan musicians to enter the *luk thung* industry. By the time Suphan Chuenchom wrote Siriphon Amphaiphong's massive 1991 hit "Bow rak si dam" (Black Love Bow), the dominance of Isan songwriters and their Isan protégés was firmly established.

During the economic boom of the 1990s, *luk thung* declined in popularity in comparison to J-pop, imported Western recordings, and Thai pop. However, when the 1997 Asian Economic Crisis hit, the genre experienced a revival because it was perceived to be an authentic Thai art form, and it spoke to the rural romanticism felt by many disillusioned urban Thais. This wave of nostalgia was accompanied by the continued assimilation of *thansamai* (up-to-date) influences into *luk thung*, with the result that the genre's appeal has broadened and its status has risen (see Amporn 2006, 25–41).

Forces Contributing to the Low Status of *Luk Thung* in Thai Society before 1997

The low status of *luk thung* in Thai society before 1997 has been referred to frequently,[8] but there has been little attempt to explain why *luk thung* developed such low status and maintained it for so long. Disdain for popular music genres is certainly not a new phenomenon—genres such as jazz, blues, or bluegrass were all once regarded as lowbrow music. In this case, various social and political forces, movements, or conditions combined to produce a negative image of *luk thung* in Thai society and in academic writing before 1997.

One of the forces that may have influenced the status of *luk thung* was its connection with Phibun. The social engineering characteristic of his first regime created the conditions that allowed *luk thung* and other popular song genres to develop. According to official Thai historians, the first *luk thung* song was written in 1938. *Luk thung* really developed as a separate genre during the 1950s and 1960s, but this earlier date is significant because it coincides with Phibunsongkhram's first term as prime minister (1938–44), when he adopted an overall strategy to weaken the monarchy's hold on Thai society and attempted to do this through modernization (Ubonrat 2000, 4). *Phleng Thai sakon* had begun to develop as part of the motion picture industry, and the Fine Arts Department under Luang Wichit Wathakan used the new song style as a hegemonic tool. Between 1939 and 1942, Phibun issued twelve cultural mandates, the eleventh of which ordered Thais to improve themselves by listening to radio news, entertainment, and arts. Commenting on Phibun and Wichit's concerted efforts to impose a popular culture upon the masses, Moro (2004, 199–200) observes that "the performing arts became a focal point in top-down efforts to create a modern, national Thai culture."

It is therefore possible that *phleng Thai sakon* and *ramwong* had higher status during the years of Phibun's influence because of government patronage and the corresponding neglect of Thai classical music. Ubonrat (1990, 63) points out that following the abolition of the absolute monarchy, Thai governments adopted Western music as the basis for a new national popular music because it "broke with the classical court music of the *ancien regime*." Both Phibun and the architect of his cultural policy, Wichit, could see that a new society needed new performance styles, and they seem to have grasped instinctively what popular music theorists only later realized—that popular music has greater potential for social and political influence than avant-garde or art music because it can generate a mass audience (Martin 1995, 128).

The preservation and classicisation (in other words, restriction and sidelining) of the royal musical tradition gave *phleng Thai sakon* and *ramwong* the space in which to grow and develop eventually into *luk krung* and *luk thung*. However, the overthrow of Phibun's government in 1957 may have resulted in a loss of status for the popular music genres associated with him. Despite the far-reaching effects of his time in office, he has completely fallen out of favor in Thailand today—the fifty-year anniversary of the name change from Siam to Thailand was ignored because of its association with his first militaristic, fascist regime (Reynolds 2002, 1). It is possible that Phibun's fall from grace, combined with the rehabilitation of the monarchy under Sarit's rule and a renewed interest in Thai classical music among the central Thai middle class, led to the decline of traditional *ramwong* and may have contributed to the lower status of some popular music during the 1960s and 1970s. This does not mean that genres such as *luk thung* and *string* became less popular but that they were regarded as having little cultural value.

Possibly the main reason why *luk thung* had such low status in Thai society was its links with Isan people and culture. Central Thai chauvinism toward Lao people extends back centuries on the basis that the Lao were never part of the original Sukhothai kingdom. Thais take great nationalistic pride in the idea that Thailand was never colonized by Western nations, yet Siam was its own colonial power in the nineteenth century, "drawing neighbouring peoples around its periphery into its sphere" (Moro 2004, 198). In 1827, the destruction of Vientiane by Rama III was accompanied by the forced migration of the population, transferring ethnic Lao to areas they had not previously occupied, including the central Chao Phraya River basin (Keyes 1971, 11). This has important implications for any discussion of Lao-Isan influence on *luk thung* because, as has already been discussed, some rural areas of central Thailand actually have large populations of ethnic Lao.

Over the past 130 years there has been a systematic dismantling of ethnic Lao identity in Thailand, in the service of nation building. In 1900, a royal decree was issued prohibiting the recording of Lao nationality in the census. In the same year, Ubon Ratchathani was officially designated as Phak Isan and then, in 1913, there was a royal decree issued by King Rama V to announce the grouping of Udon Thani, Ubon Ratchathani, and Roi Et together under the name of Phak Isan (Northeastern Region). Attempts by the Siamese authorities to control the Khorat Plateau and the Isan population, such as the centralization of education through the teaching medium of central Thai rather than Lao (McCargo and Hongladarom 2004, 222), led to a series of revolts during the early part of the twentieth century.

Although the term "Isan" was only officially employed up until 1925, it persisted in popular usage because it allowed central Thai authorities to avoid the word "Lao" and enabled the Lao-Isan to maintain a separate identity. The suppression of Lao cultural identity continued after the ending of the absolute monarchy. In 1939, Wichit Wathakan ordered that the word "Lao" be replaced with "Thai" in popular *molam* songs (Barmé 1993, 151). The assassination of Isan politicians in 1949 and 1952 by state forces on charges of promoting separatism contributed to the development of an Isan regional political identity (Keyes 1971, 34). However, Keyes identifies economic underdevelopment in the Northeast and the resultant urban migration during the 1950s as the most important catalyst for the development of a regional Isan mentality. Temporary migrants were confronted by the wealth of Bangkok and discovered that Bangkok Thais considered them unsophisticated and inferior. Feeling marginalized, they congregated together and worked in a narrow range of professions, most notably as *samlo* (pedicab) drivers. Central Thai prejudice was exacerbated during the 1960s by the Thai government's characterization of Isan as a hotbed of communist activity, even though such activity was fomented by the neglect of successive Thai administrations. The heavy Isan involvement in *luk thung* during the 1960s and 1970s led to it being classified as music for "country bumpkins" (Amporn 2006, 43).

The designation of the genre as *luk thung* (children of the field) from 1964 contributed to its identification with folk music, and this association has been confirmed by the majority of Thai commentators.[9] In a society which, up until the 1997 Asian Economic Crisis, privileged the elite, the modern, and the urban, this meant that *luk thung* was accorded low status. In 1988 and 1991, a series of concerts and ceremonies was organized by the government to mark the fiftieth anniversary of Thai country music. The wording of the official review of the concerts published in the *Thai Cultural Newsletter* is revealing:

> Some Look Thung songs, in spite of their popularity amongst the local people, have considerable influence over them and their way of life. Some remain a source for sociological studies and a mine of local wisdom. Such a cultural heritage should be preserved. ("Half a Century of Thai Country Music," 1991, 4)

Luk thung is here classified as local culture, and only useful for sociological study—not as an art form. The implication, whether intended or not, is that what is regarded as influential culture should not be popular, and any quality of sophistication is not to be considered in relation to *luk thung*. The distinction between high and low culture is clearly drawn in Sujit Wongthet's short story "Second Nature":

> [They] were dancing to the tempo of pigs or dogs scalded with boiling water. Alas and alack! ... Two of the girls ... danced together on the stage, complacently bumping and grinding their hips—oblivious to their fellow countrymen, oblivious to the Chronicles of Si Ayuttaya [the most famous Thai historical chronicle], oblivious to the inscription of the Kingdom of Sukhothai [a great early Thai kingdom] ... oblivious of King Chulalongkorn [a great Thai king who reformed the nation] (quoted in Lockard 1998, 179).

Popular music here is marked by moral transgression and animalistic behavior. High culture intrinsically takes on the values of central Thai culture, inherently denying access to people from Isan (and other minorities). A measure of the low value assigned to *luk thung* by the Thai hierarchy can be seen in the recognition of *Sinlapin haeng chat* (National Artist) (see chapter three). Considering the enduring market share and popularity of *luk thung*, it is strange that there have only been ten *luk thung* National Artists versus twenty for *luk krung*, fifty-five for Thai classical and folk music, and even nine in Western music.

The ongoing influence of the royalist-nationalist history can be seen in Lamnao's (2006, 14, 17) definition that *luk thung* is derived from Thai folk genres whereas *luk krung* is derived from Thai court music. In this he is following Anake Nawigamune's oversimplified alignment of *luk thung* with Thai folk music and *phleng Thai sakon* with the royal *phleng Thai doem*. Such a definition is questionable, since *phleng Thai sakon* acted as a conduit between *phleng nuea tem* and later genres. Furthermore, there are many *luk thung* songs that use *phleng Thai doem* melodies and melodic features. Lamnao (2006, 16) also states that *luk thung* is composed in a "simple style, as some musicians cannot read musical notation" but immediately contradicts this by writing that "the musical forms [of *luk thung*] are not very different from [those] of *phleng lukgrung*". Lamnao appears to be following Kobkul's (1985, 186) reasoning that "phlaeng luk thung [sic] have a simpler style and simpler words and are readily understandable appealing to the rural populace" but that if "a city style singer sings a country style song, the song becomes a city style song."

Throughout the twentieth century, Thai society has been influenced by Western assignations of value (see Pattana 2009a, 57–74), examples of which can be seen in the development of *phleng Thai sakon* and *string*, in the adoption of Western business dress and in the presentation of Thai culture to tourists. The impact on the status of *luk thung* of external forces such as Western ethnomusicology and the expectations of foreign tourists cannot be quantified, but is nonetheless deserving of consideration.

It is, perhaps, not surprising that Thai popular music genres were not studied by Thais until the late 1970s, since before 1970 "mass-mediated and popular culture . . . were all but ignored by [Western] historians, area specialists and most social scientists" (Lent 2000, 140). Charles Keil identifies three ethnomusicological biases that have prevented musical mediations becoming a top priority in research: "a) a traditional focus on non-Western music, b) a concern with folkish authenticity, and c) a privileging of live performance, both in descriptive work and in ethnomusicological performance group replications of traditional styles" (Keil and Feld 1994, 248). In Thailand, Western ethnomusicology may have contributed to a negative image of *luk thung* by privileging high and folk culture over popular culture. Some ethnomusicologists have blamed "the siren songs of extensively promoted pop music" for the loss of more authentic Thai folk and classical music genres (Lockard 1998, 179). Terry Miller was dismissive of *luk thung* when he conducted the definitive English language study of *molam* in the early 1970s:

> The new genre, called *pleng look toong* ("children of the fields"), however, is marked by simple poetry, direct sentiment, and a general lack of sophistication. The subjects are the lives of ordinary people, especially villagers. For singing styles the composers, most of whom live in Bangkok, plunder any and all regional folk and art forms including *mawlum glawn and mawlum moo* (1985, 54).

In contrast, he considered *luk krung* "sophisticated and highly Westernized [and] the lyrics . . . relatively polished and subtle" (Miller 1985, 54). Miller's portrayal of *luk thung* songwriters as wealthy Bangkok Thais who plunder peasant culture is difficult to sustain when the history of *luk thung* is examined. As is demonstrated by Waeng (2002, 255, 323) and Siriphon (2004, 439–40), most songwriters had rural origins (some were *Molam*) but they migrated to Bangkok in order to make a living. Miller (2005, 96–106) presents *luk thung* more favorably, albeit briefly, in a recent article, which suggests that the field of ethnomusicology has since become more accommodating of popular genres. However, his conclusion in *The Garland Encyclopaedia of World Music* that "Thailand's heart may beat to the sounds of rock and modernized regional music, but its soul rejoices in its classical tradition" (Miller 1998, 333) does not allow for class and ethnic divisions in Thailand. Isan people, who comprise approximately one third of the population, have very little interest in central Thai classical music, but even gentrified and urbanized Isan are intensely proud of traditional *molam*.

The overt commercialism and (occasionally) nationalistic lyrics of *luk thung* have possibly discouraged the attention of cultural studies. Hayes (2004, 23) identifies the reluctance of some Western popular music writers to discuss music within its commercial context—"the avoidance of commercialism" and a corresponding level of discomfort with music that does not call explicitly for revolution. For many world music listeners this has translated into a general aversion to nearly all East and Southeast Asian popular music because it is openly commercial and not obviously rebellious. The influence of Antonio Gramsci's theory of hegemony, whereby culture is viewed as a power struggle between the establishment and the oppressed, has encouraged scholars to analyze popular music genres in terms of resistance or counter-hegemony. Sometimes, as in Myers-Moro's (1986, 93–114) examination of *phleng phuea chiwit*, the genre demands this kind of analysis, but with *luk thung* such analyses have not been so successful. Tony Mitchell (2001, 19) criticizes Lockard for "trying to fit his subjects into outmoded Western sociological paradigms of rock music as 'a vehicle for social and political comment.'"

The problem for many non-Thai scholars has been accessing information. Because Thais saw that Thai classical music was valued by foreign ethnomusicologists, they were more likely to translate "high culture" texts than "low culture" texts. In addition, texts that supported the royalist-nationalist history taught throughout the Thai education system were more likely to be translated than texts which questioned central Thai cultural and political hegemony. Consequently, foreign scholars have sometimes accepted the information they were given as the only discourse. In Thai popular musicology, the Thai and English literatures have tended to operate virtually as separate worlds—Lockard openly acknowledges that his work is a synthesis of the few secondary sources available at the time in English—Ubonrat (1990), Marre and Charlton (1985), and Kobkul (1985).

The expectations of foreign tourists regarding Thai culture have also influenced the status of Thai classical music and popular genres. The importance of tourism to Thailand's economy has resulted in an emphasis on the exotic and oriental: "Classical music and dance are one of the messages foreigners want to hear about the Thai, and which the Thai are willing to tell" (Myers-Moro 1989, 193). Clewley (1994, 440) asserts that Thai popular music in general is largely ignored by tourists, who are far more likely to encounter "classical or court ensembles at restaurants or the National Theatre." Understandably, Thais want to make a positive cultural impression, and the influence of foreign ethnomusicologists and the dominance of central Thai culture have contributed to Thai classical music being viewed as the most appropriate representation of Thai culture. *Luk thung* is as representative of the contemporary cultural endeavors of Thai people as Thai classical music, but when it comes to representing Thailand to tourists, *luk thung* has been regarded as too Westernized by foreigners and *mai thansamai* (old-fashioned or rustic) by Thais.

Luk Thung's Rise in Status and Isan Cultural Dominance in Modern Thailand

In "*Lukthung*: Authenticity and Modernity in Thai Country Music," Amporn Jirattikorn (2006) argues that the 1997 Asian economic crisis propelled a rapid reevaluation of the cultural value of *luk thung*. Certainly *luk thung* had been appreciated as a unique Thai art form prior to 1997, as shown by the Half a Century of *Luk Thung* concert series in 1989 and 1991. Yet the economic crisis became a crisis point for Thai cultural identity. Governmental, royal, and cultural institutions blamed Western influence for Thailand's loss of sovereignty to the IMF, and *luk thung*'s supposed authenticity and evocation of rural nostalgia became the antidote to economic woes.

Luk thung is now a valuable cultural commodity and Isan people have benefited from that rise in status. The field is more dominated than ever by

Isan faces and traditional singing styles. Today in Thailand Lao-Isan cultural identity is resurgent and even dominant in some fields. Isan celebrities abound in popular music, film, television, and sports. The birthplaces of the biggest *luk thung* stars since 1997 constitute a tour of Isan provinces: Nakhon Ratchasima (Sunari Ratchasima, Kot Jakrapan, and Takadaen Chonlada), Khon Kaen (Phi Sadoet and Mangpor Chonticha), Udon Thani (Mike Phiramphon and Fon Thanasunthon), Buri Ram (Yingli Sichumphon), Ubon Ratchathani (Tai Orathai), Yasothon (Phai Phongsathon and Monkhaen Kaenkhun), Mukdahan (Monsit Khamsoi), and Si Sa Ket (Yingyong Yotbua-ngam). *Molam* has become mainstream through crossover stars such as Jintara Phunlap (Roi Et), Phonsak Songsaeng (Khon Kaen), Noknoi Uraiphon (Si Sa Ket), and Siriphon Amphaiphong (Udon Thani). GMM Grammy, the dominant Thai entertainment group, which initially ignored *luk thung* in the 1980s, began its own *luk thung* subsidiary Grammy Gold in 1996. In 2000, Grammy Gold claimed that the fifth album of Mike Phiramphon, titled *Yachai konchon* (Darling of the Poor), sold more than one million cassettes. Currently, the most celebrated *luk thung* songwriter are Grammy Gold's Sala Khunawut, from Ubon Ratchathani, and Wasu Haohan, born in Udon Thani. The current crop of Grammy Gold artists are exclusively Isan, including Siriphon, Tai, Phai, Takadaen, and Monkhaen, as well as newcomers Khaothip Thidadin (Amnat Charoen) and Oenkhwan Waranya (Sakon Nakhon).

Isan musicians have also been successful in other genres. Thailand's most popular soft-rock duo, brothers Asanee and Wasan Chotikul, were born in Loei. Sek Loso, the 'bad boy' of Thai rock, is from Nakhon Ratchasima. Current stars in the hybrid genre of *nu luk thung* include Chaem Chamram from Buri Ram and Vit Hyper (mother from Nakhon Ratchasima). First appearing in 2005, entertainment group Ponglang Sa-on, led by comedian Sompong "Eed" Kunaprathom (born in Kalasin), has capitalized on the popularity of all things Isan by presenting a show that blends comedy, music, and culture. Eed and his musicians dress in kilts made from *pha khao ma*, the traditional cotton cloth worn by Isan men, and play Isan instruments such as the *phin*, *khaen*, and *pong lang* (vertical xylophone).

Aphichatphong Wirasethakul, who won the *Palme d'Or* at the 2010 Cannes Film Festival for *Lung Bunmi raluek chat* (*Uncle Boonmee Who Can Recall His Past Lives*), hails from Khon Kaen. Apichatphong's multi-platform art project *Primitive* examines Nabua in Nakhon Phanom, "a land in Isaan with a brutal history," where in 1965 the military cracked down on communists (quoted in Wise 2010). In 2006, another Isan-born director, Chaloem Wongphim, produced *Khon fai bin* (*Dynamite Warrior*), which features an Isan superhero who fights cattle bandits and feudal lords with the kind of homemade bamboo rockets used every year at Yasothon's rocket festival (*bun bang fai*).

In 2003, Tony Jaa, born in Surin, became a Thai action hero through his film *Ong Bak*, which celebrated the resilience of Isan villagers through drought, poverty, and urban migration. Much of the success of *Ong Bak* can be put down to martial arts choreographer, Panna Rittikrai, born in Khon Kaen. Appearing in some of Tony Jaa's movies is "Mum Jokmok" (Phetthai Wongkhamlao, born in Yasothon), the most successful comedian in Thailand. A film star in his own right, in 2005 he wrote, directed, and starred in *Yaem Yasothon* (English title *Hello Yasothon*), a homage to the *luk thung* comedy films of the 1960s and 1970s. In a sign of the times, however, the dialogue was entirely in Isan, and for its theater screenings in Bangkok, subtitles were provided so that central Thais could understand.

On Thai television the rural musical is an established genre that has become even more popular in the wake of the Isan cultural resurgence. Recent *lakhon* (drama series) such as *Phleng rak rim fang Khong*, featuring Lao popstar Alexandra Bounxouei and Khon Kaen heartthrob Sukonwat (Weir) Khanarot, and *Dao charat fa* (*Brightest Star in the Sky*), starring glamorous *luk thung* singer Fon Thanasunthon, present a very different picture of Lao-Isan people compared to past portrayals. In sports, tennis star Paradorn Srichaphan (Khon Kaen) and 2004 Olympic weightlifting gold medalists Pawina Thongsuk (Surin) and Udomporn Polsak (Nakhon Ratchasima) have dismissed the stereotype of the lazy Isaner.

Luk Thung as a Cultural Bridge

Peter Manuel (1988, 205) has written that *luk thung* performs a mediating function between rural and urban society. Extrapolating this historical function, one can go further: the present popularity of *molam sing*, Isan films and comedians, and Isan culture in general is directly linked to Isan involvement in *luk thung* that began in the 1940s and continued throughout the 1950s, 1960s, and 1970s. The *luk thung* music industry created both employment opportunities for Isan people and a legitimate space for their language and customs to first survive and then become acceptable to the wider population. Through *luk thung*, central Thais gradually became accustomed to Isan language and culture, and when *luk thung* experienced a rise in status after 1997, other Isan cultural forms benefited.

A Musical Analysis of *Luk Thung*'s Form and Development

A song is a song. Elevating some songs in value above others is wrong. I have travelled to lots of places and I can confirm that luk thung songs are popular in every province. This is not just my songs but those of other people as well. If someone says that *luk thung* songs are low grade this means that person is looking down on singers throughout Thailand. Let me say this as an example: if you have a song competition with a high standard band for every kind of song, the luk thung songs will win.

—Suraphon Sombatjaroen (quoted in Siriphon 2004, 244, my translation)

Description of *Luk Thung*

Generalizing about the form of *luk thung* is somewhat difficult, because throughout its history many disparate styles have been experimented with and either quickly discarded or incorporated into an ever-changing synthesis. Such borrowing of melodies and rhythms has ensured that the most consistent element in *luk thung* is the tragic narrative in miniature; nonetheless, it is possible to make a number of observations on the basic *luk thung* musical form.

Luk thung follows a standard formula and a pattern of creativity within constraints. Western tuning is employed because the core of the *luk thung* band is drums, bass, organ, and electric guitar. Traditional Thai instruments are frequently added, but sometimes adapted tuning is required. Vocal and instrumental melodies are highly ornamented; the vocals are nasal and combined with techniques such as *luk kho* (heavy vibrato) and *uean* (melodic embellishment on a vocable, or melisma). Songs can be classified as either slow, usually with slow dance, beguine, or bolero rhythms, or fast, predominantly with cha-cha or Isan *soeng* rhythms. Chord progressions are influenced by the traditional pentatonic melodies, which means that the standard I–IV–V of Western popular music is seldom heard. Minor progressions such as i–iv–v,[1] i–iv–VII, and i–VI–III are more common with sudden shifts to relative, tonic, or dominant major chords. The standard structure of a *luk thung* song is introduction / verse / verse / break / verse (IAABA). Often this structure is extended by repeating the break and final verse (IAABABA). The introduction typically consists of a four-bar statement of the basic chord pattern followed by overlapping solos from two instruments, one of which is almost always organ. Part of the introduction is usually restated before each verse. A defining feature of *luk thung* is the frequent use of cha-cha rhythms, whether in fast or slow songs. Because *luk thung* lyrics conform to some rules of traditional Thai poetic forms (see chapter three) verses are composed in regular lengths: eight, twelve, or sixteen bars. Songs are usually between two-and-a-half and four minutes in length, reflecting *luk thung*'s origins as a popular mediated genre recorded on 78 rpm discs.

Cultural Heterogeneity in *Luk Thung*

The two most contested issues in studies of *luk* thung are whether the genre's origins are urban or rural, and to what extent *luk thung* can be considered Isan music. Debate on the former issue has been restricted to the Thai literature, whereas debate on the second issue initiated in the English literature and gradually spread into the Thai literature. A consistent omission from the discussion of both issues is actual content analysis of musical examples, with the Thai sources overwhelmingly concentrated on lyrics and English ones limited in scope. Since a deconstruction of the hybrid nature of *luk thung* is central to both issues, this chapter considers the musical syncretisms contained in *luk thung*.

The portrayal of *luk thung* as an authentic Thai cultural form has perhaps discouraged a consideration of the actual makeup of the genre. Thai histories often list the Thai folk genres that have been absorbed into *luk thung*, but very seldom identify clear, specific examples. Furthermore, there is very little written in the Thai literature concerning exactly what foreign influences were brought into *luk thung* and when. If the process of syncretism is discussed at all, there is seldom any distinction drawn between musical, lyrical, and cultural influence. For example, because *luk thung* is often translated as "Thai country music" it could easily be assumed that its most important musical influence has been American country and western. However, while American country may have influenced costume and lyrical content during the 1960s, it did not have lasting impact on *luk thung* musically, and there have been much more significant external influences.

Influences on *luk thung* can be divided roughly into three categories—Thai, Western, and other Asian. The Thai influences include *phleng Thai doem* and *ramwong*; central Thai folk genres such as *phleng lae, isaeo, choi,* and *lamtat*; Isan *molam, soeng, and kantruem*; Northern *phleng so*; and Southern *nangtalung* and *manora*. Western and Latin American influences include nineteenth-century brass-band music, cha-cha, rock, disco, funk, jazz, and Latin pop. Other Asian sources include Bollywood film songs and Chinese Cantopop.

Thai Elements in *Luk Thung*

Whether *luk thung* is a modern version of Thai folk or an urban acculturated genre is the subject of a lively debate among Thai scholars. Thai traditional music is divided into the urban court-centered "classical" tradition and various rural folk traditions. Musical elements from both categories can be found in *luk thung*, and the genre has also been influenced by the acculturated popular song genres that preceded it, such as *phleng Thai sakon, ramwong,* and *phleng chiwit*.

PHLENG THAI DOEM

Central Thai classical music is performed by percussion-based *piphat*, string-based *khrueangsai*, and *mahori* (which mixes the two). The *piphat* accompanies the dance-drama forms of *khon* (masked) and *lakhon* (non-masked). In televised and more prestigious *luk thung* performances, classical instruments such as *ranat* (Thai xylophone), *khong wong* (circle of gongs), or *so* (Thai violin) are often added to the Western-style band, thus representing a mixing of musical traditions that has been taking place since the introduction of Western music into Thailand in the nineteenth century. The difficulty of combining the roughly equidistant tuning system of classical instruments with Western harmonic forms may have contributed to the unstable tonality that exists in some early *luk thung* songs, and may be the reason why certain *luk thung* songs shift between major and minor tonality in a fashion unfamiliar to Western ears (for example, "Dao charat saeng" [Shining Star] sung by Kan Kaeosuphan).[2] However, the most significant Thai classical influence on *luk thung* has been through the adaptation of *phleng Thai doem* melodies.

The term *phleng Thai doem* (original Thai song) refers to the large Thai classical repertory. The oldest songs, which are grouped together in suites known as *rueang*, date back at least to the eighteenth century and the Ayutthaya Kingdom (1351–1767). During the reign of King Chulalongkorn, a number of royal composers began to use the techniques of *thao* composition[3] to create new versions of old songs, and as a result many of the most well-known classical melodies date from the period 1880 to 1930 (see Morton 1976, 15–16, 180–82). After the end of absolute monarchy and the disbanding of royal ensembles, the classical background of a number of Suntharaphon musicians resulted in many *Thai doem* melodies being set to ballroom dance rhythms during the late 1930s and 1940s.

The idea that *luk thung* is derived from Thai folk music whereas *luk krung* is derived from Thai court music (see Anake 1978, 65 and Lamnao 2006, 14, 17) is problematic when the significant use of *phleng Thai doem* melodies by *luk thung* composers is considered. The ability to compose new songs from classical melodies is considered a necessary skill and perhaps a rite of passage for *luk thung* songwriters. Celebrated songwriter Thinakon Thiphamat explains that when he is teaching students how to compose, he recommends that they first learn to add Thai lyrics to a foreign melody and next learn to adapt a *phleng Thai doem* with modern lyrics (Surin et al. 2004, 114). He stresses, however, when the melody is altered it must be done with care, taking intonation into account.

The following are just a few examples of *luk thung* songs that have made use of *Thai doem* melodies: "Ramthon," by Benjamin, follows the classical melody "Phama ramkhwan" (Burmese Axe Dance) as does Suraphon's "Phama chon kai" (Burmese Fighting Cock), and Chai Mueangsing used "Mon du dao"[4] to write "Luksao khrai no" (Whose Daughter?). In 1976, Cholathi Thanthong wrote a pair of *phleng kae*—"Kin arai thueng suai" (What Do You Eat to Get So Beautiful?) for Sayan Sanya, and "Kin khao kap namphrik" (Eat Rice with Chili Sauce) for Phongsri Woranut, using the tune "Ton worachet." Even "Srinuan," one of the revered *phleng rueang*, has been imported into the field of popular song. There are at least three *luk krung* adaptations: "Srinuan" by Charin Nanthanakhon, Suntharaphon's "Ramwong thewi Srinuan," and "Wasana khonchon" (Poor Man's Chance) sung by Rungruedi Phaengphongsai; and two *luk thung* adaptations: Benjamin's "Nok khao, Nok rao" (Your Bird, My Bird) and "Sutthai thi Krungthep" (Last Time in Bangkok), sung by Sunari Ratchasima and written by Jithakon Buaniyom.

The convoluted history of Thai melodies is illustrated by three famous *luk thung* songs that make extensive use of the *phleng thao* "Khaek Mon Bangkhunphrom"—"Rak chang thi Bangpakong" (Love Fails at Bangpakong) by Sotsai Rungphothong, and Soraphet Phinyo's pair of songs "Sansani ni cham" (Sansani Escapes) sung by Nong Nut Duangchiwan and "Tam ha Sansani" (Looking for Sansani) sung by Soraphet. This Rattanakosin-era melody, written in 1910 by Prince Paribatra (pronounced Boriphat) Sukhumbhand, has been used in other songs, most notably the *luk krung* standard "Chup yoei chan" (Kiss the Moon). Soraphet used the entire melody for his verse and chorus whereas Sotsai employed it only in the chorus section. In fact Sotsai adopted the verse of "Rak chang thi Bangpakong" from an Ayutthaya-period *phleng Thai doem* known as "Thale ba" (Crazy Sea).

If *Thai doem* melodies are just as likely to be found in *luk thung* as in *luk krung*, this suggests that melody is far less important than arrangement, vocal style, and lyrical subject matter in delineating between the genres. The difference between *luk thung* and *luk krung* interpretations of *Thai doem* melodies can be observed by comparing Chinakon Krailat's version of "Lao duang duean" (Lao Full Moon),[5] with a cha-cha beat and *luk thung*-style brass arrangement, to Got Jakrapan's recent slow and sentimental piano, *so-u*, and *khim*[6] version.[7]

Chinakon is perhaps the best-known singer for adaptations of *phleng Thai doem*. He achieved the status of national artist on the strength of his popular *luk thung* versions of classical melodies. His signature song, "Yo yot Phra Lo" (In Praise of Phra Lo),[8] released in 1967, demonstrates the method of adaptation used by many *luk thung* songwriters. Renowned *luk thung* and *luk krung* composer Phayong Mukda borrowed the melody of "Lao krathop mai" (Lao hitting poles), originally a folk song from Surin in northeastern Thailand used to accompany the traditional bamboo dance. Written in the Lao *samniang* it is an example of a *phleng phuenban* (songs of the village; i.e., folk songs) melody that has been adopted into the *phleng Thai doem* repertoire. The first half of the song is an extended *lae*-style[9] introduction. The second half of the song is identical in length to the original melody, but Phayong made a number of adaptations in order to create a popular song. The first three bars are used as an instrumental introduction, while the "la la" riff is sung by female chorus and repeated as a break between the song's verses.

Part of the song is sung as a female solo, and an instrumental break is created by omitting a number of vocal syllables.

In the case of "Yo yot phra lo," Phayong has adopted the complete melody of "Lao krathop mai" into a through-composed song.

For example, the opening vocal line (above) is turned into an instrumental introduction. It is possible, however, for *luk thung* songwriters to borrow shorter sections of *Thai doem* melodies, even down to single phrases. "Narak ching Nong" (You're So Cute) by Phloen Phromdaen uses a section of "Lao krathop mai" as a verse sandwiched between two newly composed melodies. The first of these, which acts as a chorus, is an arpeggiated melody that utilizes Phloen's wide vocal range.

A MUSICAL ANALYSIS OF LUK THUNG'S FORM AND DEVELOPMENT

Na＿en du＿ching no chao   Nat＿ khuen chao＿ ching no uan＿

Unlike Phayong, who uses the "la la" riff as a recurring break, Phloen's singing fills in these gaps. A particularly interesting example is when the riff is incorporated into the main melody:

raem＿ Song - khla wan   waem khong khlai＿＿ tha - nun＿

In the third section Phloen departs from the "Lao krathop mai" melody into a second newly composed melody. The basic borrowed melody is then restated before the chorus returns. Although the approaches of the two composers are different, in both cases the *Thai doem* material has been transformed into an effective popular song.

LIKE

Like is a theatrical form which has blended central Thai folk traditions with classical elements. Originating during the reign of King Chulalongkorn, *like* blended Muslim chant (*dike*), Buddhist recitation (*suat phramalai*), and Malay chanting (*suat khaek*) into a new popular declamatory style. Musical accompaniment is usually provided by a small *piphat* orchestra featuring the *ranat ek*, drums such as *taphon*, and percussion instruments such as *ching* and *chap*. Dialogue is declaimed in a nasal style of chanting similar to that found in many kinds of central Thai village songs. There is a long-standing tradition of *like* singers moving into *luk thung*. Saneh Komarachun, who produced the *phleng chiwit* "Like kanmueang" (*Like* Politics), performed with the famous Homhuan troupe of Homhuan Naksiri in the early 1950s. During that decade Phon Phirom, Buppha Saichon, Chaichana Bunnachot, and Jiu Phijit all entered the *luk thung* industry via *like*. Later, during the 1960s, Phiset Saengphet, Phaithun Khanthong, Raphi Rueanphet, and Roeng Pirom also came from *like* into *luk thung* (Siriphon 2004, 440). Modern *like* star Chaiya Mitchai (see figure 5.3) also sings *luk thung* and is famous for the *like* costumes and customs in his shows.

Some standard *like* songs have been used in *luk thung*. For example, Phaibun Butkhan's "Like chiwit" (*Like* Life) appeared in 1954 and was sung by Pricha Bunyakiat and Siri Khumyu. In this song Phaibun alternates sections of *Thai sakon* melody with "Ranikroeng," a *like* song often used to accompany love scenes. Dokdin Sueasanga composed "Ranikroeng" by adapting the *Thai doem* melody "Mon khruan" (Mon Person Sighs) which had long been used to accompany sad scenes ("Like song khrueang," 1994).

PHLENG THAI SAKON AND PHLENG CHIWIT

By the 1950s *phleng Thai sakon* had divided into the subgenres of *phleng chiwit* (life songs), sometimes known as *phleng talat* (market songs), and *phleng phudi* (good people's songs). After 1964 these two subgenres became known, respectively, as *luk thung* and *luk krung*, although it is a more accurate generalization to consider *luk thung* of the 1960s a hybrid of *phleng chiwit* and *ramwong*, and *luk krung* a hybrid of *phleng phudi* and Western pop.

Life songs usually use the ballad form to comment satirically on society. For example, in "Samlo khaen" (Resentful Pedicab) (see chapter five) Saneh Komarachun affects a rural accent to take on the character of a *samlo* (pedicab) driver complaining about the harshness of life in Bangkok. While this may sound like the plot of a typical *luk thung* song, *phleng chiwit* differ significantly from *luk thung* in terms of the number of verses (up to eight), melody and instrumentation (highly Westernized), and vocal character (lack of *uean*).

Some *luk thung* songs are described in the Thai literature as having *Thai sakon* melodies. This may perhaps mean that the melody is borrowed from a Thai song composed in a Western style, which appears to be the case in the above example of Phaibun Butkhan's "Like chiwit." A two-part series of songs titled "Tasi kamsuan" (Weeping Eyes),[10] also written by Phaibun and sung by Khamron Sambunnanon in 1955, uses *phleng Thai sakon* melodies interspersed with *lamtat* sections.

RAMWONG

Many *luk thung* songs from the 1950s and 1960s are based around an ostinato of two to four bars played monophonically by bass, piano or organ, and sometimes saxophone. This ostinato structure is a feature of *ramwong*, a dance genre manufactured by Phibunsongkhram (Phibun) and Wichit

A MUSICAL ANALYSIS OF LUK THUNG'S FORM AND DEVELOPMENT

Wathakan during the Second World War to rival the popularity of Western dances. The strong beat and lack of syncopation indicate that these ostinatos may have been influenced to some degree by Western brass band marches. A simple *ramwong* ostinato can be heard in "Ram toei" (fig. 2.1) by Benjamin, the most influential figure in *ramwong*. More-developed ostinatos can be heard in later hits of Suraphon Sombatjaroen such as "Nak chai" (Heavy Heart) and "Damnoen cha" (fig. 2.1), which is unusually slow for *ramwong*, and Khamron Sambunnanon's "Wao Lao" (Isan language for "Speak Lao").

FIGURE 2.1. Ostinatos from (1) "Ram toei" (Benjamin), (2) "Nak chai," and (3) "Damnoen cha" (Suraphon Sombatjaroen).

As discussed in chapter one, *ramwong*, as popularized by Benjamin, could almost be counted as an Isan genre and a precursor to the *luk thung Isan* genre of the 1970s and 1980s. Isan influence can be seen in the use of solo *khaen* introductions, *lam klon* poetry, pentatonic minor scale, fast tempo, repeated lines, and an answering chorus. Most of these features can be observed in the most popular song by an Isan artist during the 1960s—Saksri Sriakson's "Phuyai Li" (1961). A significant number of *phleng talat* and *luk thung* songs from the 1950s and 1960s employ what is described as a *"ramwong* beat," which is a fast rhythm, usually around 140 to 150 beats per minute (bpm). However, sometimes the beat seems slow because the first and third beats are stressed.

Analysis of original recordings from the period 1948–69 shows that the *ramwong* style and rhythm actually became more popular after the genre was subsumed into *luk thung*. Over 25 percent of *luk thung* songs from the 1960s are in *ramwong* style. This trend fed directly into the beginnings of *luk thung Isan* as a subgenre. For example, Saksayam Phetchomphu's "Hak sao ramwong" (Love the *Ramwong* Girl) and Phloen Phromdaen's "Nueng nai laem thong" (One of the Best) are virtually identical to the pentatonic minor pattern established by Benjamin's "Ram toei." The influence of *ramwong* can still be heard in modern *luk thung*. The fast tempo of *ramwong* mixes with funk in Nik Niranam's versions of Benjamin classics such as "Ram toei" and "Ai Chan." The riff from Benjamin's "Sat cha khong chai" is quoted in the chorus of Kratae's recent hit song "Chong ya mong" (Stir Balm). Through *ramwong*, recordings of *molam klon* made in the 1940s and 1950s, and then *luk thung Isan*, there is an unbroken line of direct Isan influence on Thai popular music from World War II to the present.

Phleng Phuenban (Folk Song)

As previously mentioned, many Thai authors regard *luk thung* as updated folk music. Even those who stress the urban origins of *luk thung* acknowledge that several characteristics of Thai folk song are also defining characteristics of *luk thung*. For example, Nidhi Eoseewong (1985, 95) asserts that the only definite way to differentiate between a *luk thung* and *luk krung* song is the folk singing styles of the former. Siriphon (2004, 27, 327) agrees that *luk kho* (vibrato) is a distinguishing feature of *luk thung* and adds that suggestive banter and the common *luk thung* practice of writing pairs of songs (*phleng kae*) are also characteristics adopted from *phleng phuenban*.

Phleng kae or *phleng to* may be translated as "dueling songs" in which male and female performers sing the same melody but with different lyrics, the female usually responding to the male's criticism. This type of gendered conversation through song is a feature of many Thai folk genres. As discussed in chapter one, Suraphon Sombatjaroen popularized the practice by singing dueling songs with his female protégés before the notorious public slanging match through song between Suraphon, Phongsri Woranut, Jinda Sombatjaroen, and Benjamin. Arguably, the most famous *phleng kae* are Suraphon's "Luem mai long" (Cannot Forget) and "Nai wa mai luem" (Don't Forget) sung by Phongsri Woranut, and Cholathi Thanthong's compositions for Sayan Sanya and Phongsri Woranut, "Kin arai thueng suai" and "Kin khao kap namphrik," respectively.

A MUSICAL ANALYSIS OF LUK THUNG'S FORM AND DEVELOPMENT

CENTRAL THAI FOLK TRADITIONS

The most significant folk influences on *luk thung* are the central Thai *phleng lae* and *lamtat* and the northeastern *molam* tradition. Although all Thai folk genres use pentatonic scales, the roughly equidistant tuning of central Thai genres contrasts greatly with the natural pentatonic minor scale of *molam*.

Traditional central Thai *lae* is derived from Pali incantations of the *Vessantara Jataka*, which were organized into poems by royal scholars between 1602 and 1627. During the Ayutthaya period the royal *lae* spread outside the palace and absorbed elements of secular tunes, but it continued to have a religious purpose. Ceremonial retellings of the *Vessantara Jataka* are still presented in temples throughout central Thailand using *lae*-style recitation accompanied by a traditional *piphat* ensemble. After 1958 *lae* became an important melodic influence on the makeup of *luk thung*, for reasons that are still unclear. However, it is quite possible that the 1957 coup, which launched the highly restrictive and royalist Sarit and Thanom regime, encouraged songwriters to make their compositions more 'Thai'. The fervent Buddhism of performers such as Chaichana Bunnachot, Waiphot Phetsuphan, and Phon Phirom (who spent the final forty years of his life as a monk) was probably significant, as was the general process of hybridization between *lae*, *lamtat*, *isaeo*, and *like* during the 1960s (see Phrakruvinaitorn et al. 2009, 485–86).

The term *lae* is now commonly used to refer to the subgenre of *luk thung* songs with melodies derived either wholly or in part from traditional central Thai folk genres. The first recorded song of this subgenre was Phaibun Butkhan's "Dok din thawin fa" (Flower in the Dirt Desires the Sky), sung by Chaichana Bunnachot in 1958, when he was just sixteen. The song begins with a brief slow *Thai sakon*-style introduction before passing into a faster extended *lae* section. Chaichana himself began to write in the *lae* style, and "Sam pi thi rai nang" (Three Years without a Woman) became a major success for the young Waiphot Phetsuphan, who soon became known as the "King of *Lae*." Other examples of this subgenre include "Mae khrua tua yang" (Exemplary Chef) written by Jiu Phijit and sung by Khwanchit Sriprachan, and Chaichana Bunyachot's "Lae Chuchok" (named for Chuchok, the colorful, inept villain of the *Vessantara Jataka*), which is described as *lae sakon* on the album cover, presumably indicating *lae* that has been adapted to Western tuning. Phaibun Butkhan's "Bangkok krung kao ton nueng" (Old City of Bangkok, Part One) features a slow and stately *kroen* or herald section in which Chaichana recites the full name of Bangkok before launching into the accompanied *lae* section. A typical *lae* introduction and melody with percussion accompaniment can also be heard in Suraphon's "Sang wiman" (Build a Palace).[11] *Lae* is considered extremely difficult to sing, and, for capable *luk thung* singers, it fulfils the virtuosic role served by cadenza in opera—Waeng (2002, 199) records that Benjamin and Suraphon chose to sing in *lae* style to compete with one another in order to demonstrate their skill. However, the best *lae luk thung* singers are those with a folk song or *like* background—such as Chaichana and Khwanchit. At present, Thosaphon Himaphan is the undisputed king of *lae*, but there is not as much competition as in the past.

Lamtat (cutting songs), is a music-theater genre which combines sections of chanted rhythmic dialogue split between two groups of men and women with combined group choruses, accompanied by *rammana lamtat* (Indian drum), *ching, chap,* and *krap*. *Phleng isaeo* are similar to *lamtat*, but are faster and require greater skill at improvising poems. *Lamtat* singing is derived from *suat khaek*, or Malay chanting, introduced by Malay prisoners during the reign of King Rama III (1824–51). In the popular theater, the original Islamic religious chanting was transformed into secular singing in central Thai language with a Malay melody (Ubonrat 2000, 9). "Khao Phra Wihan haeng khwam lang," written by Phaibun Butkhan and sung by Khamron Sambunnanon, uses a *lamtat* melody. Surin Phaksiri's "Rup lo thom pai" (Extremely Handsome),[12] sung by Buppha Saichon, is a mix of *lamtat* and Western slow rhythm (Surin et al. 2004, 35).

Phleng choi are sung at a very fast tempo, with clapping as the only accompaniment. "Kap khao phetchakhat" (Deadly Food),[13] written by Jiu Phijit and sung by Khwanchit Sriprachan, is a good example of *phleng choi* in *luk thung* (Siriphon 2004, 432). Niyom Marayat's "Rup lo khoi mia" (Handsome Man Seeks a Wife), sung by Waiphot Phetsuphan, mixes a sloweddown *phleng choi* melody with percussion, piano, and saxophone.

Phleng phuang malai (garland songs) are sung in a circle by separate groups of males and females and accompanied by clapping. *Luk thung* adaptations include Waiphot Phetsuphan's "Mae phuang malai"[14] (in folk genres the lead singers are given the titles of *mae*, "mother," and *pho*, "father"), Chalong Karaket's "Phuang malai," also sung by Waiphot, and Phaibun Butkhan's "Sakit chai dao" sung by Phraiwan Lukphet. *Klong yao* (long drums) refers to a marching drum ensemble often used to accompany dancing processions, which also include *chap lek* and *chap yai* (small and large cymbals), *krap* (woodblocks), *ching* (metal castanet), and *mong* (small gong). Although it probably originated in Burma and can be found throughout Thailand, it is today most popular in Isan (Miller 1998, 303). Some *luk thung* songs use a rhythm described as *klong yao*, such as Suraphon's "Luk thung klong yao," which seems to have been recorded live using a drum troupe and vocal chorus.

Other types of central Thai folk song that are now extinct can be found in *luk thung*. The melody of Chaichana Bunnachot's "Chom khao" (Visiting a Mountain) is derived from a *phleng aeo khlao so* (Anake 1978, 71). The slow tempo *phleng ruea*, or courtship songs between boatloads of men and women, can be heard in Waiphot Phetsuphan's "Phai ruea kiao sao" (Paddling a Boat to Woo a Girl)[15] and Phongsri Woranut's answering song "Phai ruea kae kiao," both of which were included in the 1964 television show *Phleng Lukthung*. Pradit Uttamang's "Kiao nang ban na" sung by Chaichana Bunnachot combines luk thung and phleng ruea sections. *Phleng talat* adaptations of *phleng ruea*, such as Suraphon Thonawanik's "Loi ruea kiao sao" sung by Siri Khumyu and Narit Ari, date back to 1955. Perhaps one day, mediated, Westernized *luk thung* will be seen as responsible for aiding the survival of many of these folk art forms.

NORTHEASTERN FOLK TRADITIONS

Molam is traditional Lao folk music characterized by flexible pentatonic melodies derived extemporaneously from word tones. The pentatonic melodies of *molam* are a reflection of the cultural significance of the *khaen*, a Lao free-reed mouth organ with a vertical arrangement of bamboo pipes, which usually produces the notes ABCDEFG (compatible with Western tuning), although *khaen* in any key are now available.[16] There are two common resultant scales, *lam thang san* (GACDE) and *lam thang yao* (ACDEG). For those accustomed to Western music, this means that there is a strong major feel to *lam klon*, which is primarily *thang san*, and a strong minor feel to *lam phloen*, which is always *thang yao*. A significant feature of *molam* is the *khaen* introduction known as *kroen* (herald)[17] whereby the full chord of the song is held for five to ten seconds before the player improvises a free metered section known as *lam long* before the melodic pattern begins in duple meter. In *ramwong* and early *luk thung*, piano accordion is sometimes used to provide this introduction. For example Benjamin's "Ram toei" opens with a piano accordion extended chord and then an extemporized ornamented cadenza (poorly played) before settling into the riff. Pong Prida's "Tam Nong Toi" (Follow Miss Toi) follows the same single-chord pattern as *molam klon*, but with accordion as the main accompaniment instead of *khaen*. In *luk thung Isan* of the 1970s and 1980s, organ often imitates the sound of the khaen. The most relevant subgenres for this discussion are *lam klon, lam phuen,* and *lam phloen.*

Traditional *lam klon* is performed by a pair of singers, usually two males or a male and a female, with *khaen* accompaniment. Each singer performs for fifteen to thirty minutes, but each session consists of several poems, of approximately fifty lines each, joined together (Miller 1985, 50). This length of poem has translated easily into *luk thung*. Soraphet Phinyo has been one of the most significant figures in adapting *lam klon* melodies, especially the tune known as *lam doen,* into *luk thung,* such as in the songs "Mia pa phro Sa-u" for Somphot Duangsomphong and "Namta mia Sa-u" for Phimpha Phonsiri (see chapter three). Figure 3.11 shows examples of the adaption of *lam* singing into *luk thung prayuk*. The choruses of "Namta mia Sa-u" (bars 32–41 of stave one) and "Lop na thi Malay" (bars 32–40 of stave two) are very similar pentatonic minor improvisations on the *lam thang yao* (ACDEG) scale, with extended and ornamented final notes. Phonsak Songsaeng is well known for using another *lam klon* melody—*lam toei*—in his *luk thung molam* albums.

Lam phuen are long, sung stories either of Lao-Isan origin or based on Lao versions of the Jataka stories (the body of literature native to India concerning the previous births of the Buddha). *Nithan kom* were the short stories told by traveling monks and singers that were part of the early *molam* tradition. Isan people would tell *nithan kom* to relax after the rice harvest, to remember departed friends at funerals, or to woo mates (with witty proverbs, or *phaya*). In 1973, Miller (1985, 41) wrote that *lam phuen* would probably become extinct in northeastern Thailand within twenty years. However, the style is still performed, and abridged stories from *lam phuen* and *nithan kom* can be found in *luk thung* songs. Surin Phaksiri used the text and structure of Isan *nithan kom* to compose *luk thung* songs such as "Bong kancha" (Marijuana Bong), sung by Kawao Siangthong, and "Pha khao ma" (the name of an Isan men's loincloth), performed by Royal Sprite (Waeng 2002, 110). The original story from which Phiphat Boribun drew "Phuyai Li" (see chapter one) may also have been a *nithan kom*.

A MUSICAL ANALYSIS OF LUK THUNG'S FORM AND DEVELOPMENT

Lam phloen was originally a genre of Lao theater music, but since the 1960s it has become successful as a popular song genre. During the late 1950s and early 1960s it was influenced by *phleng talat/luk thung* singing styles and, in turn, has become the *molam* style most likely to be found in *luk thung* songs. Traditional *lam phloen* was accompanied only by *klong*, *khaen*, and *phin*, but Western instruments were added in order to compete with *luk thung* and Western rock music. *Lam phloen* can thus be thought of as a compressed version of *molam* that probably developed in response to the shorter length of mediated genres such as *ramwong* and *luk thung*— it has a light mood, and the poetic form is usually not as rigid as in *lam klon*. The standard structure is a slow ornamented introduction with liberal use of *uean* and sparse accompaniment leading into the fast main section with full *luk thung*–style instrumentation. In *lam phloen* stanzas, the ending syllable of the second line should be either a falling or low tone. If a section of singing ends on the fourth line, which has no tone, a short phrase such as "la na" is added to provide the falling or low tone. This agrees with Kobkul's (1985, 188) observation that the extension of a phrase's final syllable in some *luk thung* songs is a feature borrowed from *molam*. Kobkul does not give any examples, but there are numerous instances of *lam phloen* being adapted into *luk thung* songs, such as "Baek rak chao krung" (Carry My Love to the City Dweller) sung by Sommainoi Duangjaroen (1990). Early *luk thung* songs that used *lam phloen* style were "Yak pen nakrong" (I Want to Be a Singer) by Pong Prida, "Klon sot" (Improvised Poem) by Cho Kamcha-i, and Surin Phaksiri's "Lam kiao sao," which was sung by Kabin Mueangubon in 1967 (Waeng 2002, 315–16). Recently, leading Grammy star Tai Orathai has taken to singing *luk thung prayuk*, an example of which is the highly successful and traditionally styled song "Isan lam phloen."

Molam songs are usually written in strophic *klon* poetic form (see chapter three) without variation in the melody between verses. Phiphat Boribun recalls that by the late 1950s, *luk thung* songs typically had four verses, one of which was contrasting in melody. As related in chapter one, after attending a *molam* performance with his wife Saksri Sriakson, Phiphat imitated the style of the *molam* songs, which only had three verses and no contrasting melody, to produce "Phuyai Li." Two conclusions can be drawn from this: *luk thung* songs with the structure AAA (where A is the melody of the verse) have been influenced by *molam*, and *molam* influence dates back at least to

1959. However, Suraphon's "Namta Lao Wiang," recorded in 1953, followed Chaloemchai's compositional practice of only having three verses, which shows that *molam* influence came even earlier.

As discussed in chapter one, however, there was considerable *molam* influence on *ramwong* throughout the 1940s and 1950s and therefore on *luk thung* during the period when *ramwong* was being absorbed into *phleng talat/luk thung* (c. 1953–57). For example, before experiencing success in 1958, Pong Prida worked for a number of years in Bangkok playing the *khaen* on recordings by stars such as Suraphon Sombatjaroen. Famous *khaen* player Samai Onwong was also active in the recording and film industries during this period. On recordings from the 1950s and early 1960s, the melodies of *molam*-influenced songs were sometimes described as *phuen mueang* (local or folk), such as in "Khwanchai Khorat" (Darling of Nakhon Ratchasima) by Chainarong Bunnachot, "Soeng bang fai" written by Prasit Nakhonphanom and sung by Waiphot Phetsuphan, and Saksri Sriakson's "Chai nam kham khong," which has slow and fast sections that sound like *ramwong*. The development of *luk thung Isan* during the 1970s made it increasingly possible for *molam* performers such as Dao Bandon and Phophin Phonsuwan to move into the *luk thung* industry.

In Isan, both *soeng* and *fon* are used to describe the style of dancing employed by non-singing performers on the *molam* stage. *Soeng* has developed into a group dance particularly used for the *bun bang fai* (rocket) festival. It is characterized by rhythmic hopping and raised hands accompanied by up-tempo instrumental *molam* and includes participant exclamations and responses (see Waiphot Phetsuphan's "Soeng huea suang"). The melody from the traditional "Soeng bang fai" is used in Saksri Sriakson's "Sao soeng bang fai" and also in Chai Mueangsing's "Kusanaen thaen maen." "Khun Lamyai" (Miss Lamyai),[18] sung by Luknok Suphaphon, and Rock Salaeng's "Motorsai hang" (Broken-Down Motorbike) are *soeng* mixed with *lam phloen* (Surin 2004, 37). That *soeng* and *ramwong* rhythms are often interchangeable demonstrates the high degree of Isan influence on *ramwong*. For example, "Salawan ramwong," sung by Waiphot Phetsuphan and written by Phongsak Chantharukkha, is in *soeng* rhythm and, like the earlier *ramwong* songs of Benjamin, features extensive use of *khaen*. Furthermore, the call-and-response so typical of Benjamin's *ramwong* songs is almost certainly derived from *soeng*.

Although Buddhist monks are prohibited from singing, there is a tradition in northeastern Thailand of sacred texts and sermons composed in *klon* poetic form recited in a melodic chanting style known as *thet lae Isan*. Although not from Isan himself, Waiphot Phetsuphan was the pioneer of incorporating Isan *lae* into *luk thung*, in songs such as "La Bangkok klap Isan" (Leave Bangkok to Return to Isan),[19] which features ramwong ostinato and khaen style piano accordion, and "La kon Isan" (Farewell Isan) from the early 1960s. Another example of Isan *lae* in *luk thung* is "Lae son ying" (Sermon to Teach Women) by Dao Bandon, who was a talented *thet lae* preacher before he became a singer.

Kantruem is the folk music of the Isan provinces closest to Cambodia—Surin, Buri Ram, and Si Sa Ket. It features lyrics sung in northern Khmer and Isan and, during the 1980s, developed a folk rock variant (similar to the development of *molam sing*). The rhythm is strong and fast and the signature sound is that of the *tro* (bowed fiddle), the Khmer version of the *so duang*. *Kantruem* has influenced the wider Thai music industry as one element of *rock Isan*, a blend of *luk thung*, *molam*, *phleng phuea chiwit*, and *kantruem*. According to Surin (2004, 41), the word *rock* in the name of this genre does not mean that the music uses rock rhythm, but it became common usage through the foundational band Rock Khong Khoi. The influence of this band has been so great that numerous groups such as Rock Sadoet, Rock Sadao, and Rock Joko have appeared, cementing the usage of the term *rock Isan*. One of the best-known songs of the genre is "Motorsai hang" by Rock Salaeng.[20] Several *luk thung Isan* stars have produced *kantruem*-influenced songs. Surin-born Chaloemphon Malakham, who came into the industry in 1985, has had an extensive career performing *kantruem* as well as *molam* and *luk thung*. Kantruem has remained popular; for example, in 2009, "Sao kantruem" (*Kantruem* Girl) was a big hit for Phai Phongsathon.

NORTHERN AND SOUTHERN FOLK TRADITIONS

Phleng luk thung kham mueang is northern-style *luk thung*, which may incorporate northern instruments such as *pi chum* (free reed pipe), *sueng* (plucked lute), and *salo* (bowed lute) and elements of northern folk genres such as *phleng so* and *phleng chia kom*. *Phleng so* is a repartee genre which uses a range of standard pentatonic melodies adapted for the particular texts. During the 1990s, Phensi Phongsi and Banyen Kaeosiangthong were the biggest names in the Chiang Mai music scene, incorporating Northern words and folk instruments into otherwise standard *luk thung*. The music of such popular contemporary performers as Kratae and Liu Ajariya has a strong northern lyrical and occasionally musical flavor.

Southern *luk thung* covers a large group of performers and songs, often with an Indian or Arabic flavor absorbed from nearby Malaysia, but also drawing on two significant southern folk musical styles. *Manora*, or *nora*, is a kind of dance-drama, named after a famous story of Indian origin about a heavenly bird-maiden, Manora, who marries a human prince. *Nora* instrumental melodies are highly ornamented and are based on the seven-tone scale of the *pi chawa* (double-reed oboe, used to accompany muay thai) or either *so-u* or *so duang* (two types of fiddle) with rhythmic accompaniment provided by *khong khu* (gong) and *klong chatri* (pair of small barrel drums played with sticks). As with central Thai village songs, *manora* singing is declamatory but is centered around one pitch with a narrow melodic range. Nophanan Khwanprapha and Rom Sithamarat entered the *luk thung* industry after careers in *manora*. Rom, otherwise known as Nai Roi Juinum, was a *nora* performer from Nakhon Si Thammarat who turned to singing in the Srinuan Sombatjaroen Band.

Nang talung is a shadow puppet theater genre popular in southern Thailand, similar in character to Malaysian and Indonesian *wayang kulit*. The musical accompaniment is very similar to that of *manora*. According to Surin Phaksiri, Luan Khwantham (who was himself a southerner) adapted the musical style of *nang talung* for the Suntharaphon band to create *talung*, a rhythm that purported to represent southern Thailand. Luan also designed dance steps and, for a short time, *talung* became the most popular rhythm in Thailand (Surin et al. 2004, 36). Juliam Kingthong and his daughter Salika Kingthong entered the *luk thung* industry via *nang talung*. Examples of *talung* in *luk thung* include Kingkaeo Srisakhon's "Ya luem Khorat" (Don't Forget Khorat)[21] and Suraphon's "Chan chop talung" (I Like *Talung*).

Phleng Phuea Chiwit (Songs for Life)

Songs for life is a genre that developed in the 1970s, combining Thai folk melodies and singing technique with the folk-rock coming from the United States. Myers-Moro (1986, 103) observes that *luk thung* was strongly influential in the development of *phleng phuea chiwit*, and many songs-for-life musicians originally performed in bands that played *luk thung* (Vater 2003). *Phuea chiwit* has influenced the subgenre of *rock Isan* (see discussion of *kantruem above*) and *nu luk thung*[22] performers, such as Vit Hyper and Ke Napho, who employ the picked guitar accompaniment typical of songs for life.

Western Elements in *Luk Thung*

The brass bands introduced by foreign military advisors during the nineteenth century contributed directly to the development of *phleng Thai sakon*. Early in the reign of King Chulalongkorn (1868–1910), Thai military bands began to perform traditional Thai melodies on brass instruments with simple Western harmonizations. These songs were often in the style of Western marches or dances such as the quadrille, and the brass bands gradually became an acceptable symbol of modernization in the Thai way (Ware 2006, 98–100). The very early *phleng talat* songs of Khamron Sambunnanon from the 1940s and 1950s often have brass accompaniments that sound very much like a brass band playing a march. Today the brass section, whether synthesized or made up of actual brass instruments, is a standard element of the modern *luk thung* sound.

The structural form (number of verses or sections) of *luk thung* and *luk krung* songs is often similar and reflects their common ancestry. The AABA structure, so pervasive in *phleng Thai sakon* before the 1960s, was almost certainly adopted from Tin Pan Alley songs. This form has remained popular with Thai songwriters. (See for example Soraphet Phinyo's "Num na khao sao na kluea.")[23]

The waltz, slowfox, foxtrot, and one-step were both known and part of typical dance performance in Asia before 1935. In post-1936 Thailand, the position of the Suntharaphon band as a harbinger and molder of public taste quickly cemented the position of ballroom rhythms such as the waltz, foxtrot, tango, beguine, and rumba within *phleng Thai sakon*. Eminent songwriter Surin Phaksiri (2004, 20) observes that the majority of today's *luk thung* songs fit into one of three rhythmic categories: beguine, cha-cha, and *soeng*. This begs the question as to why the beguine, introduced into Thailand during the 1940s, would still be a significant part of *luk thung* seventy years on when the other rhythms from that period are not. Precise definitions of the dance terms are sometimes difficult to determine and it is possible that Surin is using the term beguine to also cover slow and bolero rhythms, which are far more frequently cited than the beguine on *luk thung* record labels from the 1960s.

The fact that virtually all Thai classical music is in duple meter may have contributed to the scarcity of waltz and 6/8 dance rhythms in *luk thung*. Although waltzes were extremely popular in Thailand during the 1930s and 1940s, the slow three-beat rhythm is more often found in Westernized *luk krung* than in *luk thung*. That tango rhythms are common in *phleng Thai sakon* but almost non-existent in *luk thung* possibly indicates that the rhythm quickly lost popularity to the mambo and the cha-cha during the 1950s. The tango rhythm most often encountered in *phleng Thai sakon* is moderately slow and features a stressed final beat, with cells such as $\frac{4}{4}$ ♩ ♩ ♪ ♪ or $\frac{4}{4}$ ♩ ♩ ♩ ♫ .

The Thai Bolero is approximately 65 bpm, sometimes with a suggestion of swing, such as in "Ro rak" (Waiting for Love) by Prani Thanasriropkun. Phongsri Woranut's "Lok chan khao laeo" (You Tricked Me) features the rhythmic cell $\frac{4}{4}$ ♫♫ ♫ ♫♫♫ and is described as bolero on the album cover. Another interesting example is "La sao khao krung" (Farewell to Girl Going to the City) by Chaichana Bunnachot, which employs a truncated bolero rhythm in slow triple time: $\frac{3}{4}$ ♫♫ ♫ ♫ . Bolero rhythms can also be found in Kongphet Kaennakhon's "Hom klin dok kham tai" (Fragrant Cassie Flower) and Sonkhiri Sriprajuap's "Nao lom thi Renu" (Cold Wind at Renu),[24] both written by Surin Phaksiri, and "Raeng ngan khao niao" (Sticky-Rice Labor) by Cholathi Thanthong and sung by Jintara Phunlap, which is described as bolero *phuen mueang*.

Mambo is an upbeat adaptation of the Cuban danzón that became popular throughout the world during the 1950s. In 1950 Perez Prado's "Que rico el mambo" was marketed in the United States under the title of "Mambo jambo" and both the song and Prado became an international craze. Always keen to experiment, Benjamin produced a Thai version of "Mambo jambo" in 1951, and the mambo beat remained popular in Thailand throughout the decade, until the cha-cha finally gained dominance. The influence of Perez Prado can be seen in the names of bands from that decade such as Krungthep Mambo (Bangkok Mambo), Juea Rangraengjit's Mambo Rock, and Racha Mambo (King of Mambo). Racha Mambo was

A MUSICAL ANALYSIS OF LUK THUNG'S FORM AND DEVELOPMENT

led by saxophonist Suthep Sonwijit (and featured a fourteen-year-old Phongsri Woranut for a short period in 1954, and later, in 1957–58, the young star Chai Chatri). One example of a mambo-beat *luk thung* song is "Mae taeng rom pai" (Smooth-Skinned Young Woman)[25] sung by Chaichana Bunnachot, which has a medium-fast tempo with a rhythm of ♩. ♪♩♩ . During the second half of the 1950s, mambo was gradually fused with *ramwong*. In "Farang Mueang Thai," listed as *ramwong* on the label, Benjamin parodies the mambo craze in a pastiche of phrases from various languages. The always-competitive Suraphon Sombatjaroen responded with "Mot fai mambo," which is also listed as *ramwong*. During the late 1950s Suraphon also used mambo rhythm for songs such as "Khon khi mao" (Drunkard) and "Ban ni chan rak" (I Love This House) but he did not persevere with the style beyond 1960.

The cha-cha, essentially a slowed-down mambo beat, was invented by Cuban violinist Enrique Jorrin in 1954. In 1955 Perez Prado had an American number-one hit with a cha-cha version of the French song "Cherry Pink and Apple-Blossom White." That same year Phayong Mukda translated the song into Thai and released it as "Tai rom choeri" (Under the Shade of the Cherry Tree) sung by Srisa-ang Trinet. The record describes the rhythm as mambo, which may indicate that the cha-cha had not yet become part of the Thai consciousness. Suntharaphon's "Mai mi wang" (Hopeless), which came out around 1958, was described as "mambo cha-cha." Performed by the band's famous quartet of singers Woranut Ari, Winai Julabusapa, Loet Prasomsap, and Somyot Thasanaphan, this song may represent the changeover point in popularity between the two rhythms. Phayong Mukda produced a 78-rpm record in 1954 with an A-side featuring "Kliat chai khi hueng" (I Hate Jealous Men), listed as cha-cha, and a B-side of "Calypso ma laeo (Calypso Has Come). The popular band Bangkok Cha-Cha-Cha, which was led by Chuthima Suwannarat, also dates from 1958. This year corresponds with the change in the music of Suraphon Sombatjaroen and Benjamin, from *ramwong* to the style that would come to be called *luk thung*.

Usually referred to in Thai as *sam cha* (three chas) and sometimes by Isan people as calypso (Waeng 2002, 488), the cha-cha has become so synonymous with *luk thung* that, according to Surin (2004, 35), "Thais think it is a native Thai beat." The beat of most cha-cha *luk thung* songs is around 120 bpm, but the rhythm can be made faster and slower and can be mixed with folk rhythms such as *ramwong*, *soeng*, and *talung*.

A MUSICAL ANALYSIS OF LUK THUNG'S FORM AND DEVELOPMENT

The most common rhythmic cell in *sam cha luk thung* is $\frac{4}{4}$ ♪♩ ♪♩♬ . For example, Suraphon Sombatjaroen's "Hong pak hak" (Swan with a Broken Beak) and "Huachai phom wang" (My Empty Heart) are in medium-fast cha-cha rhythm and both feature the rhythmic cell $\frac{4}{4}$ ♪♩ ♪♩♬ . In the introduction to "Hong pak hak" the rhythmic cell is actually $\frac{4}{4}$ ♬ ♪♩♩ , which may indicate a tango rhythm, but it reverts to the standard cha-cha rhythm when the singing begins. Soraphet Phinyo's "Lop na thi Malay" (with a tempo of 122 bpm) features a slightly different cha-cha rhythmic cell, $\frac{4}{4}$ ♪♩ ♪♩ ♪♩ ♪♩ , which also happens to be the most common bass rhythm used in *molam*.

The cha-cha is dominant in Phongsri Woranut's "Bangkok lok luang" (Deceitful Bangkok) and "Luk khoei phu kwang khwang" (Influential Son-in-Law) by Chaichana Bunnachot, along with cha-cha rhythmic cadences. Typical rhythmic cadences are found in four *sam-cha luk thung* songs: "Thahan ken phlat song" (Private Second Class), written by Surin Phaksiri for Sonchai Mekwichian, Soraphet Phinyo's "Num na khao, sao na kluea" (Rice-Farming Boy, Salt-Farming Girl), "O.S. ro rak" (Emergency Volunteer Waiting for Love), composed by Surin Phaksiri for Saksayam Phetchomphu, and "Nang kwak maha sane" (Welcome Idol Attracts), written by Phongsak Chantharukkha and sung by Sayan Sanya.

FIGURE 2.2. Rhythmic cadences from four *sam cha luk thung* songs: (1) "Thahan ken phlat song," (2) "Num na khao, sao na kluea," (3) "O.S. ro rak," and (4) "Nang kwak maha sane."

A MUSICAL ANALYSIS OF LUK THUNG'S FORM AND DEVELOPMENT

Phleng luk thung is sometimes translated as *Thai country music*, and some Thai writers claim that significant influence from American country music can be found in *luk thung*. For example, Lamnao (2006, 16) suggests that "some singing styles of Western country music are similar to some Thai folk music singing styles, and these were easily adopted into *pleng luk thung*." Certainly American country contributed to the naming of *luk thung* (see chapter one) and performers' styles of dress, but lasting musical influence is more difficult to substantiate.

The subgenre of *phleng ho* features yodeling and is clearly influenced by American country and western. However, in terms of musical characteristics, the subgenre rests more with the category of *luk krung* than *luk thung*. One such song is "Prakai Duean" (Shining Moon), sung by the "King of *Phleng Ho* in Thailand," Phet Phanomrung; the Thai lyrics are the only feature that distinguishes it from an American yodeling song. The voice is highly cultured, lacking any nasal delivery or *uean*. The most lasting contribution of the brief craze for *phleng ho* was the use of Hawaiian guitar. "Khun nai chai bun" by Jiraphan Wiraphong features a Hawaiian guitar solo as well as clarinet. A recent *phleng ho* by Mangpor Chonticha, "Sao luk thung" (Country Girl), is very much a standard fast *luk thung* song until the yodeling interlude when Hawaiian guitar also appears.[26]

FIGURE 2.3. Phet Phanomrung. (Peter Garrity)

Perhaps the influence of country and western contributed to the change from electrified *ramwong* to *luk thung*. Benjamin borrowed the melody of Hank Williams's 1952 hit "Jambalaya" for his song "Chamdai mai la." Suraphon's songs such as "Hong pak hak" and "Huachai phom wang," which sound distinctly different from his *ramwong*-style songs, combine cha-cha beat with elements of country and western, such as off-the-beat accompaniment, piano accordion, cowbell, and bass that accentuates chord changes rather than ostinato. "Chan khiang thoe" (Together with You), sung by Buppha Saichon and probably written by Surin Phaksiri, features Hawaiian guitar over a cha-cha beat. Despite these few examples, however, it seems that American country and western did not easily blend with Thai melodies but rather was imported as a distinct genre.

Suang Santi's "Mao hai luem mia" (Drunkard Forgets His Wife), and "Phu ying yai phak song" (The Great Man, Part Two), and "Kao roi rong cham nam," (Nine Hundred Pawn Shops)[27] along with its phleng kae "Kao roi khwam rakam" (Nine Hundred Regrets),[28] sung by Tueanjai Bunphraraksa, employ musical elements that were popular in the spaghetti westerns of the late 1960s, such as twanging guitar, solo trumpet, gunfire sound effects, and whistling. Perhaps the best example of American country being successfully blended into *luk thung* is in the fingerpicked guitar film songs of Rungphet Laemsing, such as "Fon duean hok" (Rain in the Sixth Month) written by Phaibun Butkhan and rerecorded in the 1970s.

Composers such as Benjamin, Suraphon, Phiphat Boribun, and Phayong Mukda, who produced songs in all the major genres (*phleng Thai sakon, ramwong, luk thung,* and *luk krung*), were adept at following the latest international trends. Rock 'n' roll crazes such as the mashed potato and watusi almost immediately reached Thailand, shown respectively by popular songs from 1962 such as Phiphat Boribun's "Thing Nong" (Leave Her) sung by Sa-ang Thip and "Phuyai Li wathusi" sung by Saksri Sri-akson. However, although rock and rock 'n' roll were incorporated into Thai popular music as *string*, the rock rhythm did not become a major influence on *luk thung* until the 1970s. For example, "Luk thung siang thong" (Golden Sound of the Country), written by Phayong Mukda and sung by Phet Phanomrung, has a fast rock beat of 190 bpm, but perhaps this song falls more into the category of *luk krung* than *luk thung* because of the singer's Western singing style. Musically, it is American country and western with Thai lyrics, even quoting a number of American standards such as "Dixie and

"Old Susanna" in the instrumental section. Incidentally, the success of this song may have encouraged the idea that *luk thung* was Thailand's version of American country music. Following the popularity of Elvis in the 1950s, a rhythm known as offbeat or backbeat, which had an emphasis on beats two and four, typical of rock 'n' roll, was occasionally incorporated into *luk thung*. Examples of offbeat rhythm in *luk thung* include Chai Mueangsing's "Luksao khrai no" (c. 1957) and Surin Phaksiri's "Ya doen show." However, Siriphon (2004, 170) records that government censorship of rock music on radio stations between 1955 and 1957 may have discouraged early *luk thung* composers from incorporating it into the makeup of the new genre.

Waeng suggests that it was actually the withdrawal rather than the presence of most American troops from bases in Isan such as Udon Thani in 1973 that propelled the blending of rock with *luk thung* and *molam*. While the Americans were in Thailand they were entertained by Thai bands who performed Western pop music in English for the soldiers and in Thai for Thai audiences. Once the soldiers left, many of these bands had no work and returned to playing *luk thung* and *molam*, incorporating Western techniques they had learned. For example, 1970s *luk thung* Isan star Dao Bandon was the first Thai performer to incorporate distorted electric guitar into his band (Waeng 2002, 319).

Early Carlos Santana albums such as *Santana* (1969) and *Abraxas* (1970) have had an enormous impact in Thailand, such that a Latin-tinged funk-rock style is still referred to as *santana*. This style can be heard in an up-tempo version of Saksri Sriakson's "Phuyai Li" from 1970, which features timbales, congas, and funk guitar and bass.[29] "Choe pup rak pap" (Love at First Sight) by Yodrak Salakchai is a typical fast *santana* song. Medium-tempo funk is still a popular rhythm in *luk thung*. For example, Nik Niranam incorporates funk into his adaptations of old *ramwong* standards by converting the cut common time into a grinding four-four rhythm.

Because disco itself evolved out of Latin rhythms such as cha-cha, merengue, and samba, its adoption into *luk thung* was a natural move. In the late 1970s the disco craze was just as prevalent in Thailand as in the rest of the world, but it took a few years before it was successfully adapted into *luk thung*. Lop Burirat is usually credited with introducing disco beats into *luk thung* with his songs for Phumphuang Duangjan. "Phuchai nai fan" (Man in My Dream) and "Hang noi thoi nit" (Move a Little Closer) in 1984 and "Ue hue . . . lo chang" (Ah Ha . . . So Handsome) and "Krasae" (Come Closer) in

1985 used a disco beat to reinforce Phumphuang's sexually aggressive image (see Ubonrat 1998, 215–20).

Since the late 1990s, Latin pop incorporating rhythms such as salsa, samba, and merengue has become a mainstream genre throughout the world. The influence of this genre can be heard in Bird Thongchai's 2002 album *Chut rap khaek*[30] and the resultant live album *Birdfloor*, which represented the extremely successful efforts of Thailand's most famous pop artist to perform *luk thung*. A key ingredient in Bird's updated sound was the pop-salsa rhythm and instrumentation, especially montuno-style piano, typical of recordings by Ricky Martin or Jennifer Lopez at the time. This blend of Latin pop and *luk thung* has continued to be popular with recent performers such as Liu Ajariya[31] and Mangpor, who emphasize Latin-style dancing in their routines.

Japanese Influence

Considering the close ties between Japan and Thailand immediately before and during World War II and the popularity of Japanese films in Thailand at that time, it could be expected that Japanese *ryukoka* melodies were absorbed into *phleng Thai sakon*. Likewise, it has been assumed that elements of the Japanese rural working-class genre *enka*[32] were incorporated into Thai popular song during the 1950s and 1960s. This is yet to be proven, but certainly Loet Prasomsap's "Sao ngam nai Tokyo" (Beautiful Girl in Tokyo) borrowed the melody of "Otomi san," which was a big hit in 1954 in Japan for Hachiro Kasuga (dubbed the first *enka* singer). Almost twenty years later the same melody was used by Surin Phaksiri for "Ya doen show." The key figure in adapting Japanese material into early *luk thung* was Suraphon Sombatjaroen. "Rak nuea khop fa" ("Love above the Sky"), sung by his Japanese speaking protégé Chusri Thongyaem in 1961, established a pattern of Suraphon combining Japanese popular song melodies with new Thai and Japanese lyrics. He partnered this song with his own attempt to sing in Japanese on "Athit uthai ram luek" (Thinking of the Rising Sun),[33] a song about a man who must leave his Japanese girlfriend, which borrowed the melody of "Ringo hana wa saita kedo". Other hits for Chusri soon followed such as "Tokyo haeng khwam lang" (Tokyo in the Past), "Khoi thoe thi Tokyo" (Waiting for you in Tokyo), which used the melody of Kyu

Sakamoto's 1961 world hit "Ue o muite aruko", "Ring-ngo sa-uen" and "Thoe cha yu nai" (Darling, Where Are You?). Exotic costumes are a *luk thung* staple and there are frequently Japanese-themed video clips. For example, Liu Ajariya's "Kha tha kho chai" uses *koto* in an otherwise standard fast *luk thung* song, and the film clip features her clad in a green kimono-style outfit with a wide neck dancing *luk thung* style in front of a huge Japanese flag.[34] Japanese brands are regularly mentioned, such as in "Honda kikkok" by Ke Napho, in which the boy's locally manufactured Honda motorcycle is contrasted against the girl's father's imported BMW. Interestingly, the two male characters are saved from a gang by the girl's Taekwondo skills, perhaps a commentary on the current popularity of South Korean culture in Thailand.

Indian *Filmi Geet* (Film Songs)

Luk thung follows the pattern of many other acculturated song genres in that the folk vocal style is among the most fundamental traits (see Manuel 1988, 20). However, just as there are some *luk thung* singers who use Western vocal styles, there are also many sung in Indian or Malay vocal styles. The majority of these *thamnong India* (Indian melody) songs are sung by southerners, such as Ekachai Sriwichai's "Ruai laeo ngiap" (Already Rich but Keeps Quiet) or Miao Khunathan's "Luk sao chao le" (Fisherman's Daughter) (written by Chat Sinsuepphon). However, Isan-born singer Monsit Khamsoi had a big hit in 1998 with "Kosamphi," named after the ancient Buddhist city in India, and the most recent Indian-style song is Alice Chayada's "I don't care"[35] which, like "Kosamphi", was promoted by a sumptuous Bollywood-themed music video.

Luk thung composers have been borrowing melodies from Bollywood film songs since the late 1960s and perhaps earlier. As with *phleng Thai doem*, once a melody enters the *luk thung* canon it is used over and over, usually without attribution (although in the case of Thai classical music, the melodies are so well known that perhaps they do not require attribution).

Peter Doolan, the author of a blog on Thai popular music, pointed out one example, where "Neele gagan ke tale," composed by Ravi and sung by Mahendra Kapoor from the film *Hamraaz* (1967),[36] becomes "Sao na khoi khu" (Farm Girl Waits for a Partner), composed by Surin Phaksiri and sung by Buppha Saichon, from the *luk thung* musical *Mon rak luk thung* (1970).[37] The melody was also used for "Roi rak, roi monthin" (Love's Scar, Unclean Mark),[38] sung by Phraiwan Lukphet and composed by Pradit Utamang, and later by Soraphet Phinyo for "Lop na thi Malay," sung by Phimpha Phonsiri. The first three songs are essentially identical in melody, but "Lop na thi Malay" shows significant development. Soraphet has created a new melody by adapting the distinctive first three bars of the original melody using repetition and sequence typical of *molam*. Another *thamnong India* (Indian melody) song performed by Buppha Saichon is Surin Phaksiri's "Won lom fak rak" (Ask the Wind to Send Love).[39] Surin's "Ni kam" (Debt of Karma) features an introduction sung in Hindi.

Doolan suggests that *filmi geet* influence in *luk thung* can be isolated to two periods—the beginning of the 1970s and the beginning of the 1990s. These dates coincide with two eras of international success for Indian cinema (the films of Dharmendra, Amitabh Bachchan, Mumtaz, and Helen Jairag Richardson in the 1970s and Aamir Khan and Shahrukh Khan in the 1990s), and so he surmises that Thai artists have simply been following international trends in adopting Indian sounds during these times. Doolan notes that the songs from this first group of Indian films were dubbed by Thai stars to increase the films' commercial appeal, and believes that *luk thung* singers were chosen because of the popularity of the Thai rural musical genre at the time. A prime example of this dubbing is the popular and influential 1970 *thamnong India* album, *Chom nang* (*Watch a Woman*), which featured hits such as "Thorani chiwit" (Life of the Earth) and the title track, credited to Surin Phaksiri and sung in Thai by Chatri Srichon and Yuphin Phraethong.[40] All of the songs from this album were taken from the Indian film *Dharti* (1970) and were written, in reality, by the famous Bollywood songwriting duo Shankar and Jaikishan. In the *thamnong India* craze that followed, Bangkok-born Sumit Satjathep[41] became the first (and probably only) bilingual (Hindi and Thai) *luk thung* star.

Korean Song

After his posting in Korea in 1956, Benjamin produced songs such as "Aridang," "Siang khruan chak Kaoli"[42] (sung by Somsri Muangsonkhiao), "Kaoli haeng khwam lang," and "Rak thae chak num Thai" (True Love from a Thai Boy). For this popular series of Korean-themed songs he adapted and borrowed Korean folk and pop melodies and even sang some lines in Korean. Benjamin was not the only Thai musician to serve in Korea—Suntharaphon singer Loet Prasomsap spent eighteen months there in 1954–55 and in 1958 wrote "Rim fang nam Phaengma" (The Bank of the Phaengma River) using a Korean melody. However, all of these songs were predated by Nian Wichitnan's "Chiwit nai ruedu fon" (Life in Winter), sung by Somjit Tatjinda around 1955 and based on the Korean song "Sala ngae."

These Korean melodies may not have had lasting influence on *luk thung*, but the recent spread of Korean pop culture throughout the world, known in Korean as *hallyu* (Korean Wave), has had a notable impact. For example, Grammy's *luk thung Isan* star Phi Sadoet had a big hit in 2009 with "Sao Kaoli" (Korean Girl) about a Thai girl so infatuated by Korean pop culture that she forgets her poor Isan boyfriend. This is a twist on the stock *luk thung* storyline of country girl seduced by the city. The film clip, in which the dancers wear variations on the *hanbok*, replete with progressively shorter hemlines, is a sendup of every element of the Korean Wave. The girl rejects her boyfriend in favor of a K-pop lookalike driving a sports car, begins to wear skimpy Korean-style clothing, and strides through the dusty Isan village listening to K-pop. She dreams that she is in a Korean serial, similar to 2003's *Winter Love Song*, but wakes to find she is still in hot, humid Thailand. She turns up her nose at her boyfriend's Isan-style pickled vegetables (*phak dong*), preferring to eat kimchi, and goes to bed with a cardboard cutout of a K-pop star. In the end the Korean wannabe breaks her heart, and, after throwing out all her Korean Wave merchandise, she dresses (as apparently a good Thai girl should) neck-to-toe in Thai traditional clothing and sits down to eat *phak dong* with her Isan boyfriend. Although tongue-in-cheek, the message is clear—young Thais should reject Korean cultural imperialism. Musically the song is standard *rock Isan* but K-pop influence can be heard in the high-tech-sounding metallic keyboard lines.

Chinese Song and Cantopop

The significant involvement of Sino-Thai businessmen as patrons in the *luk thung* industry has, not surprisingly, led to some Chinese influence in the music. During the 1950s and 1960s a number of Chinese melodies were adapted into Thai popular song. However, since then Chinese influence has been muted due to the strength of Isan involvement in the *luk thung* industry as performers and targeted audience. During the 1970s and 1980s Isan people were keen to distance themselves from any connection to China for a number of reasons, including the perceived link between Isan and communism, and the corresponding backlash in central Thai society. In the Isan region there has been an ambivalent attitude towards immigrant Chinese. On the one hand Isan people have respected Chinese businessmen, who provided employment and local investment long before the Thai government became interested in the region. On the other hand there has been some resentment at the success of Sino-Thai businessmen when contrasted with the poverty of many Isan people.

Perhaps the most significant Chinese influence on Thai popular music was through the work of Taiwanese star Miss Khumi (Carrie Koo Mei) who stayed in Thailand from 1958 to 1961 and appeared in several Thai films. She recorded for famous bandleaders such as Pricha Mettrai, Saman Kanjanaphlin, and Sanga Aramphi and sang a famous duet with Suthep Wongkamhaeng—"Phuea thoe khon diao" (For You Alone),[43] written by Sanga. In 1956 Hong Kong star Grace Chang (or Miss Koelan) visited Thailand to act and sing in the film *Hong Yok* (*Budgerigar*). She recorded three songs for the film in Thai: "Chiwit chan khat thoe mai dai" (My Life Can't Be without You), adapted by Sanga Aramphi and Chali Inthorawijit from a Chinese song, "Mai khoei rak khrai thao thoe" (I've Never Loved Anyone as Much as You) by Chali and "Rak raem klai", also written by Sanga and Chali using melodic material from Puccini's Madame Butterfly.

In terms of Chinese influence on luk thung, Suraphon was again the key innovator. In 1964 he used the Chinese melody "Uang kim leng" in two sets of *phleng kae*: "Sae si ai lue chek nang," and "Muai cham" (Disappointed Chinese Girl)[44] sung by Pathama Na Wiangfa (words by Thongbai Rungrueang); and "Yik thao hola sua" (Moon over the Lake), and "Muai hai cham" (Chinese Girl Recovers) sung by Pathama. In each of these songs the introduction is played on solo *so duang*, which communicates a Chinese feel, and Suraphon imitates the Teochew style of speaking. Waeng (2002, 218) records that Suraphon was extremely popular among the Chinese community in Bangkok and that he used Chinese words and imagery to appeal to these fans. For example, in "Dokfa mueang Thai" (Thai flowers) he praises women of Chinese origin by comparing them to the to flower, which grows in both China and Thailand. Phongsri Woranut, Suraphon's most famous protégé, followed his lead and performed songs based on Chinese originals. "Na chuen ta ban" (Cheerful Person) by Chai Mueangsing is described as mixed Chinese style (*chin phasom*), which may mean that it is a mix of *Thai doem chin* melodies or that it is a mix of Chinese folk song melodies. "Chan khiang thoe," sung by Buppha Saichon, has a borrowed Chinese melody (Surin et al. 2004, 26).

During the 1980s Nithithat Promotion was the leading company in producing music for the Sino-Thai community in Thailand. One very talented Thai singer for Nithithat active in the 1980s and 1990s was Phimphayom (Iu) Rueangrot, who recorded *luk thung*, Chinese pop, and even Japanese-language songs, and who also spoke fluent English. Iu, who covered many songs by Taiwanese pop legend Teresa Teng, has a clear, sweet voice more typical of Cantopop than *luk thung*. Another Nithithat singer was Phaijit Aksonnarong (see chapter five), whose music is described as "*luk thung* classic: Chinese music" in the liner notes of her albums. While the music does bear some similarity to *luk thung* in terms of tempo and melodic structure, this description must also be a marketing ploy to broaden appeal among Thai listeners. With the use of rich strings, solo *erhu*, and Chinese flute, plus standard western harmonies including such techniques as cadential six-four chords and resolving suspended fourths, Iu and Phaijit's albums are very much in the style of classic Cantopop. This *luk thung*–Cantopop fusion genre is still being recorded but is much less popular than it was twenty years ago.

Import, Absorb, and Transform

One of the great strengths of early *luk thung* was the willingness of the artists to borrow from other cultures. Since its beginnings, *luk thung* has assimilated influences to the extent that identifying individual sources is sometimes difficult. However, a number of points are clear: First, it is clear that *luk thung* draws upon a wide variety of Thai musical forms, including high-status *phleng Thai doem* melodies. Second, while it is true that central Thai folk traditions have heavily influenced *luk thung* (especially through *lae*), there is also no doubt that Isan musical influence on the genre is significant and, through *ramwong*, from an early date. As an entertainment in the Northeast, *molam* is so pervasive that Isan people are universally acculturated to its scales, rhythms, and poetic forms. When the influx of Isan people into the entertainment industry is considered, it is not surprising that many of the musical characteristics of *molam* can be observed in *luk thung* (and vice-versa). However, Isan influence has also entered *luk thung* through genres such as *ramwong*, Isan *lae*, *klong yao*, and *soeng* rhythm. Third, Thai songwriters have experimented with a wide range of Western and Latin American genres but only a few, such as brass-band music and cha-cha, have become integral. Finally, as demonstrated by Benjamin, Suraphon, and Surin Phaksiri, *luk thung* songwriters have actively sought out foreign source material and have followed international trends. This shows that the *luk thung* audience has always been interested in the modern (*thansamai*) and the exotic.

CHAPTER THREE

Soraphet Phinyo, Isan Songwriter

We must put a price to our work since the music companies make so much money out of it.... Just to give an idea of the differences... [t]he company made approximately 44 million bahts (about 1.1 milion pounds) from "Num Ma Kao, Sao Na Klua" [*sic*] ("Rice Field Lad, Salt Field Girl") but the songwriter, Sorapet Pinyo, received 8000 bahts initial payments plus another 2000 bahts (approximately 250 pounds in total). When the song became a hit, the company then paid him 50000 bahts more (approximately 1250 pounds). You see the gap?

—Songwriter Cholathi Thangthong (quoted in Ubonrat 1990, 54)

One of Thailand's most eminent *luk thung* songwriters, Soraphet Phinyo is proud of his Isan heritage and is well known for including Isan material in his songs. His relatively short period of success as a singer (1982–84) positions him on the cusp of a significant change in the Thai music industry. During the 1960s and 1970s, singers and songwriters were represented by a multitude of small companies that derived the majority of their income from concerts and (during the 1970s) from cassette sales. However, after 1980, consolidation in company ownership and the importance of visual image in the promotion of celebrities became features of the industry. Soraphet can therefore be viewed as perhaps the last in a generation of successful singer-songwriters, which began with Suraphon and Benjamin and extended through to Chai Mueangsing and Phloen Phromdaen. As a singer, he experienced the same degree of success as 1970s superstars such as Sayan Sanya, Yodrak Salakchai, and Sonchai

Mekwichian, but not for as long. Soraphet's calculated incorporation of Isan musical elements into his songwriting places him within the *luk thung Isan* tradition of Surin Phaksiri and Thepphon Phetubon. Finally, his long, successful career as a songwriter for singers managed by large companies sheds light on the issues faced by the new generation of songwriters such as Sala Khunawut and Chat Sinsuepphon, who must deal with giant entertainment corporations such as GMM Grammy.

I was introduced to Soraphet at his house in January 2007 by an associate professor from Khon Kaen University. Soraphet agreed to be interviewed and drove to my house the following day. We shared a meal of *sup nomai* (spicy bamboo with herbs), *yam khai mot daeng* (red-ant eggs salad), *somtam* (papaya salad), *lap pet* (spicy minced duck), and *khao niao* (sticky rice). These traditional Isan dishes were prepared by my wife's parents, who were well aware of his songs and status in the community and were thrilled to meet him. The interview went well, and Soraphet readily agreed to further meetings. Our second and third interviews occurred the following week in Soraphet's recording studio at his house, with my wife acting as Isan-language interpreter. During these interviews he also gave me ten newly composed songs to translate so they could be sung in English. Over the next year I met Soraphet on a regular basis in order to teach him English.

Throughout our interviews and English lessons there was never any mention of payment or money. Once he knew that I was from a university, Soraphet stated that he was pleased to be able to assist in the preservation of knowledge, a sentiment often expressed by my informants. However, it certainly appears that Soraphet expected to gain from our relationship. That he raised the possibility of an English-language *luk thung* album during our first interview suggests that he was considering how he might benefit from ongoing contact. Correspondingly, I indicated my willingness to teach him English so that we would have a reason to continue meeting, and so I could partly repay the debt that I felt I owed him for granting me access to his experience.

Soraphet Phinyo's Early Career

Soraphet Phinyo was born Samoe Janda in 1950, in Bua Yai near Nakhon Ratchasima in Isan. He left school after finishing sixth grade and then joined his parents and eight siblings in the family business of rice farming. Soraphet's interest in a music career was sparked by the performances of traveling *ramwong* bands that came to Bua Yai, and he taught himself how to sing by imitating recordings by famous artists such as Suraphon and Benjamin. He also taught himself to play the *khaen* by memorizing the melodies of any *Mokhaen*[1] he encountered. During his early teenage years it was *luk thung* bands rather than *ramwong* that caught his interest. He recalls attending concerts by Banchop Charoenphon at Bua Yai Theater and the famous Jularat band fronted by Chai Mueangsing in Nakhon Ratchasima.

When he was fifteen years old he entered a radio singing competition at Chaiyaphum, which he subsequently won. The competition's *khosok* (emcee), a reasonably well-known DJ called "Dornjedi" (Sawat Sri-udon), invited Soraphet to come and live with him in Khon Kaen. Soraphet recalls that his parents were generally supportive, although they expressed concern about him living in another province because he was *"khon chonabot"* (country person). Dornjedi gave Soraphet the stage name Son Buengphralai, entered him in competitions throughout Isan, and paid for recording sessions in Bangkok. At least two of these recordings, "Na laeng na lom" (Dry Field, Failed Crop) and "Sanya muea sin duean" (Promise at the End of the Month), were broadcast by Dornjedi on local radio.

For the next three years Soraphet continued to perform in singing competitions and minor concerts in Khon Kaen and Bangkok. When he was eighteen he completed two years of mandatory military service before returning to the singing profession. While he did not experience major success at this time, he made sufficient income from singing to support himself without resorting to other employment. He began to practice composition by using famous *luk thung* songs as models. His early output was Lao-Isan in character, with titles such as "Sura lam phloen" (Whiskey Lam Phloen) and "*Lam toei* Isan." The latter was written in 1972 and, in 1974, became his first song to be bought by a record company. This initial success coincided with a move back to Dornjedi's house and radio station in Khon Kaen. It was at this time that he adopted the stage name Soraphet Phinyo—"Soraphet" because it used the same consonants as luk thung legend Suraphon Sombatjaroen, and "Phinyo" as it was the birth name of his patron. In Khon Kaen he became part of the Dornjedi *khana lakhon withayu* (radio drama troupe), which was led by DJs Daen Darathong and Thitma Miani and at one point included Samai Onwong (see chapter one). This group was well known throughout Isan because their radio plays were recorded and distributed to stations in every major city. For the next few years he wrote and pitched songs to companies with limited success, though in 1979 "Sura lam phloen" (fig. 3.1) was very popular throughout Isan, and another song, "Prap thuk kap chao thui" (Confide in the Buffalo) became a minor hit.

That year Soraphet formed a professional relationship with a young female factory worker who had applied to be a singer in the Dornjedi radio *lakhon* team. Janwimon Phansaita (b. 1959), otherwise known as Nong Nut Duangchiwan, became one of the biggest female *luk thung* stars of the 1980s by singing Soraphet's songs. However, in 1979 their first performing experience together was as part of the Thepphon Phetubon Band. During a break in touring, Nut recorded Soraphet's "Alai chai daen" (Border Lament), a song about Thai soldiers tasked with protecting the country's borders. At that time a song's popularity depended on listeners sending request letters to their radio station and, according to this measurement, "Alai chai daen" was a major success in Isan. Further hits such as "Phi cha daeng klap ma laeo" (Darling, I've come back) and "Ok sao ban na" (Heart of a farm girl) followed, and by 1982 Nut had recorded five cassette albums of Soraphet's songs (fig.3.2) and acquired a following in Bangkok and in northern Thailand.

However, she did not believe that singing would be a lasting career and decided to enroll in the well-known Ketsayam beauty therapy school in Bangkok. Later that year Soraphet convinced her to record a duet with him called "Num na khao sao na kluea" (Rice-Farming Boy, Salt-Farming Girl) and he then tried to find a company that would distribute the record. Nut recalls that she woke early one morning and was shocked to hear the song being played on every radio station. She then received a phone call from Soraphet, who wanted to tell her that the song was taking off in Khon Kaen, but he was not aware of its success in Bangkok (fig. 3.3). Later that week, the record company informed her that she did not need to stay for the last two months in the beauty school because promoter Lung Yai Ayutthaya had a band ready for her and Soraphet to go on tour throughout Thailand. This band of around a hundred performers toured constantly over the next two years—as Nut remembers it, they literally went to every province and almost every district therein.

Soraphet and Nong Nut's first cassette album as a singing duo was titled *Num na khao, sao na kluea* (figs. 3.4 and 3.5), and was issued by Longplay

FIGURE 3.1. Soraphet's first cassette album, *Sura lam phloen* (1979). (James Mitchell)

FIGURE 3.2. Nong Nut's cassette albums prior to *Num na khao, sao na kluea*. All songs were written by Soraphet. (James Mitchell)

FIGURE 3.3. Cover of *Chaophya Weekly* magazine, November 5, 1982. The writing above Nong Nut reads "'Num na khao–sao na kluea' dang raboet" (explodes loudly). (James Mitchell)

FIGURE 3.4. A promotional poster for "Num na khao, sao na kluea" from *Racha Siang Thong* magazine, September 20, 1982. (James Mitchell)

in 1982. The title track was a megahit that started a fashion for duets, as opposed to the more traditional practice of the male and female singing alternating but related songs (*phleng kae* or *phleng to*). Other popular songs from this album included "Phua mia pho pho kan" (Husband and Wife Are Really Similar) and "Num na la sao" (Farm Boy Bids Farewell to His Girl). Later that year the pair's second album, *La sao khao bot* (Leave the Girlfriend to Enter the Temple) was published by Hang Phaensiang Thongkham, featuring the hit song "Sansani ni cham" (sung by Nong Nut), and two more albums, published by Metro, followed in 1983. Soraphet then became a solo artist, releasing two successful albums, *Thui ot ya, kha ot khao* (*No Grass for the Buffalo, No Rice for Me*) (1983) and *Kang mung khoi mia* (*Setting Up the Mosquito Net and Waiting for the Wife*) (1983). From 1984 he concentrated on the more lucrative areas of songwriting and production, although he continued to sing and record his own compositions. After 1984, Nong Nut took a long break from performing but made a successful comeback in the early 1990s as part of Nophadon Duangphon's Phet Phin Thong troupe.

The cultural impact of Soraphet's most famous song, "Num na khao, sao na kluea,"[2] has been considerable. Soraphet says that the company told him

SORAPHET PHINYO, ISAN SONGWRITER

FIGURE 3.5. Cassette cover for *Num na khao, sao na kluea*. (Peter Doolan, monrakplengthai.blogspot.com)

FIGURE 3.6. Nong Nut's cassette albums after *Num na khao*. (James Mitchell)

it was a number-one hit and that six months after its release it had sold a million copies. Both of these comments are problematic because there are no official records kept of album sales—recording companies keep track of their own artists' sales and these figures are jealously guarded. Moreover, both statements are commonly used by Thais to indicate that a song has been extraordinarily popular. For example, the title of the compilation album cover shown in figure 3.7 can be translated as "Million-Selling Thai Country Songs, Year '29 [1986]." However, if the figure of 44 million baht mentioned by Cholathi Thanthong in the opening quote to this chapter is accurate, then the *Num na khao* album must have sold well in excess of one million copies and possibly up to two million. Certainly "Num na khao" was an extraordinary success—in 1982 it was awarded a Phaensiang Thongkham (fig. 3.8), a highly prized, royally sanctioned, annual honor given to the "best" song from each genre. Soraphet remembers that his life changed that year—he was suddenly able "to buy the things that wealthy people have, such as a house and car." Moreover, continued playing of "Num na khao" on radio and television demonstrates that musical elements of the song have become ingrained in the public consciousness. The introduction's rhythmic cell and cha-cha rhythmic cadence are so well known that *luk thung* fans inevitably begin the opening lyrics at exactly the right spot—no easy task

FIGURE 3.7. Compilation LP cover (front and back) from 1986, titled *Luk thung ngoen lan pi 29* (Million-Selling Thai Country Songs, Year '29 [1986]). Pictured on the front, from top left, are Dao Bandon, Sanya Phonnarai, Sayan Sanya, and Yodrak Salakjai. From bottom left are Sotsai Rungphothong, Sonphet Sonsuphan, and Soraphet Phinyo. Soraphet's song is "Num Khorat khat rak" (Boy from Nakhon Ratchasima Lacks Love), and the album is listed as a product of Mon Mueangnuea Company but distributed by RS Promotion. (James Mitchell)

FIGURE 3.8. Soraphet and Nut get the Phaensiang Thongkham from Princess Sirindhorn. (Nut Duangchiwan)

FIGURE 3.9. Soraphet with his royal award today. (James Mitchell)

with a syncopated anacrusis. Cover versions[3] and *phleng plaeng* (songs with altered lyrics) abound, and it remains a ubiquitous karaoke choice.

Translation of "Num na khao, sao na kluea" (Rice-Farming Boy, Salt-Farming Girl)

M: My village farms rice, plants rice at all times.
F: I harvest salt, sell salt to buy food to eat.
M: My village is in Kalasin.
F: As for me, Yuphin, I live in Samut Sakhon.
M: I have come to meet a beautiful girl and visit Dao Khanong.
F: I count it as good luck that when I met you you greeted me first.
M: I really want to go to live at Samut Sakhon.
F: From what you say I'm afraid that is not true.
M: I, the rice farmer, love a young girl.
F: I am a salt-field girl.
M: The rice field boy will never forsake you.
M: If I will go what will your father say?
F: I'll be very happy if you truly go ask for my hand.
M: The rice field boy guarantees I will not forsake you.
F: If you love me truly don't leave the salt field girl.

During the most successful stage of his career, Soraphet did not draw heavily on his Isan heritage. There is little overt Isan musical or lyrical influence to be heard in Soraphet's albums with Nong Nut. For example, although the male protagonist of "Num na khao" hails from Kalasin, he speaks exclusively central Thai and wants to relocate to Samut Sakhon in central Thailand. The instrumentation for the album is generally standard for *luk thung* from that period: Western sounds such as bass, "twangy" electric guitar, funky saxophone, organ and piano, drumkit, and congas. Three tracks feature *so u* (Thai fiddle); as stated in chapter two, the instrument is an element of Khmer-Isan *kantruem*, but it is also found throughout Thailand. Significantly, there is no use of Lao-Isan identity markers such as *khaen*, *phin*, or *pong lang* throughout the album. On the pair's second album Soraphet's choice of borrowed melody for the "Runaway to Bangkok" songs "Sansani ni cham" (Sansani Escapes) and "Tam ha Sansani" (Looking for Sansani) was the classical central Thai (*doem*) "Khaek Mon Bangkhunphrom."

These musical and lyrical choices contrast greatly with his choices during his songwriting developmental period and his period as a master songwriter. Soraphet insisted these lyrical differences were unintentional, and he put down the success of "Num na khao" to it being a "fun" song. He did not remember there being any industry or government pressure for songs not to include Isan elements. However, in response to a question about when record companies first became interested in *molam*-style songs, Soraphet noted that Bangkok companies were not interested in *luk thung molam* until 1985. This indicates that in the process of writing for Nong Nut prior to *Num na khao*, he adapted his musical style to produce songs with wider commercial appeal. Nut's popularity outside Isan was probably the key motivation. It is therefore possible that Soraphet may have felt the need to conform to an orthodoxy in order to achieve the elusive first success, and that, having become part of the *luk thung* establishment, there was little incentive for him to see any part of that success as problematic.

Soraphet's Career as a Master Songwriter

Soraphet's period as a top-tier singer was less than three years, but the experience he had gained in that time and the preceding decade ensured that he was soon in demand as a songwriter. Successful *luk thung* songwriters are often sought out by emerging talent, who become *luksit* (protégés) of the master *khru*, a system of social organization which frames and facilitates the transmission of traditional knowledge throughout Thai society. This system formally establishes a social relationship between the two parties via a social and ritual contract, which acts to regulate the transmission of information.

Between 1984 and 1989 Soraphet had three protégés who all went on to be major stars: Somphot Duangsomphong, Phimpha Phonsiri, and Jintara Phunlap. For Somphot, Soraphet produced two albums through Azona— *Mia pa phro Sa-u* (Wife Dumped Me because of Saudi Arabia) (1984) and *Ro rak thi u rot* (*Waiting at the Mechanic Shop*) (1985). For Phimpha, he produced *Namta mia Sa-u* (*Tears of the Wife of a Laborer in Saudi Arabia*) (1986)[4] and *Isan khiao* (*Green Isan*) (1987), and for Jintara, her first two albums with Grammy, *Thuk lok ok rong rian* (Tricked out of School) and *Wan phuean khian chotmai* (*Ask a Friend to Write a Letter*) (1989).[5]

In each of these cases Soraphet stressed that he had sole creative control over all aspects of the project. Once he agreed to be a new singer's *khru*, he would decide on a persona or theme for the album, either select from songs that he had already written or write new songs, teach his protégé to sing them, record the demos, and make a deal with a company to bankroll the recording. He would oversee the recording process in Bangkok and, finally, would sell the master copy and all rights to the recording company. The protégé would sign a contract with the company—at no stage would Soraphet actually pay the protégé—and the songwriter's involvement would then cease. Soraphet very specifically stated that he alone would decide which songs were suitable for each disciple and that, in the cases of Phimpha and Jintara, he had already written the songs before meeting them.

Phimpha Phonsiri's *Namta Mia Sa-u*

In 1986, seventeen-year-old Nithaya Suphap from Chaiyaphum approached Soraphet at his house in Khon Kaen and asked permission to become his protégé. After a short period of rehearsal and performance, he negotiated a deal with record company Metro to write and produce her 1986 debut album under the stage name Phimpha Phonsiri. The success of Phimjai Phetphalanchai's "Sai ta phikhat" (Eyes That Kill) had revived interest in *molam*-style *luk thung*, and Soraphet set out to emulate both the song and the singer's name. The result was the enormously successful *Namta mia Sa-u*, which broadened the appeal of the *luk thung prayuk* (also known as *luk thung Isan*) sound.

For the title track, Soraphet composed a response to the hit song he had written for Somphot Duangsomphong in 1984, "Mia pa phro Sa-u." In the original song, an Isan man who has gone to work in Saudi Arabia criticizes his wife for spending his remittances on other men. "Namta mia Sa-u"[6] (fig. 3.10), however, is sung from the wife's point of view. She admits that she has had an affair but says that she has been left alone with her children without enough money coming from her husband. She accuses her husband of having a *mia noi* ("My husband has a mistress waiting"). Furthermore, the money that her husband paid as a guarantee to the recruitment company came from selling her family land. The singer pleads the case for the Isan women who must remain at home while their husbands go to work overseas ("Not every laborer's wife is evil / They're evil because the husband never returns"). This pair of *phleng to*, detailing the social problems caused by labor migration through male and female points of view, demonstrates that *luk thung* provides a social space for the expression of sexual politics.

FIGURE 3.10. Cassette cover of *Namta mia Sa-u* (1986).
(Peter Doolan, monrakplengthai.blogspot.com)

Translation of "Namta mia Sa-u" (Tears of the Wife of a Laborer in Saudi Arabia)

Whenever I think, I'm sad
Because my beloved husband never sends money.
To know the news, it makes me sad
When I know that money is not coming to me.

My husband's parents have received
Lots of money from him in Saudi Arabia.
He sent it to them and they spent it happily;
But for his children and wife they must lick their tears.

Before you went you paid a lump sum—
The rice field, which belonged to me
Was used as guarantee for the dealer.
When you flew away you seemed to forget your wife.

And my heart was broken; you shouldn't tease,
Teasing your wife makes her sad.
My parents tell me to get divorced.
They hate their son in law and curse him morning and night.
I'm so sad I don't know what to do.
Whatever bad thing happens, blame the wife of the Saudi laborer.
Why does nobody know about the good things I've done?
Not every laborer's wife is evil.

They're evil because the husband never returns.
They wait but never see the husband come back.
Now later on know that I'm almost going crazy
Because my husband has a mistress waiting.

When I know this I don't want to live anymore.
This is the heart of the wife no one knows.

Soraphet's adoption of a female voice is the normal practice in a genre in which songwriters are universally male yet more than half of the singers are female. Unlike in *molam*, where female composers are common (for example, Ratri Sriwilai and Noknoi Uraiphon), *luk thung* songwriting is strictly a male profession. When I questioned Soraphet concerning his writing of songs for female singers I expected him to say that professional performers such as Phimpha or Jintara would have some input into their material, but he was adamant that in both cases he had written the songs before meeting them. He explained that the role of a singer was to occupy the character created by the songwriter. A credible match between persona and singer, grain of voice and style and image, is necessary in order to achieve success (Ubonrat 1990, 67). Thus, Phumphuang Duangjan needed to have dancing lessons, plastic surgery, and an image makeover in order to inhabit the persona created by Lop Burirat's disco-influenced and sexually aggressive compositions. In the case of *Namta mia Sa-u* Soraphet succeeded in creating a persona for Phimpha that embodied the life experiences of many Isan women.

This persona is clearly on show in the second song on the album "Sao molam chamdai" (*Molam* Girl Remembers).[7] In this charming song a young performer realizes that the man who has booked her *molam* troupe to celebrate his recent promotion used to teach her when she was in primary school. The geography of the song is focused on Isan—she relates how after the death of her father she had to move from Udon Thani to Maha Sarakham to study. Having grown into an independent and attractive woman (ten years have passed since she was in fourth grade) she intimates the possibility of a relationship ("Have you forgotten that you used to joke with me? That you would marry me?").

Translation of "Sao molam chamdai" (*Molam* Girl Remembers)

When I met you I knew you were my teacher
You used to teach me from when I was in first grade
Since that time we haven't met even once in the last ten years.
When I met you I knew you were a distinguished teacher
From a long time ago but I still remember.
My hometown was in Udon far away.
After my father passed away I moved to Sarakham.

Following my mother I went to study.
It was a long time that we were separated.
My heart didn't know that I would meet you.
I'm a fortunate person—it's a great blessing.

The host is my distinguished teacher
Who organized the party for the people.
This party invited guests from all over the *tambon*
To celebrate his promotion to *Pho Mo*.
You booked the *molam* troupe.
Teacher Buntham, I remember your face.
You booked my troupe and I came in to greet the master teacher.

I remember. Remember you taught me from first grade to fourth grade
Then you moved from the old house.
Have you forgotten that you joked with me?
That you would marry me when I used to study?

As discussed in chapter two, the third song on the album, "Lop na thi Malay" (Escape to Malaysia), demonstrates the capacity of *luk thung* to engage with processes of acculturation. The boundaries that define *luk thung* are permeable and musical elements can easily flow into *luk thung* from other genres. Indeed, Soraphet was surprised when I told him that the original song was from the Indian film *Hamraaz* (1967). He did not pretend that the melody was his invention but he believed it was from another Thai song, though which one he could not be sure. Unlike "Sansani ni cham," which follows "Khaek Mon Bangkhunphrom" in its entirety, Soraphet adapts the borrowed melody and combines it with a *molam*-style chorus. As figure 3.11 shows, this chorus is very similar to that of "Namta mia Sa-u" and, in fact, such a *molam*-style interlude is inserted into almost every song on the album. These interludes confirm the singer's Lao-Isan persona and also unify the album musically. Soraphet explained that a sense of unity in an album set was a key concern for him when deciding on new projects—he said that if any of his disciples wanted to record some of their own songs he would not continue to work with them because the album would feel fragmented.

FIGURE 3.11. These lines compare the choruses of "Namta mia Sa-u" (1) and "Lop na thi Malay" (2). For this comparison, the key of "Lop na" has been adjusted to be the same as "Namta."

The massive success of the *Namta mia Sa-u* album propelled Phimpha into the top rank of Thai performing artists, touring for "forty weeks a year, supported by 133 people and nine trucks" (Clewley 1994, 446). Soraphet wrote and produced Phimpha's next album, *Isan khiao* (1987), and also the hit song "Sao Tim dot tuek" (Miss Tim Jumps from a Building). Despite this success Metro did not retain Soraphet's services for follow-up recordings. It seems a curious decision, and Soraphet will only say that the company wanted to try a different direction. It appears that Metro later realized they had made a mistake; in 1994 they had Phimpha record Soraphet's "Num na khao, sao na kluea" (with Chaloemphon Malakham as the male singer) with some degree of success.

After parting with Metro, Soraphet's reputation as a songwriting master was cemented by two prestigious honors. In 1989 "Num na khao" was listed in the top fifty *luk thung* songs of all time by the Office of National Culture, and in 1991 "Namta mia Sa-u" was named in the next top-fifty selection.[8] Since then his career has been divided into periods of managing protégés, selling songs to companies, and attempting to relaunch himself as a performer. His songs have been hits for Yingyong Yotbua-ngam ("Rak sao Thali"—Love a Girl from Thali), and Nik Niranam. In 2009, he unsuccessfully promoted Chok Chaiyaphum, an untried thirty-one-year-old singer, through the recording company Mon Mueangnuea. When I interviewed him in January 2011, Soraphet had taken on another protégé hailing from Chaiyaphum, whom he had given the stage name of Wanchat Mueangchai. This project appeared to be progressing much better and he had to return to Bangkok the next day to oversee the production of video clips for each song. During our interview Soraphet received a call from the recording studio in Bangkok asking him to supply words for a spoken introduction to a song about soldiers, which he gave without hesitation.

Soraphet's attempts to relaunch his own singing career with new material have so far been unsuccessful. In 2007, he tried to exploit the fame of his most successful song (while avoiding paying copyright) through a self-recorded cassette titled *Num na khao man, sao na kluea*, which featured all new compositions. In 2010, he released another self-recorded album titled *Soraphet ma laeo* (Soraphet has Come), alluding to the famous Suraphon song "Suraphon ma laeo." With each of these albums he struggled to achieve distribution beyond stores in Khon Kaen and Nakhon Ratchasima, and there was not enough interest to risk touring. When I last spoke to him he had on-sold the songs from both albums to other recording companies. However, like other veteran singers such as Dao Bandon and Saksayam Phetchomphu, Soraphet regularly accepts bookings for private parties, where he sings his biggest hits to backing tracks.

Soraphet's Career and the *Khru-Luksit* Relationship

Some of Soraphet's experiences are atypical of the usual development path of *luk thung* singer-songwriters. As described in chapter one, throughout the 1950s, 1960s, and 1970s new singers and songwriters would seek out the tutelage and protection of established artists. With so many *luk thung* performers migrating to Bangkok the result was extended communities consisting of senior and junior performers working and living together. Soraphet had lived with Dornjedi in Khon Kaen, but he did not join a performers' community when living in Bangkok during the 1970s. He stated that he had one songwriter acquaintance at that time—Phon Phanaphrai, a former protégé of Suraphon Sombatjaroen—but at no stage did he live or work with other songwriters.

Unlike the majority of *luk thung* songwriters, Soraphet has never had secondary employment. Apart from helping his parents farm rice as a teenager, he has always derived his income from singing, songwriting, and producing. This contrasts with other highly skilled songwriters such as Benjamin, who stayed in the army for five years at the height of his career, Surin Phaksiri, who worked first as a hospital wardsman and then as a prison guard for over ten years, Thinakon Thiphamat, who maintained a second career as a film cameraman, and Songkhro Samatthaphaphong, who was a career public servant. The pragmatism of these composers demonstrates the uncertainty of songwriting income but also highlights the single-minded determination and aptitude for business evinced by Soraphet during his developmental period.

Soraphet's experience is also unusual in that his patron, Dornjedi, was a promoter rather than a musician, who approached him (rather than the other way round), and that he was completely self-taught. Soraphet did not have a *khru* in the usual sense of "skilled teacher" and his relationships with his many *luksit* (disciples)[9] were very much commercial arrangements. He said that he had never conducted a *wai khru* (honoring teacher) ceremony with any of his disciples, although Phimpha did telephone him each year on Wan Khru (Teachers' Day), the sixteenth of January. In its original context of Thai classical music, the relationship between *luksit* and *khru* is extremely significant. Deborah Wong's ethnomusicological study of the *wai khru* ceremony demonstrates that both musical expertise and spiritual power are passed down from teacher to disciple. Under the traditional teaching system a master musician would accept promising students into his house as disciples and provide them with food and lodging throughout their studies. Disciples were expected to do menial housework and attend all of the master's performances. Only the most devoted and skilled could become *luksit ek* (primary disciples), which might give them the chance to become master musicians themselves. For classical musicians, hierarchy is determined by ritual initiation into the *naphat* repertoire, and only the highest-level practitioners are permitted to lead the *wai khru* ceremony (Wong 2001, 67, 112–13).

After the end of the absolute monarchy in 1932, the orchestras of the royal courts were disbanded and many younger classical musicians moved into the emerging popular music industry. Some elements of the classical teaching system were likely transferred into the popular sphere as well, although they would have had to be adapted to commercial conditions. The teaching of the Western instruments used in *phleng Thai sakon* and *phleng chiwit* was not compatible with the classical system, but in the areas of songwriting and singing the *khru-luksit* relationship continued to be the key means of knowledge transmission.

In the early history of *luk thung*, young performers had to serve an apprenticeship with an established master. For example, Pong Prida (discussed in chapter one) joined the household of *Khru* Nat Thawonbut, who was in charge of a band sponsored by a tobacco factory. Pong's duties for several years included watering the garden, cleaning, and cooking, as well as accompanying his teacher to performances late at night because *Khru* Nat was afraid of ghosts (Waeng 2002, 225–26). However, when Pong discovered that the tobacco factory did not sponsor recordings he left *Khru* Nat and went to live at Sahamit Dontri, a company that employed songwriters such as Phayong Mukda and "Gungadin" Nakhon Thanormsap. After more months of cleaning and cooking Pong became a disciple of Nakhon, who recommended him to the influential band leader Mongkon Amathayakun. Mongkon was not very impressed and Pong spent a further two years playing *khaen* and providing sound effects such as leaf blowing and bird whistling on the recordings of singers such as Suraphon Sombatjaroen and Thun Thongchai (Waeng 2002, 228). As related in chapter one, Pong eventually became famous for his songs written about the Mekong River, and he featured as a singer in Mongkon's Jularat band from 1958 to 1963.

While the path to stardom was not always this difficult there are key aspects of this narrative that remain typical of the relationship between *luk thung* master songwriters and their disciples. As in the classical system, it is usually up to the student to approach the master, and disciples are expected to assist in the everyday running of the master's household or company. However, unlike in the classical system, disciples are more likely to change teachers if their expectations are not met. Perhaps this is because in the commercial environment of popular music, the reward of spiritual power that circulates between the adept and the initiate (see Wong 2001) is replaced by that of commercial success or fame. In the *luk thung* industry, master songwriters achieve and maintain their position by producing commercially successful disciples. For both classical and popular musicians the goal is higher status, but there are different means of achieving that status.

Soraphet's Recording, Distribution, and Business Dealings

Soraphet's ongoing commercial success and status as a master songwriter is conditional upon his ability to record and distribute his songs to companies and other performers. Throughout his recording career he has had to master new technologies. In the early part of his career (late 1970s and early 1980s) he would raise a small amount of money to record demos on a cassette or four-track recorder. Then he would offer the songs to companies who would pay for better recordings to be made in Bangkok. The recording of each album would often be completed in one day. For the past twenty-five years, however, he has been able to record songs to near-professional standard in his home studio (fig. 3.12), which he runs as a company called SP Sound Limited. He is capable of playing all instruments for simple demos but uses session musicians for professional recordings, apart from keyboard and *khaen* parts. In 2005 he changed over to digital recording, and he explained that parts can now be recorded separately over a period of months if the musicians are not all available at the same time. This kind of recording would also be possible with analogue recordings methods, but perhaps he meant that performers are now less reliant on professional recording studios than before, due to developments in home recording technology. Considering how adept he has been at adopting new technologies, it is somewhat surprising that Soraphet has not made use of online distribution. However, as will be discussed in chapter four, both *luk thung* artists and fans highly value personal proximity and contact with each other, so online distribution still does not appear to be a viable option for independent artists or companies marketing *luk thung* within Thailand.[10]

FIGURE 3.12. Soraphet's home studio in Khon Kaen. (James Mitchell)

The fees Soraphet has received for his songs illustrate the trajectory of his career. In the opening quote to this chapter, songwriter Cholathi Thanthong claimed that Soraphet had initially been paid 10,000 baht (USD300) for the master of *Num na khao, sao na kluea*, and that he was then paid a further 50,000 baht (USD1,500) after the album became a hit. Soraphet does not dispute these figures but he would not agree with Cholathi's implication that the payment was too little. While Jorakhe Promotion certainly made a massive profit on the album, Soraphet stresses that 60,000 baht was a large sum of money in 1982. Moreover, the success of this album changed his life and made it possible for him to charge higher fees for subsequent albums. According to Soraphet, he was paid 120,000 baht for each of the albums he produced for Somphot Duangsomphong, Phimpha Phonsiri, and Jintara Phunlap, and presumably this continued to be his set fee for many years. Going a number of years without producing hit songs appears to have reduced his commercial appeal, with his most recent album fee being 60,000 baht (though this amount may not have included his services as a producer). Soraphet's experience can be usefully compared with that of Yingyong Yotbua-ngam, composer and singer of the "Million-Selling 'Somsri 1992,'" who was paid only 12,000 baht for the song while his recording company supposedly earned fifty million baht (Sukanya 1998, 2). Again, this appears to be highly inequitable, but the effect of a famous song cannot be measured only by the immediate income. "Somsri 1992" made Yingyong's reputation as a composer and he now has a very healthy career in concert and television appearances because he has been able to capitalize on the fame of his songs.

Much of Soraphet's creative output is passed on to other artists through a network of friends and business acquaintances. During one of our interview sessions Soraphet revealed that he had accepted a booking to have ten of his songs recorded at his hometown of Bua Yai. He charged 60,000 baht (USD1,800) but gave 10,000 baht to his representative in Bua Yai. His representative protested that this sum was too much but Soraphet told him it was okay because he had hundreds of songs ready to go. Soraphet expressed the opinion that maintaining a good relationship with his representatives was more important than maximizing immediate profit. This incident and his comments suggest that he understands that ongoing income, at his age, depends on the number of songs he produces, rather than the success of those songs. From anecdotal evidence, it appears that many *luk thung* songwriters have demonstrated an uneasy relationship with the copyright system. It seems that there is a perception among Thai musicians that copyright law only functions to protect the interests of recording companies.

In a Thai luk thung retrospective volume, Soraphet wrote, "I don't like copying; the thing I most hate is people who steal other people's brains and then put their own names to it" (Committee 1991, 109, my translation). Soraphet would not give specifics on the circumstances surrounding this statement, only saying that an intermediary connected with a company had tried to pass off some of Soraphet's songs as his own. This kind of substitution is not rare in the *luk thung* industry and sometimes occurs with the songwriter's blessing. I have been told that Grammy's Sala Khunawut has promoted other people's songs as his own to help them gain a foothold in the industry. In a slightly different twist both Phaibun Butkhan and Suraphon Sombatjaroen occasionally sold their own songs under pseudonyms—in Phaibun's case because he had become so famous that during an economic slowdown no one wanted to pay the premium for his songs. In Soraphet's case it must have happened before he became famous, because, during another interview, he explained to me that he made the decision early in his career to not rely on the copyright system. He stated that the certainty of an immediate payment was better than taking the chance that a song would be so successful that it would generate income beyond the investment of the record company. He also expressed the opinion that many companies could not be trusted to pass on copyright dues to the composers. That is why, during his period as a successful singer, he always sold his songs to companies for a set fee and then capitalized on their popularity by touring. Despite missing out on millions of baht in royalties from a few extremely successful songs, he has been able to ensure a regular income by his creativity, technological skill, and business sense. As a result Soraphet is still making a good living from his art almost thirty years after reaching his peak of popularity. He is in no doubt as to the worth of his chosen field and is still looking to reach new audiences. Although he is not permitted to rerecord his most famous song because a record company owns the copyright, he is constantly producing new songs. Selling each song for a set 5,000 baht (USD160) ensures independence but means that he must maintain creativity in order to keep a steady income.

Now in his sixties, Soraphet is waiting to see if he will qualify for the status of *Sinlapin haeng chat* (National Artist), a royal honor conferred on selected eminent artists when they reach retirement age. They receive a pension of 17,000 baht per month (about USD500), meaning financial security in a country without general pensions, and an associated increase in status. However, the assignation of *Sinlapin haeng chat* is an uncertain process dependent on the goodwill of each government to provide ongoing funding (Surin et al. 2004, 34). With very few assigned in recent years, Soraphet's chances of becoming a National Artist are not good, but he has been made a regional artist and has been asked to become a local political representative for his home town of Bua Yai. Soraphet's financial future might already be assured if the copyright system dealt fairly with songwriters, but he has survived and prospered because of his skill in writing poetry and melodies that appeal to *luk thung* audiences. Despite the vagaries of the copyright system, pursuing the art of songwriting is perhaps the only way to ensure a long career in the *luk thung* industry. If Soraphet had just been a singer, his career would have ended in the 1980s, but his reputation for producing hit songs means that new singers and companies continue to approach him even as he enters the normal retirement age.

The *Luk Thung* Songwriting Process: An English-Language *Luk Thung* Album

During our first interview Soraphet expressed interest in developing a *luk thung* album sung in English. After I agreed to translate, he wrote ten new songs in four days. As I slowly translated the songs and attempted to match the English versions to the original melodies, I was surprised by the complexity and artistry of the rapidly composed lyrics, because *luk thung* lyrics are usually characterized as simplistic, clichéd, and rustic.

Ten songs is a fairly standard number for *luk thung* projects. Four of the songs—"Khit thueng khon khoei rak" (Missing you), "Khit nak" (Think Hard), "Muean khao ro fon" (Like Rice Waiting for Rain), and "Ok hak rak salai" (My Broken Heart)—are from the point of view of an abandoned lover. There are two "sights of Thailand" songs, "Mueang Thai na thiao" (Touring Thailand) and "Yak yu thi mueang Thai" (I Want to Live in Thailand)—the latter is actually a "sights of Isan" song from the point of view of a *farang* living in the region. There are two other songs from the point of view of a *farang*—"Farang phop rak" (Westerner Finds Love) and "Rak kham khop fa" (Love beyond the Sky). "Thoet thun mueang Thai" (All Hail Thailand) is a patriotic song, while "Chao na na dam" (Farmer with a Dark Face) is from the point of view of an Isan farmer who feels unattractive. The translation of each song keeps the rhyming pattern, number of syllables, and, as far as possible, the rhythm of the original. As a result the English versions are not always exact translations of the Thai.

Two of the songs were written between our first and second meetings, and the other eight were ready for our third meeting, just two days later. At the time I thought this rate of composition was exceptional, but he informed me that some songs only take ten to fifteen minutes to write and that he has been known to write a whole album in one day. Such a rate of production is a demonstration of Soraphet's extensive knowledge of the subject matter that *luk thung* songs draw upon, yet it also suggests that there is a high degree of repetition in the *luk thung* industry. Ubonrat (1990, 66) writes that "the uniqueness of the artist stems largely from his/her ability to innovate while not departing entirely from the current trend," but it is possible to go further and say that the artist relies on the similarity between songs for financial security. For most songwriters, the ability to produce songs that satisfy demand—not necessarily the ability to innovate alone—is what ensures ongoing commercial success. Soraphet said that if he did not write quickly, other songwriters would get the work. Creativity and innovation do play a role, however. For example, Soraphet had not previously written songs about interracial relationships, but he was inspired by the story of my wife and me to write "Farang Finds Love" and "Love beyond the Sky." It is a common criticism of *luk thung* that many of the songs sound the same—"one hundred songs in one tune" (Ubonrat 1990, 67)—but this could equally apply to other genres, such as blues. It is true that some phrases of several of the faster songs are quite similar but as in blues the basic melody is skilfully manipulated to fit the required syllables.

The songs follow the usual *luk thung* themes, such as rural poverty juxtaposed with urban wealth, and urban migration resulting in cultural and emotional dislocation (unrequited and lost love). Typically, however, the themes are updated with contemporary concerns and references. These include the increasing presence of *farang* in Isan ("I Want to Live in Thailand"), emigration of Isan women through overseas marriages ("Farang Finds Love" and "Love beyond the Sky"), and the continuing division of Isan society in terms of wealth and class ("Farmer with a Dark Face"). This latter song has the same title as Chai Mueangsing's famous "Chao na na dam" from 1967, although Soraphet's poor farmer resents teachers, rather than the usual rich politicians. This reflects the growth of an Isan middle class—although Soraphet did explain that for this song *khru* (teacher) was just easier to manipulate than *tamruat* (policeman) or *samachik saphaphuthaenrasadon* (member of parliament).

> My fav'rite food's the frogs I catch in bogs and hang on the door—
> *Naeo kin yang di wa ko khae khiat imo chap ma tom pon*
>
> I hold and snap the legs, then boil in kegs and dry while raw.
> *Chap ma hak kha ko kae sai khi dang pae tom wai khang phon*

I make frog dip to store when crops are poor 'cause I've got no wage.
Thai na khuen ma laeo pon na lu ton khon bo mi ngoen duean
A teacher has respect and step-by-step earns more with age.
Bo khue khru si hok chet na bo dai het tae khuen dai luean
The farmer works all year, promotion here is earthworm stage.
Chao na het yu moet pi wao phuen si mi tae khi kai duean

Soraphet's portrayal of rural poverty reflects his audience without becoming patronizing or clichéd. In the following example from "Like Rice Waiting for Rain" he extends the commonly used imagery of rice fields in drought:

Waiting for you like rice for rain	*Ro chao muean khao ro fon*
My roots dry 'n' roasted red	*Rak ton hiao phrom tai pai*
I'm alive as one almost dead	*Phi yu muean khon cha sinjai*
Just like the parched and shriveled rice grain	*Mai phit arai kap bai khao chao*

Soraphet makes frequent use of this kind of metaphorical language. In "Love beyond the Sky" a cross-cultural marriage is portrayed as a union between "sticky rice and white bread" (*khao niao kap khanom pang ma ruam pen khao tang*). In "My Broken Heart" the impact of a relationship breakup is "like a punch, like a punch, thrown back, thrown back" (*muean don chok, muean don chok, ngai phueng*).

Humorous songs are expected in *luk thung* albums and the humor is usually at the expense of outsiders, whether that be the rich city folk or foreigners. The gentle humor of "Farang Finds Love" is self-referential, imagining the smell of *pladaek* (Isan fermented fish sauce) being released on a modern airplane:

If my dear cannot leave *pladaek*	*Tha yot ying ting pladaek bo dai*
You can take back a jar or two	*Chong hiu ao hai pai nam chaem chan*
But please don't open till we're through	*Hai pladaek ya het taek ka laeo kan*
Or the whole plane will be overcome	*Diao kap tan sip ha han chi lo*

Patriotic songs are also common in *luk thung* albums. "Thoet thun mueang Thai" (All Hail Thailand) is a patriotic song in the tradition of Wichit Wathakan's best known song, "Rak Mueang Thai" (Love Thailand) (see Barmé

1993, 124). The continuing popularity of this kind of song both demonstrates and reinforces the presence of pan-Thai thinking among Thai people. These nationalistic songs are popular to a certain extent, but their presence in *luk thung* albums is also expected by the various actors in the Thai establishment (the military, royal family, government, and Buddhist leadership). Lop Burirat, a well-known songwriter, points out that "the extras are imperative for our trade. . . . It is a sort of statement of allegiance. . . . It doesn't really bother me as long as we get to do what we want to" (quoted in Ubonrat 1990, 71). Keeping Soraphet's experience with Bangkok music companies in mind, it is difficult to believe that he is not being a little facetious with lines like: "For nowhere else has air so good, air filled with ozone / Morality lives in Thai people's pure hearts / We are not deceitful" (*Mai wa cha pen phumi akat tem duai that ozone / Mai wa cha pen khunatham pracham yu nai chai khon / Mai mi wok won sap son*). As Ubonrat (1990, 71) observes, the presence of this kind of song is a commercial requirement—part of the narrow path that *luk thung* songwriters must negotiate to be successful.

The rhyme structures of Soraphet's lyrics illustrate one of the most interesting features of *luk thung*. Thai students learn to write highly complex forms of poetry in high school—*khlong, chan, kap, rai,* and *klon*. Traditional Thai poetry has tonal rules but also uses rhyme. *Luk thung* songwriters have taken these forms and adapted them for use in songs. The traditional tone rules that poets follow are not usually used (perhaps because of the distraction of instrumental accompaniment) but there is a greater emphasis on rhyme. These structures require great skill and their use differentiates *luk thung* from both songs for life and *string*. Myers-Moro (1986, 107) establishes that songs for life use the internal rhymes of *klon* but usually not the external. Thai pop though is more likely to make sporadic use of external rhyme (following Western pop music).

Soraphet's rhyme structures are far more complex than traditionally structured English poems.. In "Love beyond the Sky" each three-line stanza follows the same rhyme structure, with rhymes unrelated to tones. Each line is two bars long and contains an inner rhyme, with the third beat of the first bar rhyming with the first beat of the second bar. The dominant rhyme is the final syllable of lines one and two, which also matches the inner rhyme of the third line. The final syllable of the stanza becomes the dominant rhyme of the next stanza.

If we walk the line the wind and sky cannot accuse
Hak wa bun sang lom fa lae lom mai atcha kan
Sticky rice and white bread are joined to be wed so spread the news
Khao niao kap khanom pang ma ruam pen khao tang kon nueng diao kan
The angels won't refuse the path we choose to write.
Phrom daen haeng thep sawan mai at pit kan song rao

This rhyme structure is also used in "Touring Thailand" and "Farmer with a Dark Face." It is no surprise that Soraphet favors *klon*, the form most often used in *molam*. "Missing You" is a typical *klon paet* poem:

My heart's desire is far from me,
Naught I see can bring you to mind.
Lost forever, never to find
Hope, resigned, longing for you.
Months past seem just an hour or day,
Next spring may come, the pain is new.
God knows I still care, still miss you,
Your love too cruel, it breaks my heart.

Each four-line stanza has eight syllables per line and a similarly complex rhyme structure. The final syllable of line one rhymes with the third syllable of the next line. The final syllable of line two rhymes with the final syllable of line three and the third syllable of line four. The final syllable of the stanza becomes the dominant rhyme for the next stanza.

Soraphet is yet to find a suitable candidate to sing this album of English *luk thung*. He has recorded full demos for "I Want to Live in Thailand" and "Missing You" with himself as the singer but his experience with the failed *Soraphet ma laeo* album has dashed hopes of a performing comeback. Thus, for now the songs remain a useful academic exercise giving English speakers some insight into the subject matter and form of *luk thung* song lyrics.

Triumph and Tragedy

In February 2011 Soraphet's daughter, who had just graduated from Mahasarakham University, suddenly lapsed into a coma. The diagnosis of eosinophilic meningoencephalitis, what Thais commonly call Sleeping Beauty disease, left little hope for a recovery, and in January 2013 she passed away. For the two years that his daughter was in a coma, Soraphet put all his efforts into earning enough to cover the costs of her medical care. The case drew attention across Thailand, and one of the consequences was that the copyright owners of Soraphet's back catalog issued a compilation including "Num na khao, sao na kluea" for him to sell whenever he performed. Furthermore, in a move that is likely to lead to new career possibilities, Soraphet began recording and performing duets with well-known *lakhon* (drama series) actress, twenty-three-year-old Khemanit (Pancake) Jamikorn. He has already recorded a demo album titled *Rak tang wai*, referring to a love affair between an old man and younger girl. The album also features spinoffs of his most famous song, "Num na khao rao chai" (Rice-Farm Boy Is Excited) and "Sao na kluea buea rak" (Salt-Farm Girl Bored of Love). Soraphet's music career is thus far from over. He has also enrolled at a local university with the eventual aim of becoming a political representative for his hometown of Bua Yai.[11]

This case study of Soraphet Phinyo reveals aspects of the common practice. Many of the skills demonstrated by Soraphet are required of any successful *luk thung* songwriter: Speed of writing and the ability to adapt established forms to current trends are vital. A strong command of central Thai is required to be able to manipulate complex poetic structures, and knowledge of Isan language and culture is helpful in appealing to the majority audience. An awareness of the history of Thai song is necessary in order to be able to produce new songs that make use of "classic" material. The ability to play several instruments and make demo-standard recordings is essential for advertising one's craft.

Some of Soraphet's strengths are not so typical of other *luk thung* songwriters, although parallels can be found. Only the most skilled songwriters (such as Suraphon Sombatjaroen) are capable of creating trends, as Soraphet did with his famous duet, or of capitalizing on a new form, as in the *Namta mia Sa-u* album for Phimpha Phonsiri. His ability to write an album of songs with a consistent theme and a particular persona in mind, as in the case of his compositions for Phimpha or Nong Nut Duangchiwan, is reminiscent of Surin Phaksiri or Lop Burirat. Soraphet's decision to eschew royalty arrangements in favor of the certainty of up-front payments demonstrates a high level of pragmatism and independence. That he is still working and making a good living from selling new songs at the age of sixty contrasts with the experiences of many songwriters who have either had to return to traditional employment (such as farming) or rely on support from fellow artists. He continues to show considerable business acumen and has been able to keep pace with advances in music technology; these are also characteristics of Grammy's current master songwriter Sala Khunawut.

Despite never attending high school Soraphet is an accomplished artist who has risen to a position in Thai society far beyond his origins, following in the footsteps of a large cohort of Isan songwriting professionals, from Benjamin, Chaloemchai, and Pong Prida to Sanya Chulaphon, Surin Phaksiri, and Thepphon Phetubon. The field of *luk thung* has been greatly enriched by the Isan heritage of these songwriters.

Finally, this discussion of Soraphet's career illustrates how *luk thung* serves as a space for the exploration of contemporary social issues, including migrant and immigrant labor, gender politics, knowledge transmission, and class difference. *Luk thung* songs enable the airing of community tensions between the rural and urban, the village and the city, the working class and the elite. The remainder of this book looks at the social functions of *luk thung*—both in the close-knit, inclusive communities of *luk thung* fans and in the bitter social and political divisions of recent years.

CHAPTER FOUR

Fans, Isan Identity, and the Contemporary *Luk Thung* Scene

I can hear the sound of music.
Who is playing it?
I'm thinking of home
And it reminds me of my ex-lover.
The old people cannot control themselves.
They raise their hands and follow the rhythm.
The young people also
Move closer to each other.

—Huak Fon-ngam (in Waeng 2002, 75, my translation)

A key argument of this book is that *luk thung* has played a leading role in facilitating the regeneration of Lao-Isan identity and culture. Since the 1960s, *luk thung* has provided many Isan people with the opportunity to move into mainstream Thai society via participation in the industry as performers and songwriters. Correspondingly, Isan people have exerted increasing influence as the dominant consumers of the *luk thung* music industry. As a result certain notions of Lao-Isan identity, such as inferred equality, ethnic solidarity and determined resistance to chauvinism, have become associated with *luk thung* music and its fandom. Thus, the large Isan minority that was marginalized during the 1960s to 1980s still constituted a dominant *luk thung* fandom. Today Isan cultural identity has a higher profile in Thailand, and the status of *luk thung* has increased dramatically. Isan people are not marginalized to the same extent and are actually preeminent in some areas of society. This shift from the margins to the center has affected every part of the *luk thung* economy, from concerts to television shows to fan–singer relationships.

The Bangkok Concert Circuit

In the past, the *luk thung* concert circuit throughout Thailand revolved around temples and their festivals, but as the role of the media has grown, concerts organized by record companies, other commercial enterprises, and FM radio stations, as well as private concerts and music clubs, have become just as common. Recording companies organize concerts with radio stations and other companies in order to promote singers and sell media products. Companies such as M-150 (energy drinks), AIS (mobile phone service provider), and Isuzu organize concerts to appeal to the *luk thung* demographic. For example, the huge energy drink market in Thailand is a result of the sizeable population of laborers, the majority of whom are from Isan, and there is even a Red Bull drink named "Luk Thung." Also, Mike Phiramphon and Phai Phongsathon have advertised tractors, and Got Jakrapan has endorsed pickup trucks.

A private concert takes place when a wealthy individual or group hires a singer or troupe to perform at a private celebration. Such concerts occur nightly for funerals, as was the case for the concert described in the introduction, or to celebrate sons becoming monks, often in the presence of the initiate, newly shaven and robed in white before the ordination ceremony on the following day. Since the majority of Thai men become monks only for two to four weeks, such *luk thung* concerts, costing up to 400,000 baht (USD12,000), appear remarkably extravagant yet demonstrate the importance of the event in Thai society.

Thai music clubs, usually referred to as cafés, are restaurants with entertainment included. With popular venues such as Isan Tawan Daeng, Khaen Isan, and Isan Thoet Thoeng, the club circuit in Bangkok obviously caters to Isan audiences. The size of such cafés varies, from small thirty-seat restaurants such as the All Star off Udom Suk to huge venues such as Phra Ram IX and the recently opened Holland Brewery on Phra Ram II. The midsized cafés are where famous *luk thung* singers are most likely to appear, usually toward the end of the night. Cafés are one of the more expensive ways to view *luk thung*—an entrance fee of between 100 to 200 baht is charged and sometimes there are minimum drink orders (often whiskey) or compulsory food such as an overpriced fruit platter. The café circuit was affected by the economic downturn following 1997, with famous venues like Dara and Villa Café closing down. However, clubs such as Isan Tawan Daeng continue to be standbys in the *luk thung* scene with famous singers appearing each month.

Ground Rules for Star–Fan Interaction

As with all fan groups, *luk thung* fandom has its own rules, culture, and customs. Many of these reflect Thai society in general. For example, even though relationships between singers and their fans are extremely close and reciprocal, the usual Thai public moral code applies. Men must not attempt to kiss or inappropriately touch female singers, and risk being forcefully evicted if they do. Female fans are permitted to kiss a male singer on the cheek. Since the key age group in terms of earning potential are fans over thirty, *luk thung* singers are usually very careful to maintain their moral reputation. In 1999, Aphaphon Nakhonsawan successfully sued the editors of TV Pool magazine for spreading the rumor that she had borne the child of the owner of a music house that she had once worked for. Similarly, during the filming of *Mon phleng luk thung FM*, Rung Suriya refused to take his shirt off for a swimming-pool scene, and the planned final romantic scene was stymied when the two *luk thung* singer leads insisted "they were only willing to hold hands [because] they didn't want to harm the respectable image that their fans have of them" (Nilubol 2002, 3). The allure of availability is important, and female singers often keep their marriages secret so as to maintain (sublimated) sexual tension with their fans. For example, for many years Jintara Phunlap maintained that she was not married until a reporter saw her identity card while she was voting. She then claimed that she had forgotten that she was married despite her husband of twenty years being her manager.

A notable exception to the conservative behavior of *luk thung* stars is Ja Turbo's scandalous "Khan hu" (Itchy Ear), which attracted more than fifteen million views when it was posted on YouTube in 2011.[1] In this song coyote dancer[2] Ja declares that she has developed an itchy ear since she became a woman, and is willing to try anything with anyone to cure her itchiness, all the while stroking her groin area. That Ja Turbo caused such a controversy actually demonstrates that *luk thung* is essentially conservative. Her act was clearly modeled on Indonesian *dangdut* performances in which the female singer will work the male audience into a frenzy with suggestive and explicit lyrics and movements. Furthermore, in *dangdut* male patrons are invited onto the stage whereas in all of Ja's performances at least some distance was maintained. Compared to *dangdut*, *luk thung* lyrics are quite tame and must imply rather than confront. However, controversy has paid off for Ja, who was signed to R-Siam in 2014. Her first project with Thailand's second largest entertainment company was to accompany their number one singer Bai Toei in an album celebrating the music of veteran Chai Mueangsing, who, according to Bai Toei, was just as *saep* (spicy or risqué) in his day as she and Ja are now.

FIGURE 4.1. Chai Mueangsing. (Peter Garrity)

FIGURE 4.2. Bai Toei R-Siam. (Peter Garrity)

FANS, ISAN IDENTITY, AND THE CONTEMPORARY LUK THUNG SCENE

Interaction between Fans and Performers at Concerts: *Phuang Malai*

Luk thung concerts are community meetings and as such are structured to allow a constant stream of interaction between fans and singers. Seating is arranged to allow the audience to get in and out of their seats and a large area in front of the stage is left vacant. This is a communal space where fans are able to achieve proximity with singers through the presentation of gifts and the recording of such moments through photography and video. The main point of star–fan interaction at concerts occurs when fans present singers with red roses, gifts, and elaborately made garlands known as *phuang malai* or *malai*, a practice derived from the traditional central Thai dramatic genre *like*. *Malai* are usually made of flowers (both real and artificial) and money but can include dolls, fruit, or even groceries (such as packs of biscuits) as well as photos of the singer or the fan and singer together. Some *malai* are homemade, but most are purchased from sellers at the concerts.

FIGURE 4.3. Fans wait with presents for their favorite singers. (Peter Garrity)

The giving of *malai* and the way singers react represent an exchange of social capital. As will be identified by the singer Donut in her interview, courtesy, gratitude, and making the fans feel that the singer is still "one of them" are much-admired qualities. Singers have to be ready to collect *malai* at all times and are expected to keep holding them for as long as possible (fig. 4.4). Considerable dexterity is required to continue singing while collecting dozens of roses and allowing *malai* to be placed around the neck. Any singer seen taking *malai* home rather than discarding them is admired, although this rule does not apply to roses, which are often recycled during the show. Singers should always attempt to collect every *malai* unless the fan is abusive or behaves inappropriately. There is definitely a pecking order, however, when it comes to fans. If there are too many fans, singers will choose to take the *malai* from those they recognize rather than from strangers, and singers will always stop to accept *malai* from their "superfans."

FIGURE 4.4. *Luk thung molam* duo Job and Joy holding typical *malai*. (Peter Garrity, *Wethi Thai* concert Bangkok, April 4, 2009)

FIGURE 4.5. Fake money *malai*. (Peter Garrity, Phra Ram 2 Bangkok, June 27, 2009)

The giving of *malai* made of money is open to manipulation since popularity and respect are often measured by the amount involved. One eyewitness observed *malai* of more than 12,000 baht (USD360) given to singers who were not even top level. Singer Yodrak Salakchai is reported to have once given 300,000 baht (USD9,000) in a *malai* to a young female singer in order to outbid a wealthy fan and therefore save face. Sometimes the presentation of these *malai* is orchestrated by a singer for the purpose of building face (fig. 4.5), a tactic adopted from the *like* scene where the presentation of *malai* is a ritual with substantial bearing on status.

Interview with *Luk Thung* Singer Sasinan "Donut" Sansinee

In 2009 I interviewed a new singer on the *luk thung* circuit, known as Donut, who was unusual in that she was half Malaysian, had a PhD in education, and spoke English fairly well. In the following interview she gives her opinions on *luk thung* fan culture:

> JM: What do you do with *malai* and roses? What is considered the right thing to do with them? Have you ever received *malai* with money or photos of the fans?
>
> Donut: I keep as many of the flowers as I can. If I receive a *phuang malai* I will present it to Phra Phikhanet [a shrine] to worship (but not the money). I take the roses, dry them, and keep them in a box. When I receive money *malai*—I write down who has given the money and how much. The *malai* will always include the fan's telephone number and details about themselves. Then later I will call them back to have a conversation with them—to thank them and find out when their birthday is so I can send an SMS later on. The fans show their appreciation for what I have done, so I want to make them feel special.
>
> JM: Does your company give guidelines to their singers about the right way to act with fans?
>
> Donut: My company doesn't tell me what the right way to act is but will introduce events that are suited to me. For example, if I go to a Labor Day concert I know that I need to talk about working hard and laboring. If it's a birthday party I have to talk about the birthday person.
>
> JM: What is the best way to build up a fan base?
>
> Donut: The best way to build up a fan base is to be sincere with my words. Sometimes fans ask questions so I answer as much as I can. You cannot be proud.

Talk with them and ask them to support you. If you're not proud the fans will come and talk with you and will shake hands and appreciate your humility.

JM: How much of the singer's time is spent building up a fan base?

Donut: This depends on the media—how much time they give me and how much they promote me. I can only control the making of personal relationship with fans at concerts and through phone numbers and SMS.

JM: How much money is involved in the *malai* you receive?

Donut: The least amount is a hundred but the most is in the thousands. I keep the money and presents for myself—they don't go to the company.

JM: Have you noticed any difference in the behavior of fans from Isan compared to the southern or central regions?

Donut: Most of my fans are Isan people even though I am not Isan. Isan people like to get close to the singer, like to touch the singer, like to dance and like to cooperate with the singer. Whatever the singer asks them to do [from the stage] they will do it. In contrast southern and central people are very quiet and just sit there.

The Communities Formed by Singers and Their Fan Clubs

Luk thung differs from most Western and Thai pop genres in the level of interaction between fans and performers. Thompson's (1995, 222) observation of Western fandom that "an important part of being a fan is the cultivation of non-reciprocal relations of intimacy with distant others" cannot be applied to *luk thung*. Supanat "Off" Chalermchaicharoenkit, who entered the *luk thung* scene through the reality TV show *Academy Fantasia*, observes: "my fans regard me as a relative; a son, a brother or a nephew. Their love and care is a *rak thon rak nan* (enduring love, lasting love)" (Kanokporn 2007, 2). The conflation of celebrity and family is not surprising given the Thai perception of non-intimate distant others as threatening and unreliable. Niels Mulder (2000, 60) describes the Thai world view: "The inside is the world of near persons, of home, family, and community; the outside is the world of distant persons, of strangers, power, and suspicion." Since outside relationships are informed by the power to rule and are undertaken out of a desire for gain, it is no wonder that Thai fans wish to create a sense of inside relationship with the stars they admire, and sometimes vice versa. This is even more characteristic of Isan urban migrants who have a long history of exploitation at the hands of Bangkok employers. In his book arguing for the Isan ownership of *luk thung*, Waeng (2002, 297–305) relates a series of outrages endured by Isan migrants including the trivial example of a bus conductor from Isan who learns to swear in central Thai so he can fit in, and far more serious cases, such as rape and abuse. One young woman from Udon Thani rejected the advances of a man who then called her "Baksiao," an Isan word that becomes a term of derision when applied by others. She shot the man five times but only received a two-year sentence because she received assistance from the Isan Association, Ubon Association, the Association of Isan DJs, and the Isan Lawyers Club. The very existence of these groups demonstrates that Isan people felt they needed to stick together in a foreign and sometimes hostile environment.

Luk thung fan clubs exemplify the Thai discourse of community, which is opposed to modernity, globalization, and market-driven capitalism—the very conditions that have led to the development of modern *luk thung*. Indeed, although it might appear that the hybrid, market-driven genre of *luk thung* is an unlikely refuge from modernity, such a conception fits with James Haughton's observation that "villages and the term 'community' itself are themselves recent state constructions" (2009, 44, 53). For many urban migrants *luk thung* provides a continuous link between their rural childhood, present urban existence, and future unknown location, simultaneously fulfilling the need for familiarity and community as well as the desire to be *thansamai* (up-to-date).

Fan Club Case Study: The Mangpor Family

Until recently one of the largest and hardest-working *luk thung* concert troupes in Thailand belonged to Nopporn Silver Gold, an independent media company started by 1960s *luk thung* star Phanom Nopporn. Nopporn Silver Gold decided in 2011 to focus on television *lakhon* rather than *luk thung*, with mixed results—only the 2013 serial *Mae Pu Priao* (Saucy Miss

Pu) has met with major success. However, for the decade prior to this shift from concert organizer to content provider, Nopporn Silver Gold's biggest star was Mangpor Chonticha (fig. 4.6).

FIGURE 4.6. Mangpor Chonticha. (Peter Garrity, Lumphini night bazaar, June 14, 2009)

Mangpor (Dragonfly) was born in Khon Kaen in 1988 to an Isan mother and central Thai father. Between 2001 and 2011 she produced nine highly successful albums for Nopporn that spawned hits such as "Nu klua tukkae" (I'm Afraid of Lizards), "Tam ha Somchai" (Looking for Somchai) and "Nu yak don um" (I Want to Be Cuddled). Her popularity reached a peak in 2005 when "Nangsao Nancy" ('Miss Nancy') created a national stir with its bittersweet portrayal of a transexual's struggle to be regarded as a woman by Thai officialdom. After "Nancy" became a big hit, Mangpor decided to include similar songs on each following album and she has now built up a notable following in Thailand's LGBT communities. She was the first of so-called "dancing queens"—female stars who dance with the same skill and energy as their dance troupe. Mangpor, Liu Ajariya, and Kratae were inspired by Phumphuang's attempts to do this in the 1980s, and their success means that dancing ability is now a prerequisite for the new generation of singers, which includes Bai Toei, Alice Chayada, and Nim Khanuengphim. After falling out with Nopporn's management, she signed in 2012 with R-Siam, which required a legal name change to Mangpor Chonticha R-Siam. This move has not been a success, with only one single issued by R-Siam in her first three years. By way of comparison, within the same period Kratae has become R-Siam's second biggest *luk thung* star after Bai Toei. This could be an example of a company buying out a singer's contract simply to make space in the market for their preferred artist. The breakup of her marriage in 2013 has further compounded Mangpor's career hiatus.

She began singing professionally in her early teens, and now her fan club literally is her family—the Mangpor Family Club. Unlike Western fan clubs there is no formal way of joining. Fans who frequently attend concerts gradually become known to the singer or the singer's management and are then personally invited to events. Peter Garrity, who went with me to the concert described in the introduction, is well known on the *luk thung* concert scene as one of the most devoted fans of this traditionally working-class genre. A retired IT worker from Leicester, England, and now an expatriate resident of Bangkok, Peter and his wife were invited to become members of the Mangpor Family three years ago. They receive personal invitations to concerts, often sitting with the singer's husband and other Nopphon artists. It is not unusual for Mangpor to take the entire fan club out to dinner after a concert. Club members keep each other informed of news and appearance schedules and sit together at concerts to provide visible support for their singer. They hold up signs and LED boards with Mangpor's name and her dragonfly symbol (fig. 4.7). A sense of community is created by the designing and wearing of club shirts and a ceremonial presentation of a shirt to the singer.

FIGURE 4.7. Mangpor fan club. (Peter Garrity, Thai Cultural Center Bangkok, June 8, 2009)

Beginning in 2008, Mangpor has taken her most supportive fans on an annual bus tour—the Mangbor Family Club meeting—along with Nopporn staff and her dancers. In 2009, the excursion was a merit-making outing to a poor school in Suphan Buri which had only fifty-eight students. The company gave the school food, books, and sporting equipment, and Mangpor donated a sizeable sum for student scholarships. At the school there were games and prizes for students and competitions involving the singer, staff, and fan club. Meals and refreshments were provided on the bus, and fans received free t-shirts and memorabilia. The motivation for this kind of excursion appears to be purely relational—there is no publicity or media coverage and it will not result in further sales or bookings. However, it does demonstrate that Mangpor has progressed in her career to the point where she has become a patron rather than a client.

Superfans

It is helpful to differentiate between average fans who may attend one or two concerts per month and "superfans," such as Peter, who attend several concerts per week.[3] In the *luk thung* concert scene, the fans who attend most regularly and who are well known for their gifts achieve special status and receive special privileges. While performing, singers will sometimes point out these fans by name, especially if given *malai*, thus elevating the symbolic capital of both fan and singer. It is sometimes difficult for singers to keep all fans happy, and the complex status system in Thai society[4] must be adhered to. At a Phumphuang Duangjan memorial concert (which also featured Mangpor) Liu Ajariya accepted a bouquet from one male admirer with "*Suai mak khop khun mak mak Phi Dam*" (Very beautiful, thank you so much Brother Dam) but then had to interrupt her introduction to the next song to accept a *malai* from another male fan, who was presumably of higher status than Phi Dam: "*Oh khothot khothot Lung Kaeo*" (Oh excuse me, I'm sorry uncle Kaeo).

Lung Kaeo is a *luk thung* superfan who has achieved high status through frequent concert attendance. He is fifty-three years old, works as a food seller, and attends at least three concerts per week. He claims that he spends surprisingly little (less than 1,000 baht per month) on his hobby and that he does not give money to singers. Yet he is able to contact many singers by phone and once attended a party at Luknok Supphaphon's house. He says he feels proud when singers mention his name at concerts or telephone to thank him for *malai*.

Indeed, superfans seem to have almost instant access to their favored singers, having their personal phone numbers and sometimes visiting their homes. Siriphon Amphaiphong reportedly sets some time aside each day for these superfans to be able to call her. As previously described by Donut, singers actively court the attention of superfans through phone and text messages, even presenting them with birthday presents. As in *like*, there can be rivalry among fans over who has the longest history with the singer or who knows the most about a particular performer.

In *luk thung* the boundary lines separating fan from celebrity are extremely fluid. Occasionally superfans themselves can become celebrities, while younger singers are expected to behave as fans of older singers. For example, Mangpor still regards herself as a fan of Phumphuang Duangjan and visits the Phumphuang shrine at Suphan Buri before launching any new recording. Although singers are the focus of most fan adoration, DJs and songwriters can develop their own fan base. Jenphop Jopkrabuanwan is possibly the most famous *luk thung* fan in Thailand, but he also has a large following of fans in his capacity as a radio DJ. He is a songwriter, lecturer, and popular music historian who has helped to create a market for the *luk thung* singers and recordings of yesteryear. Although not a professional singer, Jenphop recorded an album of *luk thung* covers to present to his closest fans, and he also performs the songs in charity concerts (Chaba 2004, 5). The devotion of influential superfans such as Jenphop has played an important part in the rise in popularity of *luk thung* over the past twenty years.

Fans, Companies, and Patronage

There are a number of reasons why fan–star relationships achieve such extraordinary intimacy. The structure of Thailand's entertainment industry whereby *luk thung* singers are paid very little for their recordings has emphasized the importance of personal relationships with fans. Given the recording companies' expectations of an album every three months and the resultant high turnover in performers, fans are a singer's most reliable form of superannuation, in the sense of an informal mode of income insurance in the event of being dropped by their company. Bookings for private celebrations, which are more lucrative for singers than company-organized concerts, are more likely to result from contact with superfans than from advertising. Although there are many websites produced by record companies and fans to promote *luk thung* singers, there seems to be an overall mistrust on the part of performers in non-traditional means of promotion. In November 2009, Mangpor ceased posting on her fan-club website, reportedly because one of her fans had impersonated her on Facebook.

The high level of interaction between fans and singers exists both in spite of and because of the structure of Thailand's entertainment industry. Although major concerts are advertised through television and radio, the fan system functions as an important advertising and promotional tool. Fans swap lists of forthcoming concerts, and fan-run websites often have better information than those of the company websites—perhaps the highly developed system of personal proximity described later in this chapter has rendered the use of company websites as a tool to promote *luk thung* fan-star interaction unnecessary. The most dedicated fans are able to call their singers directly and find out where privately organized concerts are going to take place.

Contacting companies directly for concert information can be frustrating because most lack the resources to promote concerts, which occur almost every night of the week. Top Line Diamond, which manages singers such as Rung Suriya and Noknoi Uraiphon, has the reputation of being a highly professional and organized company but is very much the exception. The giants such as Grammy and R-Siam (the *luk thung* arm of RS Promotions) are usually unable to provide accurate schedules for upcoming concerts. Grammy has a website but it is used for static promotion rather than providing information about upcoming concerts or providing space for fan comments. On the other hand, the structure of Thailand's entertainment industry, whereby *luk thung* singers are paid very little for their recordings, has emphasized the importance of personal relationships with fans. Star singers are able to command big performance fees and are also booked for lucrative private concerts.

Nevertheless, it is often difficult for singers to function independently of record companies. Luknok Supphaphon, who had the huge hit "Khun Lamyai" in 2001, was unable to relaunch her career once she left Grammy, with independent distribution proving impossible. Similarly, Nok Phonphana ran into problems with her record company when she attempted to arrange her own concerts. A select few of the highest-profile singers are able to work both independently and within the company system. Jintara Phunlap organizes her own appearances yet continues to work with R-Siam and previously for Grammy and Master Tape.

A significant feature of Thai society is its organization along the vertical lines of patron-client relationships. Unsurprisingly, industry and fan relations in all Thai popular musical genres are also organized according to this system. However, *luk thung* differs from the other main genres of Thai popular music in the degree to which singers function as both patron and client in their relationships with fans. The *luk thung* fan system allows singers an element of independence in a highly hegemonic industry by boosting their bargaining power within the company and by providing alternative patronage; having fans confers status on singers and makes them more valuable to their company. The company system functions as a patron and client relationship in which the company as patron takes on more risk and consequently can claim a greater share of the profit. Furthermore, when the company helps the singer out of a hopeless situation (that of being an unknown), *bunkhun*, or moral obligation, enters the relationship and loyalty is expected from the singer. As singers gain fame, the balance between patron and client shifts and, very occasionally, the roles are reversed.

Within the *luk thung* fan system, singers and fans alternate between the roles of patron and client. When fans provide additional sources of income through private concerts and *malai,* the singer is a client. Certainly many singers regard fans as their patrons, as the following quote from Aphaphon Nakhonsawan shows: "It's a lighter example of the patronage system, which is entrenched in our society. As patrons, *mae yok* [see the following section] and other fans are instrumental in keeping *likay* and *luk thung* alive" (Kanokporn 2007, 3). However, when Mangpor takes her fan club out to dinner or on an excursion she takes on the role of patron. This progression from client to patron is the reason why money *malai* can be important income for minor singers whereas big stars will usually donate all such stage money to charity.

Influence from *Like* and *Molam*

The central Thai folk drama genre of *like* is famous for the obsessive behavior of some audience members. The most dedicated fans, known as *mae yok* (*mae* means "mother," and *yok* "to lift up or worship") are wealthy, elderly women who worship the youthful *phra ek* (hero) because of his good looks, small body, high voice, and exquisite manners—an image of non-threatening masculinity. As Mulder (2000, 62) states, "the deepest . . . *bunkun* occurs in the closed personal relationship with one's mother," and it appears that *mae yok* are seeking to fulfil the role of mother in their relationship with the *phra ek*. In addition to giving flowers, garlands, cash, jewelery, and other presents, *mae yok* frequently cook food for the singer, clean his house, and wash his clothes. The extreme possessiveness of some fans leads to fighting with other fans and also with their husbands because affairs between *mae yok* and *phra ek* are not uncommon (Mae 2009, 48–50). As the main source of revenue, *mae yok* constitute the dominant *like* fandom, but they are often held up to ridicule in the Thai media and therefore constitute a marginalized fandom within the field of Thai music.

Unlike *like*, the dominant *luk thung* fandom is split more evenly between men and women, with men possibly in the majority. Whereas *mae yok* attempt to emulate the mother–son relationship, in *luk thung*, sex is a key element of attraction for fans. Ubonrat (1990, 69) claims there are two features which make *luk thung* politically and culturally contentious: its unfailing identification with the peasantry, and its expression of sexual desire. The earthy sexuality of *luk thung* may be derived from several folk genres (*isaeo* comes to mind), but the word play and explicit jokes contained in *molam* have certainly been most influential. For example, *Molam* Ken Daolao sings: "I am an old man; my testicles have turned yellow with age. Please keep the old buffalo until it dies. . . . Please touch my dung, for this may be better than smelling my gas" (quoted in Miller 1985, 301). In *luk thung* the bawdy humor of *molam* is sublimated to a certain extent so as to be acceptable for a wider audience, but the expression of sexual desire is still too open for elite Thai society. In 2003 the Ministry of Culture issued a list of twenty songs that were to be banned, including classics such as Suthep Wongkamhaeng's "Phit thang rak" (Wrong Way to Love) and Chai Mueangsing's "Mia phi mi chu" (My Wife Had an Affair).[5] Veteran *luk krung* singer Suthep was shocked at being included in this list and advised the government to "think about banning newer songs, particularly those in the *luk thung* genre."[6] After public outcry the ministry backed down and only banned three *molam* songs "loaded with immoral content and improper language ... and in the Northeastern dialect" ("Blacklist" 2003). Oddly enough, one of the singers caught up in this moral panic was eighteen-year-old Yingli Sichumphon, who adopted the role of a scarlet woman in her song "Bor yan bap" (Not Afraid to Sin).[7] The government censure threatened to destroy her career, but she is now signed to Grammy and has the most popular YouTube *luk thung* song in Thai history, "Kho chai thoe laek boe tho" (Your Heart for My Phone Number).[8] Thus, sexuality in commercial *luk thung* is watched carefully by government organizations, but writers and singers regularly test the boundaries.

Superstar from the 1980s Phumphuang Duangjan is lauded (or blamed) for having allowed female *luk thung* stars to embrace their sexuality (see fig. 1.3). Her career only took off after her first television appearance in 1978, which publicized her name change from Namphueng Mueangsuphan (Honey of Suphan) to the more suggestive Phumphuang (Bountiful Fruit) Duangjan (Moon). Some older fans prefer the traditional demure beauty of Tai Orathai to the extrovert sensuality of Bai Toei R-Siam (fig. 4.2), who has become notorious through her crossover dance hit "Rak tong poet (Naen ok)" from 2013, performed with dance group 3.2.1. Kamikaze, which consists of male idol Gavin, male rapper T. J., and female singer Poppy.[9] While "Naen ok" means "heartburn" and refers to being weighed down by troubles, the dance moves and Bai's buxom appearance draw attention to the literal translation of "full breasts." However, the song is still typically *luk thung* in the way it combines sexual content with humor. In the video clip, T. J. masturbates (hence the English title "Splash Out") to pictures of naked Western women but fails to find release until he changes to pictures of naked male bodybuilders. The crossover character of the song is played out literally when the touring buses of Bai Toei and 3.2.1. Kamikaze collide, with Gavin, T. J., and Poppy attracted to Bai, and the male *luk thung* dancers attracted to Gavin. An official parody clip moves the location from luxury tour bus to a *song thaeo* (small open air bus with two rows of seating) in a rural setting and has the singers dancing outrageously while the village children watch bemused.[10] The part of Bai Toei is taken by a very masculine transvestite named Jenny, who, in a typical Thai play on words, is described as *mai san samoe hi* (not short up to the vagina) referring to Bai Toei's reputation for very brief costumes, or *san samoe hu* (short up to the ears).

FIGURE 4.8. Tai Orathai. (Peter Garrity)

The Impact of Isan Cultural and Social Identity on Thai Society

One of the clearest statements of Isan identity within a *luk thung* song is found in Phai Phongsathon's 2009 hit "Khon ban diaokan" (People of the Same Village), which was written by Wasu Haohan. Phai (fig. 4.9) is rapidly becoming the biggest male *luk thung* star in Thailand, and his songs communicate a high level of class consciousness and ethnic pride, despite his being signed to the dominant entertainment company Grammy. Hesse-Swain's (2006, 261) observation that competition "has driven Thai media operators to create programming that appeals to ethnic and regional tastes of their audiences," can certainly be extended to the recording and concert industries. The lyrics of "Khon ban diaokan" join past expressions of Isan solidarity such as Thepphon Phetubon's version of Phongsak Jantharukkha's "Isan ban hao" (Isan, Our Home) in placing local allegiances above cultural nationalism. The fact that Phai's songs are written by Grammy's in-house songwriters, such as Wasu Haohan and Sala Khunawut, shows either that Grammy is adept at manipulating and commodifying such troublesome concepts as ethnic identity or that its songwriters have strong beliefs on such issues. The idea that an agenda may exist among senior songwriters to advance Isan cultural identity is not necessarily fanciful. One Grammy insider informed me that the status of established *luk thung* songwriters is far higher than that of their pop equivalents, with the former receiving the title of *khru* (teacher) and being accorded greater independence in artist choice and subject matter, as long as they remain successful.

FIGURE 4.9. Phai Phongsathon at *Wethi Thai* concert Bangkok, May 16, 2009. (Peter Garrity)

'Khon ban diaokan" starts with the traditional call of "Oi no no" signaling that a *Molam* is ready to sing. The chorus sums up the singer's identification with his Isan audience through the local community:

We from the same village just look at each other's eyes and we understand.
I know how tired you are and how hard you must struggle.
We have words of encouragement,
We have words of comfort.
We have the Isan greeting, "Sambai di bo," to always give each other—the people of our village.

The song and accompanying film clip[11] casts Phai as the owner of a *lap* (Isan spicy minced meat dish) shop, who greets his customers with Isan blessings:

Hai sok hai man hai mang hai mi (May you have good luck and lots of money)
Hai yu di mi haeng, yu daeng mi hi, doe khrap phi Nong. (May you have good health, my brothers and sisters)

In this last line the consonants are swapped to create a typically bawdy Isan play on words. *Yu daeng mi hi* has no particular meaning but *hi* can mean "vagina" depending on the tone. This is a good example of the *luk thung* songwriter adapting explicit Isan humor so that it does not offend the wider audience.

The verses present two snapshots of Isan migrant workers in Bangkok. In verse one Mr. Thitkhen from Roi Et has left his debt-ridden life of rice farming to try his luck driving taxis in the big city. In verse two Nong (Younger Sister) Takadaen (played by fellow Grammy singer Takadaen Chonlada) has left high school to work in a Bangkok sewing factory but is unable to get ahead. This clever cross-promotion is a case of multi-layered mirroring: the young Isan migrant is actually the famous *luk thung* singer. In real life Takadaen worked as a Bangkok bus conductor and was rejected many times by companies before she won a competition and was signed by Grammy. The *lap* seller's exhortation to Thitkhen and Takadaen to "keep on persevering" can be applied equally to Isan migrant laborers and aspiring Isan *luk thung* singers. The taxi driver and factory worker are able to endure hardship and discrimination through the support of the wider Isan migrant community, and the successful *luk thung* singer does not forget where he or she comes from. The Isan self-image combines "a sense of marginality" with "a strong sense of ethno-regional pride" (McCargo and Hongladarom 2004, 221). This duality, so apparent in "Khon ban diaokan," is what binds Isan fans and *luk thung* singers together. Perhaps because they are so sensitive to disparagement and marginalization, Isan people are more emotionally and physically responsive to singers' overtures than other groups.

Signs of Tension in the *Luk Thung* Fandom

Undoubtedly, Isan fans still constitute the dominant *luk thung* fandom. Yet there are tensions that indicate a struggle for dominance within the *luk thung* scene is taking place. First, some fans have reacted negatively to the modern subgenre of *nu luk thung* and a perceived loss of authenticity. Wanit Jarungkitanan, a writer and *luk thung* fan, argues that Thai entertainment companies have killed *luk thung* by blending it with other genres and promoting actors who look good but cannot sing in the traditional style. Wanit protests the proliferation of recordings by *luk khrueng* celebrities at the expense of career *luk thung* singers, most of whom hail from Isan (Amporn 2006, 25–26). This blurring of the boundaries between genres is concerning to older fans especially, and a common subject of discussion at concerts is a nostalgic comparison between the modern *luk thung* scene and the past. Fans are constantly judging singers' behavior; one area where some modern singers are found wanting is in the collection of *malai*. At a *Wethi Thai* (*Thai Stage*) concert in May 2009, one teenage singer caused offense when she passed on two expensive *malai* with money attached even though she had nothing else to hold. Fans inevitably contrast this with an iconic picture of Yodrak Salakchai from a 1986 concert in which he is wearing so many *malai* that his face can hardly be seen. The success of Channel Nine's schools competition show, *Ching cha sawan* (*Ferris Wheel*), has fostered interest in *luk thung* among Thai youth, but the show's emphasis on *luk thung* as a national art form effectively dilutes the Isan-ness of the genre. Thus the issue of authenticity works against the dominant Isan fandom through the alienation of older fans and the gentrification of the genre in the eyes of younger fans.

Second, with *luk thung*'s rise in status, class difference is beginning to become an issue at concerts. Roses are a cheaper alternative to *malai* and, if singers neglect to collect them, the roses are sometimes thrown onto the stage in disgust. Recently, increased television coverage has resulted in fans at some concerts being asked to only give *malai* between songs. This has irritated fans and exacerbated the roses issue because singers have less time for interaction with the audience. The lowly *malai* sellers are complaining of being undermined by companies who hand out free *malai* to their singer's fan club to "ensure" popularity. Some upper-class fans have been heard deriding other audience members as *ban nok*—roughly translated as "country bumpkins." Before *luk thung*'s rise in status and acceptance as a symbol of central Thai culture these signs of tension were not as common, simply because the audience was far more homogenous.

The Voice and *Doe Woi*

The struggle for dominance is also apparent in mainstream television. Most readers will be familiar with *The Voice*, a reality TV contest that is supposed to emphasize singing ability over appearance. The four judges are not allowed to see the contestants until after they have heard them sing. If the judges like a singer's voice they indicate their approval by swinging around to face the singer. In most countries *The Voice*'s repertoire is similar to that of Idol or Academy Fantasia—a variety of popular music genres. But for the Thai version which premiered in October 2012, there was an obvious focus on lounge room jazz and *phleng wan* (sweet songs). The king's jazz compositions were sung frequently, as were *Thai doem* favorites such as "Lao duang duean." Thai folk-song genres did not feature at all and one of the few *luk thung* songs was a smooth jazz version of "Sao Isan ro rak." The judges included hip-hop singer and producer Joey Boy and singing teacher and former pop star Jennifer Kim. This combination of judges, choice of song style, and purported emphasis on vocal excellence meant that the show became an exercise in defining high culture. However, this overall aim was undermined by the poor singing of some contestants, perhaps indicating that the Thai talent pool for this style is too limited (which is definitely not the case for *luk thung*).

The relative absence of *luk thung* from *The Voice* became a target for satire through a regular skit on Channel Three's comedy show *Kon Bai Khlai Khriat* (Relaxing before Afternoon) called *Doe woi* (which sounds like "The Voice" spoken in a thick Thai accent). The skit parodied every element of *The Voice*, including the overacting of the judges before they swing around. *Woi* is a Thai exclamation of shock, equivalent in meaning to the Australian slang use of "bugger." The judges included comedians Tak Siriphon Yuyort and her husband Nui Choenyim (this surname is actually the name of a comedy troupe), and *katoei* performer Mam Laconic. In the first episode[12] of season one, the performance was a *phleng wan* typical of *The Voice*, sung by the vocally and physically challenged Suthep Sisai. Apparently impressed by the singer's vocal ability, the judges turned around together but, horrified by his appearance, they quickly swung back. In episode three[13] Yong Choenyim and Phuang Choenyim delivered a truly awful *lae* performance which entailed blackmailing the judges to turn around. For example, they sang, "If Tak doesn't turn around she'll find out that her husband has a second wife," and then, "If Nui doesn't turn around his wife will find a new husband." Episode five[14] featured a more than competent rendition of an up-tempo *luk thung* song "Laeo laeo" by comedian Chomphu Konbai. The judge's comments were particularly satirical in that they criticized Chomphu's actions and appearance rather than her voice. Tak's description of the singer as "Na ta ko chonabot, taeng tua boran" (rural face, in an old fashioned dress) is amusing not only because it mimics the snooty tone and pretentious atmosphere of *The Voice* but also because Chomphu is actually a very attractive young woman. In response Chomphu then recognizes Tak's real-life husband, Nui, as her old teacher who used to hit on her and complain about his wife not taking care of his needs. In episode six[15] Bongneng Choenyim presented an off-key and off-tempo performance of the recent Suthirat Wongthewan hit "Thephi ban phrai" (Jungle Beauty Queen) before pulling out a gun and threatening to shoot the judges unless they turn around. The bawdy, uproarious, and comically violent atmosphere of *Doe woi* was completely different to that of *The Voice*, clearly communicating the cultural gulf that was developing between middle- and upper-class Bangkok and Thailand's aspirational working class throughout the country.

Nang Baep Khok Kradon

The hit *lakhon* titled *Nang baep Khok Kradon* (model from Khok[16] Kradon) reflects the political power shifts that have taken place in Thai society over the past decade. Broadcast on Channel Seven in May 2012, the drama draws comic contrast between Ban Khok Kradon—a dry, dusty Isan village—and the high-society fashion scene in Bangkok. Initially, the standard *luk thung* and *lakhon* trope of a *ban nok* person lost in Bangkok is played out. When we are first introduced to the heroine Khamlao, she is dark skinned (thanks to ridiculously orange fake tanning cream), foul mouthed, and feisty. After fighting off the *nak leng* (criminal) who tries to rape her, she is sent to Bangkok by her parents with the idea of her becoming a model. At first she is tricked into serving as a maid at the model agency, but after clashing with other aspiring models she is accepted into the agency. Her unlikely transformation into an international model named Laura is actually convincing because the character is played by Thai-English model Panthita "Sammie" Cowell.

When Laura decides to return home, the action shifts back to Ban Khok Kradon, as an assortment of city characters with dubious motives descend on the sleepy village. The model agent follows Laura to convince her to return, a *khunying* (aristocrat), always talking about her restaurant in Australia, seeks to marry off her daughter to the hero, In (played by heartthrob actor Phathit Phisitkun), and unscrupulous businessman James plans to develop the area into the glitzy Khok Kradon City. Although *Nang baep Khok Kradon* appears to present Isan characters as comical and unsophisticated and the urban central Thai characters as wealthy and sophisticated, the storyline gradually reveals that the city folk are desperately in need of help. Not only are the country folk happier but they are also financially and culturally superior to their city counterparts. The model agent and the *khunying* compete for the affections of the village's *phu yai ban* (village head), who is played by *luk thung* star Monsit Khamsoi. The *khunying* hopes that she can regain the money she lost through her Australian investment by marrying the wealthy village head. Her daughter imagines that the hero ("Indy," as she calls him) is in love with her when he is really in love with Isan girl Laura. When James brings Khun Albert, a Western investor, to look at the proposed development site, Albert asks to see the area's culture. James cynically produces a couple of coyote dancers but is humiliated when the villagers appear as a traditional *klong yao* troupe and Albert joins In and Laura in dancing *soeng* to the sound of *molam*. Even the showgirls change to dance in the traditional Isan style. In each case the city characters end up being subservient to the Isan villagers they were trying to manipulate.

The music of *Nang baep Khok Kradon* follows the normal *lakhon* pattern of endlessly repeating variations of the title song. However, considerable thought and effort have been put into the song and its film clip, so the repetition is not as jarring to Western sensibilities as is often the case with *lakhon*. "Khok Kradon City"[17] is sung by the three actresses who play the young female characters in Khok Kradon village, with a cameo by Monsit Khamsoi. It is somewhat surprising that Sirintra Niyakon, a former *luk thung* star who plays Laura's mother, is not given any lines to sing, but perhaps the producers wished to project an image of a new, *thansamai* (modern) Isan. Veteran Isan actor Thongchai Prasongsanti, who plays Laura's father, is also not featured in the video. The video clip is presented as a live *luk thung Isan* performance with a gyrating *hang khrueang*, light show, and high-fashion costumes. The band is in the style of Ponglang Sa-on (see chapter one), featuring *pong lang*, electric *phin*, *wort* and a *nang hai*—a beautiful girl who dances while pretending to play pots used to store *pla ra* (fermented fish). The two young comedians who play the role of villagers interject throughout the song with "Wai bo, wai bo" (Is it okay?), while the hero In struts in the background in front of the backup dancers.

Following standard *luk thung* practice, central Thai is interspersed with Isan words and phrases such as "muan lai" (lots of fun) and, perhaps to emphasize Laura's international transformation, she begins the song singing in (broken) English, "Hello, hello, everybody. Welcome to my city, *thang* [both] ladies [and] gentlemen." The lyrics compare the simple life of Isan villagers with globalized Thai urban culture. *Somtam pla ra*, Lao-style papaya salad made with fermented fish, and *khua wakutchi*, roasted bugs found in buffalo manure, are contrasted with pizza and suki; a traditional bamboo field shelter (*thiang na*) is declared to be better than lights, pubs, and bars; and *lam phloen* is the preferred music, rather than the K-pop band Wonder Girls. This theme of local triumphing over global pervades the *lakhon*'s storyline and reflects the reality that Isan culture has not only survived decades of "central Thaification" but is beginning to dominate in twenty-first-century Thailand.

Political Fandoms

The above examples of tension and change become especially significant in the context of the ongoing class-based political turmoil in Thailand. Since 2005 the political scene has been dominated by the conflict between red-shirted supporters of former prime minister Thaksin Shinawatra and successive opposing groups. While there is no direct link between *luk thung* fan clubs and political persuasion, such as that found in Tamil film star fan clubs (see Rogers 2009, 63–85), there is a strong correlation between the dominant Lao-Isan *luk thung* fandom and the red-shirt movement, and it is clear that a link exists between Isan political identity and the Isan cultural identity expressed through *luk thung*. After the Thaksin-aligned political party Phuea Thai won a majority in the July 2011 election, cases could be made both for and against the proposition that the red shirts were still a marginalized fandom in Thai politics, but the fact that Isan people were heavily represented and invested in a powerful political movement demonstrates the progress that was made by the largest ethnicity in Thailand. It is somewhat ironic that as Isan people attempt to move towards mainstream participation in Thai politics their position as the dominant *luk thung* fandom is being threatened by media commodification and cultural nationalization.

If the dominance of any particular fandom is to be judged according to the level of influence it exerts on society, it certainly appears that Isan people have become more dominant in Thailand in recent decades. Within the *luk thung* concert scene the desire of performers and companies to attract fans has made Isan identity a valuable commodity. In the Thai political scene Isan identity has long been exploited for votes, but the convergence of *luk thung* and Isan identity in the red-shirt movement is a more recent phenomenon.

CHAPTER FIVE

Luk Thung and Political Expression

The only friend I have is a buffalo.
The buffalo smell is a perfume that makes me dream when I'm asleep.
The scent of the buffalo is mixed with the scent of the young farmers.
It's not upper class like the people of heaven.
The smell of this perfume is sweet every day;
It's like a fragrant herb.
Don't look down on farmers as if they are poor things.
One hand holds the scythe while sitting on the ground,
To feed us from the past till now.
Human life has value except for the farmers—
Honor the smell of buffaloes.

—Excerpt from "Klin khlon sap khwai" (Muddy Odor and Stinking Buffalo) by Phaibun Butkhan

Anyone who followed the turmoil in Thailand that started in 2005 is probably aware that music played an important role in the protests. Ten years of political turmoil and ten years of protest music—the recent history of Thailand has shown that even the most commercial pop music can become a political tool. The increase in social protest in Thailand since 2005 has been marked by a dramatic rise in the use of music in a political context. Unlike the leftist movement of the 1970s, which entrenched the view of *phleng phuea chiwit* as the accepted Thai protest genre, the People's Alliance for Democracy (PAD), or "yellow shirts" (and successive groups of various colors), and the United Front for Democracy against Dictatorship (UDD), or "red shirts," together made use of almost every kind of music found in Thailand. Remarkably, this outpouring of rebellious sounds took place against a backdrop of increasing state censorship, self-censorship by media and recording companies, and punitive lèse majesté laws. Why this has been possible is not straightforward. Certainly, advances in the areas of satellite television, home recording equipment, and the Internet have made censorship easier to overcome. Part of the answer also lies in the messages and memories communicated both lyrically and musically, consciously and subconsciously, through the songs and music used by each group.

Music and the Yellow Shirts

The PAD's combination of free-to-air satellite television coverage and continuous demonstrations centered around a performance stage, resulting in a blend of protest and entertainment that was simultaneously activism and media content. Just as the proliferation of cable television networks around the world has led to a massive increase in demand for content, so the twenty-four-hour format of PAD leader Sonthi Limthongkul's satellite television station, ASTV, meant that musical content was essential. Furthermore, the pro-monarchy PAD appears to have had high levels of support from Bangkok's entertainment industry. This was clearly seen when well-known musician, actor, and film director Phongphat Wachirabanjong accepted the award for best supporting actor at the Nataraja Awards (for Thai TV) ceremony in 2010. To a standing ovation he orated, "If you hate Father [i.e., the king], insult Father, and have thoughts about chasing Father out of this house, I would say, if you do not love Father anymore, you should leave, because this is Father's house." At a concert held in Bangkok in July 2010, *luk krung* legend Suthep Wongkamhaeng referred to Thaksin's exile in the classic Phaibun Butkhan song "Lok ni khue lakhon" (This World Is a Play), which reminds the wealthy that all must finally leave their homeland. To great applause Suthep interrupted the song to declare, "there are some people who do not have a home anymore" (Jaiser 2012, 75). Another elite artist to come out in support of the PAD was the artistic director of the Bangkok Opera, Somtow Sucharitkul, who famously proclaimed that "having returned to the country of my birth after having spent some fifty years abroad, I had never felt more free" (Somtow 2006) just weeks before the junta's Ministry of Culture censored his opera *Ayodhya* for fear of bad luck. As a result of this industry support, a constant stream of celebrities was available to perform at PAD protests. These included model Kanchanit "Phrik" Sammakun, *lakhon* actresses Phecharada "O" Thiamphet and Wannaphon "Rai" Chimbanjong, 1990s pin-up Champen Ex (best known outside Thailand for the music video to Peter Andre's 2004 UK Number 1 hit "Mysterious girl"), Miss Thailand 2004 Sirinthaya Satyasai, Phimra "Namwan" Jaroenphakdi (an actress who was formerly a member of Grammy tweens group ZaZa), Sino-Thai actor Satawat "Te" Setthakon (who had a short singing career with Grammy, both in Thailand and Taiwan), veteran film and *lakhon* actor Aphichat Halamjiak (who died in 2008), and comedian Di Dorkmadan. Correspondingly, well-educated middle- to upper-class viewers with an interest in the fine arts did not want to watch hours of uninterrupted speeches. Consequently, variety programs on ASTV, such as *Cho lueang* (*Yellow Screen*) hosted by well-known actor Sarunyu Wongkrachang, became key drawcards for the PAD.

Many of the genres favored by the constituency of the PAD and PDRC (a successive group with similar ideology),[1] such as *phleng plukchai* (patriotic marches), Thai and Western classical, *luk krung*, jazz, electronica, and Thai alternative rock, can be described as elite—genres which signify high status and are produced by and for the most affluent segment of urban society.[2] A number of other genres are not elite culture per se but are usually followed only by niche audiences. These include the central Thai folk genres of *lamtat* and *lae* represented by Wang Teh Lamtat ensemble and the pastiche folk group Farmer's Son. Illustrating the close relationship between the PAD and the majority of the Sino-Thai community, the 2006 and 2008 PAD protests featured the Teochew Chinese opera genre of *ngiu* with academic and former student activist Wirot Tangwanit leading the Ngiu Thammasat troupe.

However, not all of the PAD's music was so easily classified as elite culture. Many *phleng phuea chiwit* musicians campaigned for the PAD, including Muslim group Hammer, top Southern band Malihuanna (which sounds like marijuana but means "blossoms of song") led by Khothawut Thongthai, Saeng Thammada (also from the South), the Hope Family of Suthep Thawanwiwathanakun, husband and wife duo Khitanchali, and Folkner. Songs for life's heavier cousin, country rock, has been featured at many protests through artists such as Sek Saksit and Nasu Raphin Phuthichat and the Su Su Band. The most celebrated endorsement for the PAD came from the leader of the prototypical songs-for-life group Caravan, Surachai "Nga" Jantimathon, and his band member Mongkhon Uthok. Several of these songs-for-life performers composed songs specially for the protests, with Nga producing "March Phanthamit mai klua daet" (PAD Isn't Afraid of the Sun March) and a group improvisation called "Sanam Luang," named for the site of many PAD protests in Bangkok. Saeng Thammada wrote the scornful "Yik Thaksin" (Pinch Thaksin), Blue Issara wrote "Ao man ok pai" (You [rude form] Get Out) after one of the PAD's favorite phrases, and Sek Saksith and the Su Su band came up with "Ying kong ying ruay" (The More You Cheat, the Wealthier You Get) and "Doen doen" (Walk, Walk) (Veena 2006). Northern folk singer Suntaree Vechanont, most famous for the 1978 song "Chiang Mai Girl," first appeared for the PAD in 2006, along with her pop-star daughter Lanna Commins. Suntaree's political stance reportedly led to a grenade being left outside her restaurant in Thaksin's home city of Chiang Mai (Kelley 2009). Other popular music performers include a power trio of rock artists—Sip Lo (Ten Wheels), Rang Rockestra, and Sukanya Miguel, who first became famous as a nude pinup—as well as 1980s popstar Alice Kristan and Ort Khiribun, who had a long pop career with RS Promotion and Grammy. The PAD have even made use of *luk thung*, via crossover *luk krung* singer Ophat Thosaphon from RS and Nithithat Promotion, southern *luk thung* star Sonthaya Chitmani from Grammy Gold, actress and *luk thung* singer Sirilak "Joy" Phongchok, referred to on the protest stage as *nang ek khwanchai phanthamit* (darling heroine of the PAD), and veteran National Artist Chinakon Krailat, who is famous for incorporating central Thai folk genres such as *lamtat, phleng choi, ruea,* and *isaeo* (see chapter two) into his performances. It is significant that none of these singers is from Isan, and all are known for more than *luk thung*.

The PAD claimed to be waging a "holy war . . . to protect the three institutions of Thailand, namely the state, the religion, and the monarchy" (Palphol 2009), so it is not surprising that royal music and *phleng plukchai*, or patriotic songs, featured at demonstrations. Rang Rockestra's stirring "Rak thoe prathet Thai"[3] (We Love You, Thailand) has been a regular selection for PAD concerts, university graduations, and nationalistic advertisements alike over the past decade. Songs written by King Bhumibol, such as the anti-communist anthem "Rao su" (We Fight) and jazz tune "Chata chiwit" (Destiny of Life), and songs in praise of the king were especially popular at yellow- and pink-shirt protests. In September 2008, Australian folk singer

Kelly Newton performed her own song "Long Live the King of Thailand" on the protest stage at Government House to rapturous applause.[4] One of the PAD's leaders, Naowarat Phongphaibun, was a National Artist for poetry who, in 2007, wrote new lyrics for "Mahachai," a song currently associated Princess Sirindhorn and first composed by Prince Paribatra Sukhumbhand (see chapter two), a son of King Chulalongkorn. With such an emphasis on royal and elite culture, the yellow shirts consciously differentiate themselves from the working class. A PAD video accompanied by a 2004 rock version[5] of an old *phleng plukchai*, "Rak kan wai thoet" (Please Love Each Other), draws a clear distinction between pro-Thaksin thugs who smoke, drink, and expose themselves, and peaceful, orderly yellow shirts who participate in central Thai folk arts and customs. The video ends with a shot of the phrase, "Muea khon thoi pen yai, khon Thai yom dueat ron" ("When scum become big, Thai people are naturally in trouble"). This strong demarcation of boundaries of heritage and status was inevitably reflected in the PAD's attitude toward working-class music. Both the PAD's demographic and its assumed mantle as the protector of the monarchy led to an expressed preference for elite culture and tradition.

Music and the Red Shirts

After the Thaksin-aligned People's Power Party was dissolved and the Democrat Party came to power in December 2008, there was a proliferation of UDD media content, including a dramatic increase of music. Over the course of 2008 the UDD had learned much from the PAD regarding organization and use of media technology. Soon after the Democrats began governing, the UDD launched DTV (Democracy Television), a repackaging of the earlier PTV (People's Television) that was clearly intended to emulate the role played by ASTV in coordinating protests against the People's Power Party governments. The channel followed the same infotainment format and featured such programs as political talk show *Khwam ching wan ni* (*Truth Today*) and *Khui Kap Adison* (*Talk with Adison*). The latter was a music variety show hosted by Adison Phiangket, who composed songs for the Communist Party of Thailand (CPT) during the years of the Isan insurgency before embarking on a political career in which he rose to be MP for Khon Kaen and a minister in Thaksin's government. In one typical episode (February 18, 2009) Adison was joined by *Molam* Sathian Noi and his son, as well as *Molam* Wanida. In the studio they discussed the political situation, and improvised traditional *lam klon* and *kham soi*—ribald jokes that begin with the call to attention "soi soi." For example, Sathian Noi's son joked, "Soi soi, the red shirts throw eggs and that is illegal but the yellow shirts occupy the airport and plant bombs and they say it is for the country." Accompanied only by *khaen*, Sathian Noi sang, "Pity the poor cow owners because at the moment they sell and get hardly anything, unlike when Thaksin was there. Now they sell and come home and have to argue with the wife because they got so little for the cows." This blend of humor and politics was typical of the red shirts' music.

However, perhaps illustrating the difference in demographic, the key medium for mobilizing support for the UDD was radio rather than television. A large network of community radio stations interspersed political rhetoric with *luk thung* and *molam*, the preferred genres of the UDD demographic. The mixing of political and commercial content in such radio programs effectively appropriated these genres to the UDD cause. Demonstrations featured entertainment spots, karaoke sing-alongs, and, occasionally, specially composed political songs. VCDs and MP3s of red shirts' music and speeches were distributed at protest sites and through the internet. After their April 2009 demonstrations were dispersed by the military, the UDD consolidated support throughout Thailand via a series of fundraising concerts that became progressively more polished and professional and typically featured *luk thung*, *molam*, *kantruem*, and country rock.[6]

While there was no apparent industry-led censure of performers who supported the yellow shirts, the same cannot be said of artists who support the red shirts—no then-contracted *luk thung* or *molam* star performed at red-shirt rallies. R-Siam's Bai Toei (discussed in chapter four) attracted widespread disapprobation when it was revealed that she had been paid a million baht to perform two concerts for Thaksin overseas in 2012, even though the booking was made through her company. The appearance by Grammy star Takadaen Chonlada at Thaksin's sixtieth birthday party in 2009 is probably the closest that a top-tier contracted singer has come to declaring for the red shirts, especially since she performed her 2007 hit "Prot chuai kan dulae khon di," which was written by Sala Khunawut.[7] I learned from Thanat Khrueama, the manager of Red Shirt Radio in Khon Kaen, that this song (which can be translated as "please help one another take care of the good people" or "the good person") was one of the most frequently played and requested songs on the red-shirt community radio network because it is widely interpreted as referring to Thaksin. Lyrics such as "But then the good person could not stay long with us / There was friction until he was weakened," confirms this interpretation, and the fact that the song was not self-censored by Grammy confirms the suggestion made in the previous chapter that there is widespread support among Grammy's *luk thung* songwriters, led by Sala Khunawut, for the promotion of a strong Isan political identity, which they could believe is best served by supporting Thaksin.

Many major stars of the past, such as Phloen Phromdaen, Rungphet Laemsing, Phongsri Woranut, and Dao Bandon, were reportedly seen at rallies, and both 1970s superstar Sayan Sanya, who was a member of Thaksin's Thai Rak Thai political party, and veteran *luk thung Isan* star Phonsak Songsaeng occasionally appeared onstage. Although Sayan was probably the most famous living *luk thung* star up until his death from cancer in 2013, Phonsak was the bigger drawcard as he had been constantly touring as an independent artist for the preceding twenty years. Sayan, having begun his career in Phongsri Woranut's band during the 1960s, had his 2007 album banned by the Public Relations Department after he made a speech critical of the junta that seized power from Thaksin's government in 2006. Thereafter he kept a very low profile, although he recorded some political interviews and songs for Taxi Community Radio in Bangkok. The *Manager* website, a news organization owned by PAD leader Sonthi Limthongkul, reported that Sayan lost faith in the red-shirt cause after the violence of 2009–10, but his low profile may also have resulted from his bizarre questioning of fellow legend Yodrak Salakchai's terminal cancer, which caused Sanya to lose face throughout Thai society after Yodrak died in 2008.

The UDD leadership itself boasted a formidable quartet of musicians— Phaijit Aksonnarong, Phaijit's husband Wisa Khantap (songs for life), politician Adison Phiangket (*molam*/country rock), and 1980s pop heartthrob Arisman Phongruangrong (*phleng wan*), who took part in the May 1992 protests. Phaijit had a considerable commercial career during the 1980s and 1990s, singing Chinese-flavored *luk thung* and *phleng wan* for Nithithat Company, and even had a song temporarily banned by Thaksin's Ministry of Culture—"Pratu nip mue" (Hand Jammed in the Door)— on the grounds that it supposedly promoted adultery. She also courted controversy when she allegedly asked red-shirt supporters to vote for her (and first husband Nik Niranam's) daughter Onson in the Miss Thailand Universe 2010 competition. This sparked an online backlash with forums titled, "Don't let peasant blood become Miss Thailand" (*Ya hai lueat phrai ma pen nangsao Thai*)[8] and Phaijit referred to as *Mora kaki*, the Thai literary archetype of female promiscuity.

A particular feature of the red-shirt movement has been the number of non-professional musicians who have produced their own CDs for distribution at protest sites. One of these musicians, Pae Bangsawan, was able to forge a career out of performing and selling his red-shirt material—even becoming successful enough to play standalone concerts (Tausig 2013, 98–101). His best-known song, "Rak khon suea daeng" (Love the Red Shirt People),[9] was probably the most popular song of the 2010 protests. One of the most popular red-shirt songs after the violent clashes that marked the end of those protests was former communist activist Jin Kamachon's "Naksu thulidin" (Fighters of Dust and Dirt), which valorizes the fallen protesters.[10] Perhaps inspired by the PAD's successful use of satire, there also appears to have been a concerted attempt to produce lowbrow satirical *phleng plaeng* (songs with altered lyrics) in various popular genres by artists such as Nakara and Lorlian.

Phleng Chiwit

It may seem that this level of activism from working-class performers has been only a recent development, but in the history of *luk thung* and its predecessors, many recording artists have expressed anti-establishment political views. For example, Phloen Phromdaen, who appeared on red-shirt stages, produced many political commentaries during the 1970s in the form of *phleng phut* (speaking songs) such as "Mon kan mueang" (The Magic of Politics), which evoked other famous song titles such as "Mon rak luk thung," and "Khuekhrit khit luek" (Kukrit thinks deeply), which criticized the policies of then Prime Minister Kukrit Pramoj in 1975. Phloen even produced a song during the 1997 Asian Economic Crisis, "Ngoen baht loi tua," (The Baht Depreciates) which contrasted the elite who travel and are educated overseas with ordinary Thais who cannot afford such things and yet were expected to pay for the rich's mistakes because they are "part of this community and this family." Another example is Chai Mueangsing, who produced the song "Phuea prachathipatai" (For Democracy) during the 1973 student demonstrations, only for it to be censored by the radio and television industries:

> When the common people do wrong, they must be jailed;
> When others do wrong, they must do favour to the authorities;
> When others do wrong, they may be transferred at the most;
> When others do wrong, they may stand above the law.
> For Thai people to unite, we must not allow corruption.
> Who can help if a bad start leads to a worse end?
> (translated in Kobkul 1985, 190)

Other examples go back even further to Phot Phanawan's "Phaendin mai sin khon di" (This Land Is Not without Good People) from 1957, and Benjamin's "Phleng khaen" from 1958, both of which were banned, presumably for the same reason as Pong Prida's "Klap Isan"—insinuating class difference. Thus the tradition of *luk thung* being used for protest can be traced back to its very origins during the 1950s as *phleng chiwit* or life songs.

In his second term as prime minister (1948–57), Phibun was not in the same position of ultimate power he had experienced during his first term. Among the problems he faced were growing charges of economic discrimination from northeastern politicians (which he combated by having a number of them assassinated), an uneasy alliance with ambitious elements within the armed forces, and the maintenance of a democratic façade while still hanging onto power (Keyes 1971, 36–43). It is not surprising therefore that a range of satirical works surfaced at this time. For example, Dao Hang's novel *Pattaya* satirized the social engineering policies of Phibun's government (Thiraphap 1998, 62), while Malai Chuphinit protested Phibun's simplified Thai writing system by halting his famous novel *Phaendin khong rao* (Our Land) before its conclusion (Ubonrat 2000, 13). Malai, in *Thung maharat* (*The Field of the Great King*, 1954), and Seni Saowaphong, in *Khwam rak khong wanlaya* (*Wanlaya's Love*, 1951) and *Phisat* (*Ghosts*, 1953), abandoned the conventional aristocratic hero in favour of ordinary protagonists who fought for the underprivileged (Klausner 2004). At a nationwide *like* competition organized by Radio Thailand in 1955, the most popular performers, Homhuan, were disqualified because they deviated from the approved script in order to criticize the political situation at the time (Ubonrat 2000, 15).

The earliest incarnations of *luk thung*, variously known as *phleng chiwit* or *phleng talat*, were renowned for their biting social criticism and popularity among the working class. Songwriters such as Saengnapha Bunrasri and Nakhon Mongkhlayon, who according to Phayong Mukda were the first to use *phleng plaeng* for protest (Siriphon 2004, 114), as well as Saneh Komarachun, Chalor Traitrongson, and Phaibun Butkhan, decried the exploitation of farmers and extolled the virtues of the common man. When Phaibun's "Klin khlon sap khwai" (Muddy Odor and Stinking Buffalo) was first broadcast in 1953, it created a sensation, selling a then-unheard-of 5,000 records in one week (Wat 2003, 251). It was banned by Phibun's government for drawing unhelpful comparisons between rural and urban conditions. The most controversial lines were "The scent of the buffalo is mixed with the scent of the young farmers / It's not upper class like the people of heaven," which referred to the residents of Bangkok (Krungthep, the city's Thai name, means "City of Angels). The song implied that peasants received no help from the central government, and warned listeners not to "look down on farmers as if they are poor things" (Wat 2003, 254). Unfortunately, Phaibun died just before the October 1973 student uprising, a movement that was inspired by and affirmed the messages of *phleng chiwit*.

Saneh Komarachun and "Samlo Khaen"

One of the *like* actors responsible for the 1955 protest by Homhuan was the famous songwriter Saneh Komarachun. One of the true renaissance men of Thailand, Saneh began acting in *chamuat* (slapstick drama), *lamtat*, and *like*, singing lead and backup for an orchestra, composing for the Navy band, dubbing voices for foreign films, and acting in radio plays and film. He was a star for Homhuan's renowned *like* troupe and also led his own ensemble known as Saneh Niyomsin, which, for a short time in 1952, included Phon Phirom. Later he popularized the horror film genre when he produced and directed the iconic slapstick ghost story *Mae Nak Phra Khanong* (1959). Saneh seems to have borne a grudge against Phibun on at least two counts: Saneh had royal blood through his mother's line, and, like many other musicians, he was angered by the restrictions placed on the royal music traditions during Phibun's first regime.

During his life-songs period, his signature performance was a medley called "Suphapburut Pak Khlongsan" (Gentleman of Khlongsan Asylum). Wearing a waistcoat and shirt, with burning incense sticks inserted into a colored bandana. and sometimes holding a portrait of Phibun, he would begin by praising nature with his popular navy band song "Ngam chaihat" (Beautiful Beach), then pass through *phleng choi, lamtat,* and *ho* before finishing with "Phleng sansoen phra barami" (Song in Praise of the Royal Majesty). After singing the last line, "Dutcha thawai chai chayo" (Praise the victory), he would then tell the audience that he was a gentleman from the mental asylum. Apparently the performance was so manic and hilarious that even politicians identified by name would not take offense.[11]

Saneh's most influential song was "Samlo khaen" (Resentful Pedicab), written in 1950 to express the frustration of pedicab drivers who were threatened with expulsion from the streets of Bangkok. In this song Saneh takes on the character and accent of a pedicab driver and uses his typically humorous approach to describe the hardship of life for economic migrants in Bangkok:

> It might be my karma that led me to pedal pedicabs.
> Life is really tough having to pedal for a living.
> It is hard work but I must persevere, the road will be my death.
> Pick up, send women and men, make it comfortable for everybody . . .
> Get home late; hurry to cook fish-head soup—
> One head, salty and sour, wife and children, altogether fifteen people eating
>   in a circle.

Through its playing by these drivers during a campaign of protest stretching from 1950 to 1960, "Samlo khaen" became linked to the emerging Isan regional identity. A contemporary ethnography recorded that the majority of drivers came from the Northeast and that "the degree of interest in parliamentary politics [among them] is probably greater than that found among other working people, in Bangkok or elsewhere in Thailand" (Textor 1961, 44). This interest in politics may have been the real reason why by both Phibun and Sarit attempted to ban the pedicab drivers from Bangkok. Other famous songs by Saneh included "Phuthaen khwai" (Buffalo Representatives), which criticized politicians, and "Police thue krapong," which compared the newly adopted police truncheons to kitchen pestles. The latter spelled the end of his career in life songs because the notorious Phao Sriyanon, Phibun's head of police and right-hand man, issued Saneh with an ultimatum to cease singing or cease living. Saneh chose life and took on the role of spokesperson during Phibun's next election campaign (Wat 2009, 7).

Despite the pragmatic decision, the cultural memory of "Samlo khaen" has persisted. In recent years the song and its lyrics were shared online by red shirts. Today's equivalent of the *samlo* drivers is the Isan-dominated, pro-Thaksin Taxi Drivers Protection Association,[12] led by red-shirt leader Chinawat Habunphad. Similarly, the involvement of professional members of the Bangkok entertainment industry on the side of the PAD evokes the memory of Saneh and other *phleng chiwit* composers. Indeed the atmosphere of Phibun's second regime bears some similarities to Thaksin's final term. Both governments attempted to win support via populist measures, both made use of mass communications, and, while each was criticized for attempting to censor opposition, both periods were marked by an outpouring of satirical protest music.

Phleng Phuea Chiwit and *Luk Thung* during the Communist Insurgency

In 1973, massive demonstrations by students led to the overthrow of the military regime of Thanom Kittikachorn and Praphat Charusathien. One significant element of the student protests was *phleng phuea chiwit*, a song genre influenced by the protest music of performers such as Bob Dylan, Joan Baez, Joni Mitchell, and Pete Seeger. Fingerpicked acoustic guitar was the main accompaniment for traditional-sounding pentatonic minor melodies. Although the influence of American folk was paramount, the performers drew also from Isan melodies, eschewing central Thai folk genres such as *lae, lamtat*, and *isaeo*, which figured prominently in *luk thung*. The art-for-life (*sinlapa phuea chiwit*) ideology of the Thai communist writer Jit Phumisak can be observed in the students' choice of music. Jit differentiated between art for imperialism, which imposed vulgar popular culture on the masses, and art for the people, which protested injustice and offered solutions for society's problems.[13] In the early 1970s, *luk thung* appeared to fit Jit's description of art for imperialism. It had developed from *phleng Thai sakon*, a product of Phibun's era of social engineering, and had recently produced Thailand's first popular music superstars in Suraphon Sombatjaroen and Phongsri Woranut. By 1973, the traveling bands of artists such as Sayan Sanya and Saksayam Phetchomphu featured troupes of dancing girls, amplified instruments, and huge sound and lighting systems. The students of Bangkok's elite universities clearly did not see *luk thung* as a form of music useful for protest.[14]

Following the October 1973 revolution, many urban Thai students from the upper and middle classes were committed to political change. The massacre of students at Thammasat University on October 6, 1976, forced many student activists and songs-for-life musicians to flee to Laos and northeastern Thailand, where they found refuge with the Communist Party of Thailand (CPT). Since they were unsuited to the hardship of life in the forests, the students were organized into teams and assigned to the Isan villages under communist control. Their duties included the creation and dissemination of propaganda via pamphlet, radio, and tape cassette (see Wat 2003, 396–424). This created a situation in the Northeast whereby the majority of the foot soldiers were Isan peasants, but the propaganda units were made up of Bangkok students directed by the CPT leadership, who were themselves influenced by China. It is not surprising that a cultural disjunction developed between these three groups—a disjunction that has had important implications for the recent political struggle.

Communist *Luk Thung*

Because *phleng phuea chiwit* has become institutionalized as *the* Thai protest genre, it is often assumed that the CPT only used songs for life. However, publications by Waeng Phalangwan (2002) and Wat Wanyalangkun (2003) show that, despite the CPT leaders' preference for Chinese-style marches and the students' preference for *phleng phuea chiwit*, the most popular genre among the rank-and-file insurgents was *luk thung*.

The experiences of Adison Phiangket and Wisa Khantap vividly illustrate this cultural divide. As an undergraduate Adison used to play the *khaen* on stage with Caravan at Thammasat University, but after the 1976 massacre he and Wisa (a Ramkhamhaeng University student who cowrote Caravan's most famous song, "Man and Buffalo") fled to the forest, where they were placed with propaganda unit A30. Their first attempt at writing communist propaganda had a melody pieced together from three *Thai doem* songs, and their first composition to be broadcast was "Ramwong nueng Thanwa," (December First Ramwong), which was accompanied by guitar and piano accordion. They recall they were then encouraged to write in Chinese styles, such as the song "Chet Singha su bon thang puen" (August Seventh Fight on the Gun Road), which used a melody written by Jin Kamachon,[15] or Chot Wongchon, and was accompanied by *khim* played like a piano (Wat 2003, 397, 404).

Both Wisa and Adison were most comfortable writing songs-for-life. Since the end of the insurgency Wisa has become a mainstay of the genre, and Adison's song written in memory of his communist comrade Chuwit Owathawong in 1978 was later recorded by modern songs-for-life star Phongsit Khamphi.[16] However, during the insurgency Adison realized that the best way to inspire Isan insurgents was to use *molam* and *luk thung*. He had written *luk thung* songs with altered lyrics (*phleng plaeng*) before entering the forest and decided to compose a *phleng plaeng* using Suraphon Sombatjaroen's "Rueang khong faen phleng" (Story of Song Fans").[17] He changed the famous lyrics of the chorus "Fang, fang, fang, siang phleng roem dang ik laeo ... Suraphon ma laeo" ("Listen, listen, listen, the loud sound of song has begun again ... Suraphon has come") to "Pang, pang, pang, siang puen dang chet Singha / Pluk muan pracha / Luk khuen ma chap puen" ("Bang, bang, bang, the loud sound of guns on August seventh / Stir up the people / Stand up and take a gun") (Wat 2003, 405).

Waeng records that there were many other Isan insurgents who put communist lyrics to well-known *luk thung* songs sung by popular singers such as Salika Kingthong and Yodrak Salakchai. The most prolific writer of *phleng Phuphan*,[18] or communist *luk thung*, was "Phloeng Nalak" a forest guerrilla who wrote more than two hundred songs criticizing the government, with such lines as, "The government's power comes from the barrel of a gun." Sonchai Mekwichian's popular song "Khon ngam luem ngai" (Beautiful Girls Soon Forget) was changed into "Tuen thoet chao na Thai" (Please Wake Up, Thai Farmers) (Waeng 2002, 495, 500). Yutachak Charali used the slow and sad melody of "Faen cha yu nai" (Where Are You Darling?) by Saengsuri Rungrot for his song "Pha chan" (Sheer Cliff), which celebrated the exploits of his company against the Thai soldiers:

This sheer cliff has a story.
It is a story about arresting thieves who came to make trouble.
The enemy came to the cliff like a crazy man.
They wanted to kill people on the cliff.
The sound of the gun never disappeared ... pity the people who are slaves.
The master uses the slaves but never sees the truth.
The sheer cliff bit the enemy and they rolled down like monkeys.
(Waeng 2002, 501)

Yutachak sees the Thai government soldiers as invaders of peaceful communities and portrays the guerillas as enforcing the law—an inversion of the establishment history. An excerpt from *The Musical Compositions of His Majesty King Bhumibol Adulyadej* reveals the royalist nationalist view of songs for life and the October conflict:

> They [songs for life] were particularly apt at a time of social and political awareness in the 1970 [sic]. The songs accompanied students as they travelled upcountry to participate in volunteer development camps and for the government officials, soldiers and police assigned to protect and patrol the borders the songs strengthened their resolve to carry out their duties. (1996, 110)

Apart from the startling suggestion that the students and soldiers were on the same side, there is no mention of Isan people or the peasant class. In this version of Thai history the students have been rehabilitated and their music officially celebrated. The lower classes and their music have been ignored.

Ironically, the communist *luk thung* songs were banned not only by the government, but also by the senior members of the CPT, who decreed that only Chinese songs were to be sung. The *luk thung* songs were thought to be too commercial and the cha-cha rhythm unsuitable for marching. Nevertheless, many insurgents defied orders not to listen to "enemy radio" so that they could keep up-to-date with the latest songs (Waeng 2002, 500–505). *Luk thung* was used both to boost morale and to mourn. Writer Khaen Salika asserts that the insurgents were more motivated when they listened to *luk thung*:

> When the young people at Ban Suankhorp sang "From the ricefield" in the style of *ramwong* or *luk thung* (with lyrics like "Get him to cut off

his head / Receive the karma that he's made") and you heard what they were singing it made you feel more courageous than the marching songs. (Wat 2003, 459)

Khaen also recalls that his time in the insurgency began with the song "Ramwong su rop" (Fighting *Ramwong)*, with lyrics like "From the ricefields we will say goodbye to our parents / Go far away to the jungle with hatred in our hearts," and ended with the song "Yu kap khwam phitwang" (Living with Disappointment) by Sayan Sanya: "to leave and never go back to your hometown." He remembers his friend "sitting and humming the famous song by Phi Bao (Sayan's nickname) on the sad day when the female fighters of the artists' unit no. 32 surrendered to the authorities" (Wat 2003, 457–58). These recollections hint at the function that I believe *luk thung* performs in Isan society—that of channeling oppressive history and memories into a joyful present.

The tragedy of the October 6 massacre at Thammasat University in 1976 had seemed to create a climate for full scale rebellion, but the ensuing period was in fact an Indian summer for the CPT. The wider Thai population, including in Isan, did not want to abandon the king or the Buddhist sociocultural order for an alien social structure. Events in China, Laos, and Vietnam, combined with local factors such as government amnesties and investment, strangled the insurgency, which was effectively over by 1982. After a period of introspection the Thai left transferred its fight for better living and employment conditions into the NGO sphere, "neither confronting nor acquiescing to state power" (Haughton 2009, 45). Organizations such as the Assembly of the Poor and the Thai Farmer's Association became the face of Isan activism. However, it was not until the arrival of Thaksin Shinawatra on the political stage that Isan political identity turned into a force with the potential to reshape Thailand.

Ensconced as the official Thai protest genre, *phleng phuea chiwit* was absorbed into the Thai popular music industry, and the use of *luk thung plaeng* by the insurgents was forgotten. The rise of *phleng phuea chiwit* as the designated Thai protest genre placed additional pressure on socially minded *luk thung* songwriters. After the communist insurgency came to a close it appeared that commentary within songs for life was to be tolerated, but censorship of *luk thung* continued. The consolidation of the recording industry during the 1980s and an increase in royal patronage, such as through the Half a Century of *Luk Thung* concert series in 1989 and 1991, further discouraged counter-hegemonic content in *luk thung*. As the economy improved and the status of *luk thung* increased, there was even more incentive for songwriters to toe the establishment line.

Over the past thirty years ideological lines have become increasingly entangled. Since the end of the insurgency, many on the Thai left have become ardent royalist nationalists, while Samak Sundaravej, adjudged to be one of those most responsible for inciting the 1976 Thammasat massacre, joined forces with Thaksin and ended up serving as prime minister. Thirayut Bunmi, an iconic leader of the historic 1973 and 1976 student uprisings, attacked red-shirt supporters—many of whom embodied the working-class Isan interests Thirayut once purported to represent—by saying that "those who voted for the Yingluck Shinawatra administration have forfeited their rights by accepting a corrupt and dictatorial government, which would have to be removed through a 'people's revolution'" (Pravit 2014).[19]

This confusion of ideology was reflected in the strange juxtaposition of ultra-nationalist anthems such as "Nak phaendin" (Scum of the Earth) and leftist songs like "The Internationale" together on the PAD stage (Thongchai 2008a, 5). However, perhaps even more startling than the return of the right-wing nationalist anthems of the 1970s was the PAD's preference for *phleng phuea chiwit*, and the overall preference of *phuea chiwit* artists for the PAD. While covering the PAD rallies of 2006, Clewley (2007, 43) wrote: "The one songs-for-lifer not seen at all—Ad Carabao—said he was too busy to make it, but it is more likely that his being co-opted to many Thaksin government projects had compromised his position." The overwhelming commercialization of the Carabao brand, which has seen Carabao's face advertising all manner of working-class products, may also have rendered the group personae non gratae with the yellow shirts. However, the real irony here is that these populist government projects, which have been the key behind the continuing appeal of Thaksin's political parties, are perceived by many working-class Thais to fulfill what the original generation of *phuea chiwit* musicians called (and fought) for. To most red shirts, and indeed many songs-for-life fans, the idea of Nga Caravan campaigning to bring down a democratically elected populist government is incomprehensible. Chuwat Rerksirisuk (2007), editor of the independent (and anti-PAD) news website Prachatai, referred to songs for life when he drew a satirical distinction between the yellow shirts and red shirts: "There would not be any life music or protest songs from the intellectual bands for you to listen [to], since there will only be country music songs and [easy-to-understand] sentences from those giving the speech on the stage." Chuwat clearly believes there has been a shift in the position and function of *phleng phuea chiwit* in Thai society and that the aspirations of the Thai working class are now represented by *luk thung*. A generally pro-PAD article from 2006 suggested that a key motivation for the songs-for-life performers was the thrill of appearing in front of tens of thousands of people instead of in a half-empty pub (Veena 2006). It is possible that some were caught up in the atmosphere of mainstream protest, but it is still difficult to fathom how so many songs-for-life musicians ended up provoking and defending a military coup against a government that was supported by the majority of Thailand's working class.

Satirical Music of the PAD and UDD

"AI NA LIAM"

The involvement of many professional songwriters in the PAD movement resulted in a regular flow of original, professionally recorded satirical songs. "Ai na liam" (Mr. Square Face), which appeared in March 2006, was perhaps the most influential protest song produced by either side.[20] It was instrumental in mobilizing support against Thaksin's government, who were so frustrated by the song's rapid distribution through the internet that they asked the songwriters to identify themselves so they could be arrested (Clewley 2007, 43). The lyrics exhaustively catalog Thaksin's faults and attack populist policies such as the thirty-baht health scheme and "One Million Houses across the Country" project before lampooning everyone associated with him. Perhaps the most bizarre accusation in the song was concerning the Thai national anthem: "He may permit A Khu to change the national anthem and get a copyright for this life and the next life." A Khu is the nickname of Phaibun Damrongchaitham—the Sino-Thai owner of the dominant Thai entertainment company Grammy. While it is highly unlikely that he ever approached Thaksin to make such a change, the suggestion fits the song's overall theme that Thaksin wants to sell out Thailand.

The music is a blend of funk and rap with a chorus typical of the central Thai folk genre *lamtat*. This use of one of the building blocks of *luk thung* can be interpreted as an attempt to widen the appeal of the PAD's message beyond Bangkok and also to increase the "Thainess" quotient of the song. However, the choice of *lamtat* over *molam* or *kantruem* confirms the pattern of struggle for cultural supremacy between the people of central Thailand and Isan. The increasingly dominant identification of *luk thung* with Isan culture by both Thais and non-Thais acts as a threat to central Thai cultural hegemony. Thus, for the PAD, *lamtat* is a folk genre that confirms central Thai hegemony and does not reference the main areas of support for Thaksin in the North and Northeast.

THE PHOTOSTICKER MACHINE

One artist who demonstrates both the close links between the PAD and the entertainment industry and the eclectic musical preferences of some within the PAD constituency is Wichaya "Nong" Vatanasapt, a member of legendary Thai ska band T-Bone. Wichaya writes soundtracks for commercial Thai films and is also a freelance producer, working for Grammy on a regular basis. He describes his solo vehicle, The Photosticker Machine, as lounge-room jazz electronica usually produced for a limited circle of industry insiders and friends.

In 2005, Wichaya wrote and recorded a song to support the emerging protest movement against then Prime Minister Thaksin. "Corruption" is an extremely hard-hitting piece of social commentary that could be about Thai society in general, although the song's subtitle "FTA (Fucking "TS" Agency)" made it clear who was being targeted. The song was distributed at PAD protests and through the internet via chain letters that cursed anyone who did not forward it. Wichaya says that the recording of "Corruption" was a cathartic process that allowed him to express the anger he felt at Thaksin's betrayal of Thailand's three institutions. The first verse addresses the greed of politicians: "Day after day you think, think what law can make returns on your money / If you cannot find it then you write your own law to fill your pockets." The second verse contrasts this greed with the faithfulness of a dog: "Even dogs know the goodness of the people, poor or rich, never proud, faithful to their owner ... get the dog to teach you." The comparison to a dog is an obvious insult, yet this verse also invokes both the royal self-sufficiency program ("the land's goodness") and the king's famous children's book about his favorite dog, Thong Daeng.²¹ The final part of the song is a rapped curse which calls upon "sacred spirits anywhere in the universe" to give suffering to this thief: "Stay around, pay your karma, in the prison of the dark place / Forever the fire of hell burning you."

The song is an impeccably assembled piece of social criticism in which the musical elements have been consciously chosen to reinforce the composer's message. For example, the spoken curse is echoed by wah-wah guitar stabs, which, the composer explains, were supposed to sound like *yet mae* (motherfucker). However, the eclectic, cosmopolitan nature of the musical elements, as well as the English title, serves to narrow the song's appeal and its influence mostly to the urban elite. The opening Led Zeppelin–like riff is then meshed with reggae rhythm guitar and record scratching. The vocal melody, sung in a Western fashion, descends from the minor seventh through the notes of the major scale, in a very un-Thai melodic contour. A heavy blues guitar solo precedes a rap break, reminiscent of the Beastie Boys, with psychedelic falsetto backup vocals. Thus, musically the song is a pastiche of Western styles that would be unfamiliar to most working-class Thais.

NAKARA

Unlike the PAD, the red shirts have almost exclusively used already-famous songs as their vehicles for satire. These *phleng plaeng* are generally poorly recorded and tend to be more humorous and lowbrow than their PAD counterparts. For example, Nakara's "Mi na hak," which questions Abhisit's achievements as prime minister, is an altered version of "Family mi phaenda" (Panda Family) sung by Nong Benz Jr. The original song was a surprise independent dance hit featuring a cute Thai girl singing about the cute pandas on loan from China to Chiang Mai's zoo. Nakara's version changes the title to "Mi na hak" (sounds like either "vomit bear" or "cute bear") in order to suggest that Abhisit's achievements have all been insubstantial publicity stunts. The title also references a common red-shirt play on words used to insult the then prime minister—"Mark na hi (pussy-faced Mark), mi na hak."

Verse one describes the competition to find a name for the baby panda, which is code for Abhisit: "Ask the villagers, they answer straight away / That this panda's name is 'Na Hak.'" The second and third verses are concerned with two cases that dominated the general interest news during May and

September 2009: Keigo Sato, an abandoned Thai boy who was looking for his Japanese father,[22] and Mong, a stateless Burmese-Shan boy who was eventually given a temporary passport so he could take part in a paper-airplane competition in Japan:[23]

> Kid named Keigo came looking for his father—
> At first no one was interested until it became big news on the TV.
> Then Mark hurried to help immediately and sent money to him,
> Enough for a plane ticket to fly here . . .
>
> A Burmese boy named Mong entered Thailand to look for food.
> He's excellent at making paper airplanes and won every competition.
> He wanted to go to compete in Japan but he didn't have money or a passport.
> Mark hoped that helping this time would be as popular as the baby panda.

The fourth verse criticizes the cost of security for Abhisit's visit to Ubon Ratchathani to deliver a cheque to Yai Hai, an elderly Isan woman who was owed compensation from the government:[24] "Gave it only to one person / You don't care about other people / Then you fly away in a helicopter / Not brave if compared to the cute panda." The fifth verse edges into dangerous territory by criticizing government policies designed to increase unity through nationalism:

> Mark wants Thais to love each other, to be united all over Thailand,
> Doesn't know how to do this, so let him go sing a song.
> He thinks it will help if we sing the Thai anthem every day.

Plays on words abound: "Man chop Oxford rue ok lek wa" (Did he graduate from Oxford or as a welder?). For the most part the tone is good humoured and down-to-earth, even figuratively describing urine as a yellow-shirt version of Isan fermented fish sauce (*pla ra*), but in the last verse the song descends into pure vitriol: "Don't you know that they hate you like shit? / If you are so stupid go take care of buffaloes." As with the majority of red shirts' video clips, the production quality is low, featuring crudely manipulated pictures of Abhisit dressed as a panda.

DISTASTEFUL ATTACKS

To a Western liberal mindset, one of the more distasteful elements of the red shirts was the persistent attacks on the sexuality of Privy Councilor Prem Tinsulanonda, who is blamed by the red shirts for orchestrating the 2006 coup. In June 2006, Thaksin gave a speech to officials claiming "the intervention of an extra-constitutional power, or figure" who was seeking to damage his government, and following the coup, Prem's house at Sisao Thewet was targeted by several red shirt protests. While both sides engage in personal attacks, the targeting of Prem's alleged homosexuality has sat uncomfortably with many foreign supporters of the UDD, especially considering that he turned ninety in 2010. "Premikha" (female version of "Prem") is a satirical song sung by Nakara which details the many complaints of the red shirts against the privy councilor. For example, Prem is charged with organizing a series of coups to benefit the elite: "The coups revolve, press down the heads of the poor for the aristocrats." The writer attacks Prem for having delusions of grandeur ("Wherever you go you want people to bow") and for seeking to control the annual military reshuffle, "You move the soldiers around so only your people are happy." These accusations are embedded within a diatribe against Prem's alleged homosexuality: "One day Sunday Premikha puts on makeup / He's pretended to be a man for so long" is one of the mildest insults. However, the overall lyrics show that Prem is regarded by the red shirts as the symbol of the *amat* (aristocracy):

> Your house is in Songkhla but you think you are royalty.
> Wherever you go you want people to bow.
> I want to let you know you are the same level as them.

Not only does this allude to one of the red shirts' key catchphrases—*song matrathan* or "double standards"—but it edges towards republican thinking by suggesting that a day of revolutionary reckoning is coming: "The day when you have no power / Be careful; you will stumble from your feet." The lyrics also allude to tension between Thais from the North and Northeast and those from the South, yet do not express any sympathy for Thai-Muslim insurgents: "When you fight with the southern thieves / Can't see anyone who is good." This is because Prem is a southerner (born in Songkhla) who has at times attempted to negotiate with southern insurgents, and the red shirts remember that the Democrat Party's main supporter base is in the South.

If red-shirt attacks on Prem were distasteful, so too were many yellow-shirt attacks on Yingluck Shinawatra. During PDRC rallies, Thailand's first female Prime Minister repeatedly had her intelligence, appearance, mental state, and sexual history called into question. In one particularly appalling speech a male medical doctor offered to give her vaginal repair surgery and to change her sanitary pads, and said she could become a nude model because she had not yet reached menopause.[25] Such misogynistic abuse has also been incorporated into song form. In one of the more mild satires, "Khon ban diaokan," the Phai Phongsathon song analysed in chapter four, provides the melody for a yellow shirt *phleng plaeng* titled "Phi nong kan" (Brother and Sister).[26] The video clip includes a poster widely circulated on social media showing Yingluck with the thought bubble "Choen khit luek kap Pu si kha." This phrase translates literally as "Please think deeply with Pu" (Yingluck's nickname is Pu, meaning "crab") but "khit luek" also intimates the possibility of a sexual liaison.

"KHWAI DAENG"

Directly after the military crushed the red-shirt protests at Ratchaprasong intersection on May 19, 2010, which resulted in many deaths and the burning of the Central World shopping mall, there was an outpouring of anti–red shirt invective on social networking and video-sharing websites. The professionally produced rap song "Khwai daeng"—meaning "Red Buffalo" but translated by the songwriter as "Red Shit"—is representative of the sentiments expressed during those days.[27] In hindsight, the extreme abuse contained in this song shows that the seeds for the totalitarian PDRC were sown in the flames of Ratchaprasong and Central World. A significant proportion of the Bangkok middle class were sufficiently shaken and offended by the 2010 red-shirt protests that they began to openly ascribe to the racist view that northern and Isan Thais were stupid peasants who should stay in the fields where they belonged. This chauvinistic attitude is on display in the first verse, which accuses ordinary red-shirt supporters of being gullible and greedy:

> You dumb water buffaloes, how much did they pay you per day?
> You rushed to take it, to admit that you are low peasants .
> You hurried to become the slaves of that asshole Thaksin.
> I want to tell all of you that you are shit in every way.

Class difference is a key concern of the song—the rural red shirts who follow Thaksin are referred to as *bia rapchai* (slaves).

The second verse gloats over the death of Major General Khattiya Sawasdipol, better known as Seh Daeng, who was shot on May 13, 2010, as he was being interviewed by a reporter from the *New York Times*: "Mr. Seh fucked quick by karma / You weren't able to show off for long; you took a bullet in the head." The third and fourth verses are devoted to the core red-shirt leaders Nattawut Saikua and Jatuporn Prompan. On one level Jatuporn and Nattawut may be considered traitors by Democrat supporters because, unlike most of the red shirt leadership, they were born in southern Thailand. However, their inclusion here is also significant because, along with Seh Daeng, they were supposedly among those responsible for rejecting a negotiated settlement to the 2010 Ratchaprasong standoff. The song's omission of the third core leader, Wira Musikaphong (also a southerner), strengthens this interpretation. On May 10, 2010, Wira and the artists' faction of the red shirts led by Wisa Khantap, Phaijit Aksonnarong, and Adison Phiangket announced that they were ending their political connections with the other UDD leaders because of a disagreement regarding the government's overtures for peace. In a memo posted on Facebook, Wisa explained that the decision of Wira and his group to end the rally would have prevented further loss of life and allowed the ordinary red shirts to return home safely.[28]

The fifth verse addresses another red-shirt hardliner, Arisman Phongrueangrong, who fled to Cambodia after an unsuccessful attempt by police to arrest him in April 2010:

> Ki [Arisman's nickname] is another one, you were not brave enough—
> Father Liam [Thaksin] gave you a million per day,
> You said "yes… I'm brave enough"…
> "Out in front I am high ranking;" when the time came you disappeared.
> Ki you are the vilest scum, you lolly-sucking dog.

The songwriter's knowledge of his subjects is impressive—he plays on the title of one of Arisman's biggest hits "Chai mai dan phor" (Not Brave Enough) and alludes to the popular story that Arisman's indistinct singing style was the result of constantly sucking Halls lozenges.

When it comes to Thaksin, however, the songwriter is completely overcome by rage, alternating accusations with chants of "sat Maeo, hia Maeo." Red shirts often refer to Thaksin affectionately as Lung (Uncle) Maeo—his nickname—whereas *sat* means "animal" but could be translated as "bastard." *Hia* means "lizard" but can be translated as a range of insults (e.g., asshole). Thaksin's alleged crimes include attacks on the monarchy, a desire to be president and therefore turn Thailand into a republic, payments made to *phrai* (serfs), the bribing of Thailand's government assembly, and living in comfort while his followers are killed in the streets. In the final section the singer curses Thaksin ("may you have cancer in your testicles") and urges the red shirts to follow their leader and "move to Montenegro," one of several countries in which Thaksin found refuge and of which he holds citizenship.

The two main insults (*khwai daeng* and *phrai*) applied by this songwriter to the rank-and-file red shirts have actually been embraced by the movement as badges of honor. *Phrai* can be translated as "peasant" but more particularly as "feudal serf." Hats, shirts, signs, and buttons emblazoned with this word from Siam's feudal past were a common sight at red-shirt protests. Popular singer Om Khaphasadi distributes her music under the label Phleng Phrai (Tausig 2013, 116). By calling themselves *phrai*, the red shirts were telling the elite that the age of the *amat* was over, and the future belonged to those who formerly had no voice, who worked in the fields like *khwai* without complaining. *Luk thung* was their music before they gained political consciousness, and it remained their music once they had awakened.

Political *Luk Thung* of the UDD and PAD

Even though Thaksin was elected on a populist platform in January 2001, many in the Thai elite and political classes were still shocked when he actually implemented the promised policies. Politicians had long promised Isan voters that things would get better, but few believed that anything would ever change. Thaksin's championing of the poor and working class turned their music, *luk thung*, into a site of political struggle. In September 2002 he announced that he would like to stay in power for sixteen years, alluding to Suraphon Sombatjaroen's most famous song, "Sixteen Years of Our Past," from 1968. The editor of *The Nation*, Thanong Khanthong, responded with a discussion of Suraphon's life, which subtly made the point that sixteen years of Thaksin could be more bitter than sweet for Thailand's people.

For decades *luk thung* has been the preferred music of Thailand's poor. Rural peasants and the urban working class have found common ground in the stories and melodies of *luk thung*. Even though *luk thung* is embedded in a political context through its music, lyrics, and subject matter, the seeming absence of overt social protest in a working-class genre has discouraged the attention of Western scholars and surprised the few writers who have delved into the popular music of Thailand. Craig Lockard (1998, 191) surveyed the popular music genres of Thailand for counter-hegemonic discourses and concluded that *luk thung*

> could probably not serve as a model for musicians interested in more overt protest music, owing to its frequently lavish, almost circuslike stage productions (often involving elaborately clothed dancing girls), its progressive commercialization (and perhaps increasing co-optation) and the conspicuous consumption of its wealthy superstars.

Although Lockard's summary of the political uses of Thai music is otherwise excellent, he did not have sufficient information available to him to truly understand how *luk thung* has been used for the purpose of resistance in the past, and that during the most recent conflicts a wide range of hegemonic (affirms establishment views) and counter-hegemonic (challenges the institutions of sociopolitical power) elements of *luk thung*, including even the most commercial, have been used for protest.

In terms of hegemonic elements, there are many *luk thung* songs that praise the institutions of king, country, and religion or glorify the military. Up-tempo *luk thung* songs and concerts are unifying sites of community celebration that affirm the Thai tradition of collective *sanuk* (fun). The commercialism and extravagant performance style of *luk thung* qualifies it as bourgeois culture, as was shown by the CPT leadership's reaction to the "communist *luk thung*" songs. *Luk thung* has been increasingly viewed as authentic Thai culture since the 1997 Asian Economic Crisis and has been appropriated as a symbol of central Thai superiority.

In terms of counter-hegemonic elements, many songs deal with themes of separation and mourning and the social dislocation resulting from economic migration. The discussion of fandom in chapter four shows that *luk thung* often presents a more frank discussion of sexual matters than the establishment would like. In commercial *luk thung* indirect social criticism is common, and direct satire, though rare, does occur. Class difference is communicated through the music—the vocal styles of *luk thung* singers usually include rural accents and the vibrato (*luk kho*) and embellishment (*uean*) found in folk songs. Despite the genre's semiofficial appropriation as central Thai culture, *luk thung* is considered by many Thais to be part of Isan identity, due to the high degree of Isan involvement within the industry.

However, any assessment of music according to theories of hegemony versus counter-hegemony is problematic because musical elements are ambiguous and can act simultaneously for and against the dominant culture. In the recent Thai political conflict, the ambiguity is further complicated by the changes in government. For example, while Thaksin, Samak, or Somchai was in power, the PAD could be designated counter-hegemonic, but under the post-coup regime (September 2006–January 2008) and Abhisit's government (December 2008–November 2011), the PAD became part of the hegemony. Under the subsequent Phuea Thai administration, the PAD became marginalized,[29] but so did some elements of the red shirts, such as those calling for reform of the lèse majesté laws or those seeking justice for crimes allegedly committed by the military. For these reasons, classifying the use of *luk thung* during this struggle as hegemonic or counter-hegemonic is difficult. However, it is certainly possible to observe which musical elements and cultural memories are tapped into by each side, and their implications.

Luk Thung and the Red Shirts

The ongoing Isan cultural resurgence and the dominance of Isan people within the UDD ensured that *luk thung* and *molam* were the most-performed genres on the red shirts' protest stages. *Kantruem*, northern *Lanna* folk music, central Thai folk music, rock, and songs for life were also featured, but far less frequently. The problem with regional genres such as *molam* or *kantruem* when performed for televised protests or those held in Bangkok was that the lyrics were inaccessible to some of the audience. This is one of the strengths of *luk thung*—the use of central Thai language mixed with certain words of class and ethnic identification such as *bo* (Isan and northern dialects for "no") appeals to the largest possible audience.

Despite the gaudiness of its commercial concert presentation, *luk thung* music is suited to certain counter-hegemonic circumstances. Slow and melancholy songs function effectively as laments for loved ones lost through death or separation. The theme of longing and separation taps into cultural memories such as the unfulfilled political objectives of the CPT insurgents, fifty years of seasonal migration to Bangkok, and almost two hundred years of separation from Lao people on the northern bank of the Mekong. Reaching further into the past, *luk thung* echoes the ancient Siamese travel literature genre *nirat* (literally "separation," or departing from something that is dearly desired). The definition of *nirat* as a poetic expression of love-separation melancholy with a journey in the background aptly describes the lamentation found in many *luk thung* songs. Up until the second half of the nineteenth century, travel was not a desirable activity, and pleasure was not its primary purpose (Thongchai 2000, 42). For the Thai working class this is still the case: for them the purpose of travel is to find employment, and so *luk thung* songs are full of accounts of loss and forced separation.

Whenever these channels to the past are accessed, a deep emotional investment is created. In an interview with the BBC, Kwanchai Praipana, who led the Khon Rak Udon group from Udon Thani in the heart of Isan, described himself as *luk thung* in the literal sense that he is a "child of the field" (i.e., a country boy). This description is not accidental though, as Kwanchai is a DJ and a longtime friend of the legendary singer Sayan Sanya. Kwanchai states that he used only to care about music but that the degree of political participation made possible by Thaksin's government inspired him to become involved with the red-shirt movement (Ash 2009). The influence of *luk thung* on the red-shirt movement extends to the terminology used by UDD academics and leaders, as well as their personal musical preferences. In the introduction to an anti-coup book edited by Thanapol Eawsakul (2007, 11), the civil society activists and NGOs who joined PAD leader Sonthi Limthongkul are dismissively referred to as *hang khrueang*—the team of dancers who remain anonymous and silent while the singer receives the attention. This very scenario was acted out on the main PAD protest stage in 2008. During one of Sonthi's speeches, several of the female PAD leaders appeared, dancing to *luk thung* music, and proceeded to present him with a birthday cake and *malai*. Most red-shirt rallies include karaoke sessions in which the leaders sing their favorite *luk thung* songs and accept *malai* and roses from the audience. Nattawut, for example, usually sings

"Nong sai suea daeng" (Girl in a Red Shirt), a *phleng plaeng* of "Rak sao suea lai" by Saengsuri Ruengrot, while Jai Prasit sings "Namta cha Prasit" (Dear Prasit's Tears), an adaptation of Lukphae Uraiphon's "Namta cha noi" (Police Sergeant's Tears),[30] Thus *luk thung* has become a political statement and a rallying point.

SINGER: MUK METHINI

A survey of the songs of Muk Methini demonstrates that *luk thung* has been used by the red shirts to lament, praise, and celebrate. Muk, who had a minor singing career with Topline Audio before becoming the face of UDD entertainment, is one of the most polished red-shirt performers. "Rueang sao muea chao ni" (Sad Story This Morning) is a lament for Narongsak Krobthaisong, who died during a clash between PAD and government supporters in September 2008. The singer adopts the persona of the dead man's wife, who learns of his passing on the morning news. Narongsak is not mentioned by name; rather, his story is that of all Isan migrants: "You said you wouldn't be gone for long / You went looking for work in the big city." In the chorus, which proclaims "You died for all of Thailand / And great democracy; you joined the protest until death," the singer's individual loss is linked to the wider political struggle. Thus, Narongsak's death is connected to the sacrifices of past Thai protesters: "My loved one has died, just like last time."

Another common use of lament by the red shirts is to mourn the absence of Thaksin. "Khon di thi na nueng" (Top-Rate Person) is a hymn of praise to Thaksin that echos the title and content of Takadaen Chonlada's 2007 hit "Prot chuai kan dulae khon di" and numerous other red-shirt songs such as Nut Phojaman's "Khit thueng samoe" (Always Miss You), "Dr. Thaksin" sung by Nanny, and "Khit hot Thaksin" (Isan language for "Missing Thaksin") sung by Porm Krongthong and written by Adison Phiangket. All of these songs employ the *luk thung* trope of separation from one's lover to declare Thaksin's righteousness and superiority over those who forced him to leave. It is, of course, ironic that a working-class genre and its theme of separation caused by economic migration are being used to serenade a fugitive billionaire. It should be noted that other red-shirt leaders have been the subject of such paeans, as in the case of "Nattawut Saikuea," a polished, almost sultry, songs-for-life performance given by Orm Khaphasadi during a series of concerts in late 2010.[31] However, the sheer number of odes to

Thaksin and their continuing popularity demonstrated that the red shirt movement remained his fan club, as much as some commentators hoped that it had outgrown him.

In "Khon di thi na nueng," Muk lauds Thaksin's efforts to help the poor through populist schemes such as the *Paomai nueng lan lang thua prathet* (One Million Houses across the Country) cheap-housing scheme (which was criticized in the song "Ai na liam") and wonders why he was exiled when he was only doing good:

> At the time you were here, you took care of people and had mercy.
> For those with no place to sleep *Ban uea athon*[32] was the answer to their desires.
> This Thaksin did many projects, he got rid of Thailand's debt,
> But was vilified and had to flee into exile.

Thaksin's repayment of the IMF debt is a common refrain in red-shirt songs, with perhaps the most popular being Nut Phojaman's "Ku ku khun nu chat hai" (Loan Recovery I Provide for You).

The perceived usurping by Thaksin of the king's place in society has been one of the key drivers behind the yellow-shirt movement. Considering that *luk thung* songs are often written to praise the king, Thaksin was here seen to be assuming the position of the king in providing care for Thailand's most needy. The chorus of "Khon di thi na nueng" makes this point explicitly: "Since the day you left, the villagers have been waiting intensely / For you to come back to heal the poor." Later in the song Muk prays that "Phra Sayam Thewa will give you a way out to come and help Thai people." This reference to the statuette commissioned by King Mongkut (Rama IV) to protect the nation, the king, and the royal family again implied that Thaksin was an exalted personage in Thai society who merited the divine protection of the nation's guardian deity. This spiritual dimension of the political struggle was not always apparent to foreign observers. On October 29, 2008, PAD leader Sonthi Limthongkul announced that the power of several sacred sites, including Phra Sayam Thewathirat, "had been suppressed by evil people using magic" and that the yellow shirts had conducted rituals to rectify the situation, rituals that even included using menstrual blood donated by female PAD members to block the return of the evil spirits (see Chang Noi 2008). The idea that Thaksin had employed the services of a Khmer black magician was common in PAD circles during the period 2006–8 and is one of the many accusations cataloged in the song "Ai na liam" discussed earlier. Many up-tempo commercial *luk thung* songs, which are otherwise celebratory, assume a background of separation forced by economic migration. At red-shirt rallies Muk often sings "Sao Udon cham dai" (The Girl from Udon Remembers), a *phleng kae* of Sotsai Rungphothong's "Sao Udon chai dam" (Hard-Hearted Girl from Udon). This is somewhat ironic because Sotsai served in the Democrat government headed by Abhisit. "Sao Udon cham dai" has the simple premise of an Isan girl declaring that she will definitely return to her country boyfriend after she finishes working in Bangkok. Separation is an established part of everyday life for Isan families and the theme of waiting and enduring through prolonged absence was easily applied to the political climate of December 2008 to June 2011, during which many red shirts felt disenfranchised and abandoned by Thailand's elite.

As with blues, *luk thung* is able to fulfil the seemingly contradictory functions of lament and celebration. At a Valentine's Day 2010 fundraising concert titled "Day of Love for Democracy," Muk performed "Ramwong prachathipatai" (Democracy *Ramwong*). She adopted the role of entertainer by addressing the protesters as an audience ("You are the players, I will be the singer") and seeks to include speakers of all ages ("I invite friends, aunts, and uncles"). A traditional central Thai folk "ho" section—"Chan cha ho la na, Chan cha ho la noe, Chan cha ho la wa, Ao chan cha ho la woei " ("I will sing *ho*")—invites audience participation, and active participation in the song is equated with fighting for democracy ("Don't be tardy, come and listen to the truth"). The lyrics introduce the main red-shirt leaders, Jatuporn, Nattawut, and Wira, and continue the theme of waiting for the good person—Thaksin. Throughout this upbeat *luk thung* song, Muk is accompanied by the customary dancing revue costumed in red and also collects *malai* and roses from the protesters. Thus the commercial elements of *luk thung* (such as elaborate costumes, dancing girls, and *malai*) identified by Lockard as discouraging to overt protest musicians have actually been embraced by red-shirt performers (see fig. 5.1).

SONGWRITER: SOMJIT DAOPRATHAI

Somjit Daoprathai is a native of Khon Kaen who works part-time as a songwriter, DJ, and head of a minor *molam* troupe. During the 2009 and 2010 protests he was heavily involved in the red-shirt radio station and the

Khon Rak Thaksin '51 club in Khon Kaen. He did not travel to the protests in Bangkok but attended every night of the parallel protests held in Khon Kaen from March to May 2010. He composed and performed songs for these protests and also recorded songs for other DJs to play on their Red Shirts programs.

FIGURE 5.1. Red shirt *hang khrueang* (dancing revue). (Nick Nostitz, Khao Yai, November 15, 2009)

His most celebrated song was written for Tap Bunluea, the founder of the Khon Rak Thaksin '51 club in Khon Kaen. "Thahan kla" (Brave Soldiers) was composed in March 2010 when the first reports were coming back from Bangkok of soldiers attacking the protesters. He recalls that to that point all the red shirt songs seemed to be slow and mournful so he decided to write an up-tempo martial song. A cross between *luk thung* and *phleng plukchai*, the song satirizes the "brave soldiers" who are attacking women and children and lauds the protesters as the real "brave soldiers." Somjit intended the song to be a crowd chorus but he ended up performing it himself at the Khon Kaen Wethi Rachada (Townhall Stage) almost every night that protests were held there. He says that the song spread throughout Isan because people would stop over at the Khon Kaen protests on their way to deliver food and supplies to the main protest site at Ratchaprasong. While the trucks and buses were driving to Bangkok the Isan red shirts would sing together, and "Thahan kla" was one of the most popular songs.

Somjit sometimes writes political songs to order, such as "Thanayon phuean faen," composed for a local politician to use in his election campaign.

"Phom mai poet pratu" (I won't open the door) is a *phleng plaeng* of Maithai Jaitawan's "Phom mai dai chao chu" (I Am Not a Playboy), which satirizes the Bhumjai Thai party of Newin Chidchob. "Ham hon nam Thaksin" (Isan for "Considering Thaksin") and "Won Thaksin khuen ban" (Beg Thaksin to Come Back) are "missing Thaksin" songs in the vein of Muk's "Khon di thi na nueng." Consisting of Isan vocals with *khaen* accompaniment in the style of *molam klon*, they were written toward the end of 2010, when the Abhisit government appeared to be firmly in control. When Yingluck Shinawatra's candidacy for prime minister was announced, Somjit decided to write a song for Phuea Thai to use in campaigning around Khon Kaen. "Ying Pu phu nam Thai" draws a parallel between Yingluck and the heroines of Thalang, Thao Thep Kasattri and Thao Sri Sunthorn, who rallied the people of Phuket to defeat invading Burmese in 1785.

For Somjit, the red-shirt protests represent a fundamental shift in Thai society. He claims that in the past, ordinary people were only concerned about the price of goods or lifestyle issues, but now those ordinary people were concerned about society and political philosophy. He says that ordinary red shirts really began to mobilize when Abhisit was made prime minister because they wanted to force the Thai government to respect their right to choose political representatives. In other words, the basis for the red-shirt movement was political rather than economic. What is particularly interesting about his observations is that the 1992 protest movement does not figure into his worldview, whereas, while he is not old enough to have participated in the 1970s CPT insurgency, he does see the insurgency as a prequel for the red shirts.

SONG: "NUM SUEA KHAO, SAO SUEA DAENG"

The collective meaning and memory embodied in *luk thung* is aptly demonstrated by a red-shirt version of "Num na khao, sao na kluea" (Rice-Farming Boy, Salt-Farming Girl). As discussed in chapter three, this famous duet was perhaps the most popular song of 1982 and earned its writer, Soraphet Phinyo, a Phaensiang Thongkham, a highly prized honor from the royal family. In 1989, "Num na khao" was listed in the top-fifty *luk thung* songs of all time by the Office of National Culture. Its enduring popularity among karaoke singers has inspired a number of *phleng plaeng*, such as an amusing version in which the male and female singers declare their love for alcohol of all kinds.[33]

A key factor in the original's appeal is the ubiquitous nature of the characters—the peasant boy and girl are hard-working urban migrants who are drawn together by their humble origins. The girl is identified as "Yuphin," a traditional peasant name which can also be used to refer to any woman whose name is unknown. A second factor is that *luk thung* provides the comfort of tradition to those who are most confronted by the alienation of cosmopolitan life (see Amporn 2006, 40–41). Although tempted by their independence, the characters choose to conform to societal expectations by seeking parental blessings on their relationship and returning to live in the girl's hometown. Finally, the song itself is a well-known symbol of the inequality of modern Thailand. As discussed in chapter three, in 1990 songwriter Cholathi Thanthong complained that Soraphet was paid only sixty thousand baht by his company for a song that made well over 44 million baht. Soraphet is unable to rerecord his most famous song because he does not own the copyright. Each of these channels of identification resonates with the red-shirt constituency on deeply emotional levels.

Translation of "Num suea khao, sao suea daeng"

M: My village is white shirted. I've met a strong woman.
F: I am a red-shirt woman of the strongest kind.
M: My house likes to watch Nattawut.
F: As for me, Nong Nut, I follow everyone.
M: I came to meet my red-shirt sister and have visited Dao Khanong.
F: So it is my good luck to meet you before you turn into a yellow shirt.
M: I am interested in the red shirts—you must help to teach me.
F: From what you say I'm afraid you are not truly red.
M: I want to go to the protest. Can you come as my friend?
F: So you must wait till the end of the month.
M: If you're my friend, don't leave me.
M: If I change to become a red shirt are you going to tease me?
F: I will be very happy if you become truly red.
M: This white-shirt man guarantees that I will not go back on my word.
F: If you love me truly, don't leave the red-shirt girl.

"Num suea khao, sao suea daeng" (White-Shirt Boy, Red-Shirt Girl)[34] draws on these collective meanings and memories while adding new layers of meaning in a political context. Firstly, it purports to be sung by the original female singer, Nong Nut Duangchiwan, even though Nong Nut has told me that she did not sing it. The ubiquitous peasant girl of the original is individualized in the lyrics as the Isan celebrity Nong Nut and acknowledged as politically stronger and more aware than the male protagonist. Her acceptance of him as a partner depends on his acceptance of and active participation in her politics. This is in marked contrast to the circumstances of the original song (see chapter three). In the recent conflicts, "white shirt" was often been used to indicate someone who had no political leaning.[35] Soraphet himself used this phrase to describe himself when I questioned him about politics. So, although the male songwriter originally dominated the female co-singer, he has remained static and undeveloped, while she has developed a political ideology and cultural strength. The subtext is clear—those who were formerly subservient, whether read as the Isan people or region, Thai peasants or women, or even Nong Nut herself, now are part of a significant nationwide political movement. Secondly, some elements of the song are informed by new realities. The villagers in the original are identified by the kind of labor they provide, whereas in the red-shirt version they are identified according to political persuasion. At the time of the original song Dao Khanong was a new, vibrant marketplace, but now it is run down and out of favor. The characters of the red-shirt version go to Dao Khanong to attend a protest, rather than for social or commercial reasons.

Luk Thung and the PAD and Pink Shirts

The occupation of the Bangkok's airports in November 2008 initially appeared to be a major victory for the PAD, but the hardline activism actually signaled the beginning of a steady decline in support for the group. By 2009 many protests that would have previously been promoted by yellow shirts were instead conducted under the guise of pink or multicolored shirts. The wearing of pink shirts by royalists became popular after King Bhumibol left the hospital in November 2007 dressed in pink. In March 2009, the idea of a pink-shirt group was presented humorously in a music video for the song "Mob si chomphu" (Pink Protest Group), by Isan *molam/luk thung* singer Jintara Phunlap. This song imagined a pink-shirt political party preaching a doctrine of love and peace and for a while Jintara's fan club turned up at her concerts dressed in pink shirts. Palitano (2010) assumes that Jintara and the pink political grouping are connected although since there is no evidence of this, it is more likely that "Mob si chomphu" was intended as a satire of the various color-coded groups. The adoption of the more politically neutral pink shirts coincided with more overt attempts by the PAD to make use of *luk thung*, perhaps indicating that the royalists had realized that the genre had been a major motivational force for the red shirts.

Logically, there would have been significant advantage for the yellow and pink shirts in employing *luk thung* and *molam* to spread their message. *Molam* was used beneficially by the United States Information Service during the Vietnam War and the Thai government during the CPT insurgency (see Miller 1985, 56–57). However, up until the 2010 campaign by the red shirts, the PAD ignored *molam* and tended to send the wrong messages when attempting to use *luk thung*. In concentrating on hegemonic and satirical elements from a broad range of musical genres, the PAD missed an opportunity to engage with the working class on a visceral level. For example, Joy Sirilak became a popular *luk thung* star after her appearance in the 2000 soap opera *Sao noi café* (*Young Girl in the Café*). Yet, when appearing for the PAD in July 2008, rather than any of her own hits she sang only Phumphuang's "Siam mueang yim" (Siam, Land of Smiles) which begins "Khon Thai rak chat lae sasana" (Thais love the nation and religion), thus honoring the three institutions.[36] Similarly, patriotic *luk thung* songs from the late 1950s and early 1960s (see chapter one) have been popular choices for PAD protests at Preah Vihear temple near the Cambodian border. Furthermore, in order to connect to the *luk thung* demographic, the background of the singer is just as important as the song. Having former Suntharaphon crooner Saken Sutthiwong singing "Klin khlon sap khwai," which decries the elite's treatment of poor farmers, did not make sense.[37] Another incongruous and perplexing sight was Singha Brewery heiress Chitpas Bhirombhakdi lipsynching[38] the most popular *luk thung* song of 2013, Yingli Sichumphon's smash hit "Kho chai thoe laek boe tho."

Most of the *molam* and *luk thung* on the PAD side occurred after the beginning of the 2010 Songkran protests in the context of YouTube videos satirizing the red-shirt demographic. Such belittling of working-class genres revealed the ethnic divide that mirrored the political one. Many members of the Bangkok middle class, which is mostly of Chinese origin, believed that they work harder and are better educated than rural Thais, who are mostly of Lao ethnicity. As Pasuk and Baker (2014, 6) note, "Soap opera starlets, speaking from the protest stages, argue that governments should be chosen by people like her, not Thaksin's provincial and rural supporters, because she is more intelligent."[39] This prejudice explains why the term *khwai* or "buffalo" circulated so freely at PAD and PDRC protests and why these organizations have adopted *luk thung* as a protest tool. For example, the mocking "Khwai, khwai, khwai (daeng)" is fast *luk thung* to the melody of Suraphon Sombatjaroen's early hit "Khamen lai khwai" (Cambodian Rides Buffalo),[40] which dates back to the Preah Vihear protests of the 1950s, accompanies simple animation of Thaksin riding the other red-shirt leaders, and Folkner's "Mob Weng," referring to red-shirt leader Dr. Weng Tojirakarn, is a cross between *luk thung* and *molam*.[41]

Not surprisingly, attempts by the pink shirts and the Democrat government to capitalize on the popularity and ubiquity of *luk thung* have usually come across as forced and heavy handed. On December 27, 2009, the long-running televised *luk thung* concert show, *Wethi Thai* (*Thai Stage*), diverted from its usual programming to broadcast a pink shirts rally featuring then prime minister Abhisit Vejjajiva. When long-term fans of the show arrived at the alternative venue they discovered that about a thousand pink-shirted supporters had already arrived by bus, along with a sizeable security presence. The stage featured a huge backdrop of the king, with a halo effect, looking over farmers planting rice. An introductory film interspersed footage of the king with footage of Abhisit and his government. Before the prime minister made his appearance, Grammy artist Mon Khaen sang *molam* accompanied by ten dancers all holding *khaen*, the musical symbol of Isan. Abhisit and other dignitaries then sang Phloen Phromdaen's classic "Chom thung" (Admiring the Rural Scenery) (fig. 5.2), before being presented with garlands and roses by a procession of poor people. The choice of song was curious considering Phloen's well-known preference for the red shirts, but perhaps it was a case of reclaiming enemy territory. Despite being carefully designed to appeal to the *luk thung* demographic the overall effect was undermined by Abhisit's obvious discomfort and lapses in memory during the song.

An exception to the rule that the PAD was far less likely to make use of *phleng plaeng* than the UDD shows what the unifying force of *luk thung* might have achieved. At a PAD rally in May 2008, Nga Caravan sang a *phleng plaeng* of "Fon duean Hok" (Rains of the Sixth Month) composed by Phaibun Butkhan in 1968 for Rungphet Laemsing. The choice of song hints at compromise—Phaibun being honored by both the establishment, as central

Thailand's greatest songwriter, and by former Communist Insurgents, as the father of left-wing protest (Wat 2003, 251–53). The original evokes the spirit of rural Thailand with the sound of frogs calling in the rice fields during the rainy season. Nga's version[42] retains the wistful, lilting singing style and some of the lyrics of the original, which suited the inclement weather in which the protest took place:

FIGURE 5.2. Abhisit singing next to famous *like* and *luk thung* singer Chaiya Mitchai. Behind them is then finance minister Korn Chatikavanij. (Peter Garrity, Bangkok, December 27, 2009)

Now entering into the sixth month, rain falls—drip, drip.
The frogs are singing in the rice fields.
In our capital city the PAD meet again
Against the evil government who only benefit themselves.

Changed the law to protect investors of billions,
Those who bully the villagers like thieves,
The prime minister is like a whining bear
Who uses words to lift himself up and makes the news reporters sick.

I ask the question why it has to rain.
You answer it rains because the frog is asking the rain to come from the sky.
Ask the frog why he has a sore tummy and why he has to cry—
The answer is the price of the rice has risen and he has to eat uncooked rice.

The restrained altered lyrics attacked corruption and bullying of the press without resorting to the extreme invective characteristic of later PAD songs, although the assumption that rural folk were starving and would rise up against Thaksin proved to be wildly optimistic. Overall it was a well-performed and credible piece of propaganda that could have appealed to the working class, if it had been accompanied by an awareness and acceptance of the working class's desire to rise within a changing Thai society. Activism that sought to maintain the old sociopolitical order while making use of a musical genre that decried the injustice of that order could only appear as cynical and scheming in the eyes of the red shirts.

The Battle Lines for Thai Culture

Though they have followed different approaches, both sides have been conscious of music's importance in maintaining morale and image, and both have claimed musical superiority. A 2010 article on the *Manager* website parodies the red shirts' catch cry of "song matrathan":

> We don't intend for there to be two standards in the Thai music industry but if we compare the artists that have graced the yellow shirts' stage [with the red shirts' artists] and if we talk about "quality" rather than about various genres, try looking at the following names . . .[43]

As if to answer, red shirts leader Thida Thawornset declaimed in a speech in 2011:

> This is not just regular entertainment at the concert. It is the battlelines for Thai culture. . . . The red shirt group has a lot of music and . . . many melodies. We have international and local and village music. We use this music to reach the people (the poor). And we use it to get the response from the middle class. . . . There used to be yellow shirt musicians. Now the interest is not there and they are not producing new songs anymore. . . . Yellow shirts musicians need to go back to playing the old music of the ammat to persuade people to feel loyalty to the monarchy. (Tausig 2013, 171–2)

Both sets of claims are open to criticism. The artists listed in the *Manager* article appear to be chosen for their links to "high culture" as much as for their quality. The first three names (Suthep Wongkamhaeng, Umaphon Buaphueng, and Saken Sutthiwong) are *luk krung* singers who may be icons of high society but whose best performance days are far behind them. In terms of quality, the red shirts certainly have the edge when it comes to *luk thung* and *molam*. On the other hand, not many red-shirt songs qualify as international music, unless Thai country rock is counted (but it is really a hybrid genre like songs for life). Also, Thida's assertion that the yellow shirts stopped producing original songs after 2010 cannot be supported. While it is true that the PAD and PRDC increasingly reveled in royal songs and *phleng plukchai*, the number of songs attacking Yingluck Shinawatra during her term as prime minister showed that composers sympathetic to the PAD were still creating songs.

Both academic and popular writers have complained that Thais are not interested in professionally written history (see Jory 2003). Whether this is still true or not, both sides of the recent conflict anchored their positions in differing historical interpretations. Just as the Thai elite claim superiority on the basis of being descended from either the Sukhothai Kingdom (1238–1438) or the Ayutthaya Kingdom (1351–1767), red shirts are increasingly referencing the ancient kingdoms of Lanna (1292–1775), which was located in northern Thailand, and Lan Xang (1354–1707), which consisted of most of Laos and Isan. That the key constituency of the PAD and PDRC is middle-class Bangkokians descended from nineteenth-century Chinese immigrants does not prevent yellow shirts from looking down on the red shirt "*phrai* and *khwai*" who supposedly came late to the Kingdom of Ayutthaya. The Sino-Thai middle class connects to this mythical past using Thai classical music, including many melodies that are less than one hundred fifty years old. Similarly, despite centuries of intermarriage, some red shirts have argued for more power in Thailand via an ancient past when "they" were free of the Thai in the kingdoms of Lanna and Lan Xang.

However, by leaving the red shirts to draw on the emotional and historical resonances contained in *luk thung*, the PAD may have made a key tactical error. The red shirts have often been characterized in PAD media as un-Thai, whether as communists or republicans or rampant capitalists. Red shirts have sometimes been referred to as Isan people and northerners—not

Thais—thus bringing ethnicity into play. The presentation of *molam* at red shirt protests has lent credence to such characterizations because *molam* is only performed by Isan people. However, the use of *luk thung* implicitly refutes these characterizations because, as Amporn (2006, 25–26) shows, the genre has become a key marker of authentic culture for modern Thais. Today, *luk thung*, more than any other genre of Thai music, bridges ethnic and class divisions and can be participated in by all Thais.

The opening quote of this chapter is from "Klin khlon sap khwai," Phaibun Butkhan's 1953 *phleng chiwit* that was banned because it criticized class inequality. Today, the confrontation between the "farmers smelling of buffalo" and the "people of heaven" has become the key political and social issue in Thailand. Even before the arrival of this political turmoil, *luk thung* did not just have the potential to be political but was consistently used for political purposes throughout its history. *Phleng chiwit* and *phleng Phuphan* were explicitly counter-hegemonic in their respective periods, and the use of *luk thung* by the red shirts continued this pattern. *Luk thung* provides the rural with a voice, audible in both rural and urban contexts, which implicitly and explicitly contests the unequal distribution of power.

In the recent political conflict, the relationship between Isan regional identity and *luk thung* became highly significant. The theme of longing and separation that is expressed so prominently in *luk thung* taps into Isan cultural memories such as seasonal migration to Bangkok, the CPT insurgency, and separation from Laos. In contrast, attempts by the PAD and Democrats to capitalize on the popular appeal of *luk thung* usually failed to genuinely engage with the working class.

Coda

> Thais have abandoned their own entertainments.... Both men and women now play laokaen [*molam*] throughout the kingdom.... We cannot give priority to Lao entertainments.... Laokaen must serve the Thai; the Thai have never been the Lao's servants.
>
> —King Mongkut (quoted in Miller 1985, 39)

It is now a matter of history that the disruption of the Yingluck government by the PDRC resulted in Thailand's twelfth successful coup. In May 2014, army chief Prayut Chan-o-cha took control of the country and soon had himself proclaimed prime minister. The atmosphere in Thailand is now reminiscent of the 1950s and 1960s: once again a general is in charge, hyper-royalism is in the ascendency, and criticism of the establishment is strictly prohibited. Prayut has launched a program of "Returning Happiness to the People," ironically including free *luk thung* concerts. These events have brought a lull to almost ten years of protest and political song. It remains to be seen whether the observation of Eyerman and Jamison (1998, 43) that "Music, and song... can maintain a movement even when it no longer has a visible presence in the form of organizations, leaders, and demonstrations" will apply to *luk thung* and the red shirts post-2014. Will *luk thung* "be a vital force in preparing the emergence of a new movement" (1998, 43) or will its practitioners once again retreat into commercial hibernation to await a thawing in the political climate?

CODA

This book has been shaped by the extraordinary nature of the recent extended period of political upheaval in Thailand and the complexity of understanding the position of a hybrid mediated genre such as *luk thung* in a modern Thailand divided along ethnic and class lines. As discussed in chapter five, some Western writers have wondered why *luk thung* has not been more overtly dissident considering its working-class demographic. Certainly the seeming absence of protest in commercial *luk thung* should have led to a discussion of why it was not able to serve as protest music—because of the fragile socioeconomic position of Isan musicians and because of the strict censorship that the music attracted, largely due to its strong Isan origins.

That is why this book discusses the Isan involvement in the Thai musical genre of *luk thung* and issues that have arisen from such involvement. Beginning with the invention of *ramwong* in the 1940s, Isan cultural activity has been constantly and increasingly incorporated into the field of *luk thung*. The rise in status of *luk thung* during the 1990s supported a concurrent Isan cultural revival, accompanied by a rise in mainstream political participation by Isan people. After the 2006 military coup removed Thaksin Shinawatra as prime minister and Isan political participation became concentrated on the red shirts movement, *luk thung* became the soundtrack of their movement.

Another theme of this book is that what might be regarded as oppressive hegemonic structures can sometimes provide the means for a marginalized culture to survive and grow. The close relationship between *luk thung* and the regulated, state-controlled Thai entertainment industry has assisted the large Isan minority in establishing a new identity and achieving cultural independence while still remaining Thai. Ella Shohat and Robert Stam (1994, 354) have written that "disempowered communities can [only] decode dominant programming through a resistant perspective ... [if] their collective life and historical memory have provided an alternative framework for understanding." For most of the twentieth century, Isan language and culture was suppressed and denigrated in the service of Thai nationalization, but the mass production and dissemination of *luk thung* songs came to provide this "alternative framework for understanding." Thongchai Prasongsanti, the Isan entertainer who appears in *Nang baep khok kradon* (see chapter four), accounts for the "Isan renaissance" quite simply: "Our lives are portrayed in a lot of songs" (Kreangsak 2005, 2). Isan talent in the areas of music and comedy has been exploited for commercial profit by Thai entertainment companies, but in the process Isan culture has survived and flourished.

CODA

In contrast, for Isan entertainers' ethnic cousins in Laos, the situation is different. Phuwiang Watthalisak, the acknowledged queen of Lao *luk thung*, has had to leave Laos to live and record in the USA, not because of government restriction, but because rampant piracy has made recording in Laos untenable.[1] The absence of vertically integrated entertainment companies in Laos means that financial rewards for the best singers are simply not there. Grammy stars may be underpaid by Western standards but they make a very good living by Thai standards. Even for Laos's foremost pop star, Alexandra Bounxouei, the Thai entertainment industry has been far more appealing than its Lao counterpart.

The development of *luk thung* is one example of a collision between globalization and localization in which the global has been exploited by the national and the local. Although no longer confined to the poor and working class, the *luk thung* audience provides a snapshot of non-elite Thai society adapting to the modern mediated world. Likewise, Isan cultural identity has come to dominate the *luk thung* scene. As a result, singers without any Lao-Isan heritage have learned how to appeal to the Isan *luk thung* audience without patronizing them. The effort that established singers such as Mangpor and new singers such as Donut put into creating and maintaining fans holds lessons for the next wave of authorities and politicians, who will have to bridge the rift that has emerged in Thai society.

FIGURE 6.1. Adison Phiangket mourns his younger brother.
(Nick Nostitz, Khao Yai November 15, 2009)

At a red shirts concert at Khao Yai on November 15, 2009, Adison Phiangket broke down while singing about his younger brother who was killed during the Isan insurgency (fig. 6.1); the poignancy of this moment shows why the red shirts succeeded in becoming a nationwide movement. As Adison and Wisa Khantap discovered thirty years before, real change in the Thai social order could not be brought about by weapons or ideology. The cultural disjunction that developed between the CPT leadership, Bangkok students, and Isan farmers showed Adison that a common purpose is best promoted through a musical genre that is accessible to all Thais. A significant factor in the cultural unity of the red shirts was that their favored genre, *luk thung*, allows for regional and ethnic differences while maintaining a high degree of Thainess.

Although the PAD used a much wider variety of music than the UDD and produced music of better quality, their choices acted to exclude the majority of Thais. Perhaps this issue of agency is what truly connects the three periods of protest examined in chapter five. During the era of *phleng chiwit*, talented, highly educated songwriters protested on behalf of the muted lower classes, but the state was eventually able to stifle their criticism by force. During the struggle of the CPT, the rank-and-file insurgents had songs written for them by Bangkok students in genres prescribed by the CPT leadership but were also able to produce *phleng plaeng* in their preferred genre of *luk thung*. In the most recent conflict, both sides made use of *luk thung*, but only the red shirts were able to successfully appeal to the working class on a large scale. Perhaps, for the first time in Thai history, working-class Thais were making their own political choices.

The words of King Mongkut that opened this chapter resonate with the cultural conditions of modern Thailand. In 1865, the king proclaimed a ban on Lao musical performance because he was afraid that Lao musical culture would completely supplant Siamese genres. Today, through the forms of *luk thung*, *luk thung molam*, and *molam sing*, Isan musical culture has achieved a position of prominence in Thailand that is approaching dominance. And, just as Isan cultural identity has come to dominate the *luk thung* scene, so Isan political identity has threatened to overwhelm the established Thai power structures. Throughout the recent political turmoil, *luk thung* served as a repository of cultural memory that was able to strengthen and sustain the red-shirt movement. This role of *luk thung* should not be forgotten. Through *luk thung*, Isan people have been able to contribute to Thai culture, and, in doing so, they have made strides toward taking control of their political destiny.

Appendix I
Who's Who

Artists are listed in their most active decade. Only artists mentioned in this book are listed. M = male. F = female. NA = National Artist.

1930s and 1940s

Kaeo Atchariyakun (1915–81) Bangkok. *Suntharaphon* lyricist. M

Khamron Sambunnanon (1920–69) Bangkok. Singer of life songs/*luk thung* and actor. M

Luan Khwantham (1912–79) Thon Buri. Southern songwriter who invented *talung* rhythm. M

Narot Thaworabut (1905–81) Ratchaburi. Songwriter and pianist. M

Phranbun [Juangjan Jankhana] (1901–76) Phetchaburi. Songwriter for *lakhon rong* and films. M

Uea Sunthonsanan (1910–81) Samut Songkhram. Songwriter and leader of *Suntharaphon*. M

Wet Sunthonjamon (1901–83) Ratchaburi. Songwriting partner of Kaeo Atchariyakun. M

Wichit Wathakan (1898–62) Uthai Thani. Phibun's propagandist and playwright. M

1950s

Benjamin [Tumthong Chokchana] (1921–94) Ubon Ratchathani. "King of *ramwong*," actor. M

APPENDIX I: WHO'S WHO

Chaloemchai Sriruecha (1927–87) Roi Et. Ramwong songwriter and performer. M

Chan Yenkhae (1926–88) Bangkok. Singer of life songs and *phleng Thai sakon*. M

Charin Nanthanakhon [Charin Ngammueang] (1933–) Chiang Mai. *Luk krung* superstar. M (NA)

Latda Sriworanan (1936–) Thon Buri. Thailand's first Muslim singing star. F

Mongkhon Amathayakun (1918–89) Bangkok. Songwriter and owner of Jularat band. M

Nakhon Thanormsap [Gungadin] (1932–) Bangkok. Singer who adapted Western songs. M

Phaibun Butkhan (1918–72) Pathum Thani. Thailand's most celebrated songwriter. M

Phayong Mukda (1926–2010) Ratchaburi. Songwriter in many different styles. M (NA)

Saneh Komarachun (1923–71) Thon Buri. Renaissance man, actor, singer, director etc. M

Somyot Thasanaphan (1915–86) Bangkok. Singer and songwriter from Navy band. M

Suthep Wongkamhaeng (1934–) Nakhon Ratchasima. *Luk krung* singing legend. M (NA)

Somjit Tatjinda (1925–74) Thon Buri. Early *phleng Thai sakon* singing star. F

1960s

Chaichana Bunnachot (1942–) Chachoengsao. NA - Songwriter/pioneer of *lae* style *luk thung*. M

Chai Mueangsing (Man City Lion) [Somsian Phanthong] (1939–) Singburi. Innovator. M (NA)

Jinda Sombatjaroen (c. 1933–) Suphan Buri. Suraphon's younger brother, songwriter/ singer. M

Kan Kaeosuphan (1939–2013) Suphan Buri. Singer and leader of Prakai Dao band. M

Ken Dalao (1930–2014) Ubon Ratchathani. *Molam klon* known for spicy lyrics. M (NA)

K. Kaeoprasoet. Leader of a group of mainly Isan songwriters during the 1960s. M

APPENDIX I: WHO'S WHO

Kuson Kamonsing [Rung Phadungsin] (1934–) Bangkok. Benjamin's only protégé. M

Loet Srichok (unknown–1990) Nakhon Nayok of Lao origin. Lyricist for K. Kaeoprasoet. M

Mueangmon Sombatjaroen (1938–70) Suphan Buri. Songwriter - Suraphon's protégé. M

P. Chuenprayot. Bangkok. Songwriter especially for Kan and Thun and bandleader. M

Phet Phanomrung (1941–) Buri Ram. "King of *phleng ho*," Thai country and western. M

Phiphat Boribun (1936–2013) Bangkok. Bandleader and writer of "Phu yai Li." M

Phongsri Woranut (1939–) Chainat. The first "Queen of *luk thung*" and bandleader. F (NA)

Phon Phirom (1948–2010) Ayutthaya. *Like* actor who brought Thai doem into *luk thung*. M

Phraiwan Lukphet (1941–2002) Phetchaburi. Suraphon's protégé. Singer for *luk thung* films. M

Pong Prida (1930–2011) Khon Kaen. High-pitched vocalist and *khaen* player in Jularat band. M

Rungphet Laemsing (1942–) Phetchaburi. Singer of Phaibun's "Fon duean hok" and actor. M

Saksri Sriakson (1937–) Ubon Ratchathani. Singer of "Phu Yai Li." Married to Phiphat. F

Sombat Bunsiri (1937–) Prachin Buri of Lao descent. Pioneering Isan songwriter. M

Srinuan Sombatjaroen (c. 1935–) Suraphon's wife and leader of Sit Suraphon after his death. F

Suraphon Sombatjaroen (1930–68) Suphan Buri. "The king of *luk thung*" and songwriter. M

Samniang Muangthong (1926–) Suphan Buri. Songwriter and leader of Ruam Dao Krajai. M

Thun Thongchai (1929–95) Samut Songkhram. Singer of sweet love songs. M

Waiphot Phetsuphan (1942–) Suphan Buri. "King of lae songs," discovered Phumphuang. M (NA)

Yongyut Chiaochanchai (1935–92) Lopburi. One of Suraphon's first protégés. M

APPENDIX I: WHO'S WHO

1970s

Banchop Charoenphon (1940) Chon Buri of Lao descent. *Luk thung* singer and bandleader. M

Buppha Saichon (1948–) Chon Buri. Singer of Indian-style *luk thung* songs with Chatri. F

Chatri Srichon (1949–) Chon Buri. Singer of Indian-style *luk thung* songs with Buppha. M

Chinakon Krailat (1946–) Sukhothai. Singer of popular adaptations of *Thai doem*. M (NA)

Cholathi Thanthong (1937–) Chon Buri (Lao) Singer and songwriter for Sayan Sanya. M (NA)

Dao Bandon (1947–) Yasothon. A monk who became a famous singer and songwriter. M

Doi Inthanon (1947–) Surin. Successful *luk thung* and *luk thung Isan* songwriter.

Khwanchit Sriprachan (1947–) Suphan Buri. Famous performer of central Thai folk music. F

Nophadon Duangphon (1951–) Ubon Ratchathani. Leader of Phet Phin Thong band. M

Phanom Nopporn (1946–) Chon Buri (Lao) Sweet-voiced singer and actor. M

Phloen Phromdaen (1939–) Prachin Buri (Lao) Songwriter, "king of speaking song." M (NA)

Phongsak Chantharukkha (1937–) Ubon Ratchathani. Veteran Isan songwriter. M

Rom Sithamarat (1948–) Nakhon Si Thammarat. Southern *luk thung* singer. M

Saengsuri Rungrot (1953–) Nakhon Ratchasima. Singer named by songwriter Somrit Rungrot. M

Saksayam Phetchomphu (1952–) Mahasarakham. Biggest Isan star of the 1970s. M

Samai Onwong (1933–96) Phetchaburi of Lao descent. *Khaen* player and bandleader. M

Sangthong Sisai (1948–84) Suphan Buri. Singer and comedian who died in car accident. M

San Silaprasit [Sanya Chulaphon] (Loei). Veteran Isan songwriter who started in Jularat. M

APPENDIX I: WHO'S WHO

Sayan Sanya (1953–2013) Suphan Buri. Biggest *luk thung* star of the 1970s. M
Sonchai Mekwichian (1953–) Nakhon Ratchasima. Protégé of Chalorng Phusawang. M
Songkhro Samatthaphaphong (c.1940–) Chaiyaphum. Phloen's songwriting partner. M
Suang Santi (Dao Morakot) (1945–82) Sukhothai. Singer-songwriter who used heavy rock. M
Suntaree Vejanond (1955–) Chiang Mai. Northern folk singer and mother of Lanna Commins. F
Surachai (Nga) Jantimathon (1948–) Surin. Leader of archetypal songs for life group Caravan. M
Surin Phaksiri (1942–) Ubon Ratchathani. Leader of Isan songwriters in the 1970s. M
Thepphon Phetubon (1947–2014) Ubon Ratchathani. Songwriter for Saksayam and singer. M
Thinakon Thiphamat (1936–2011) Isan songwriter, "father of love songs." M
Yodrak Salakchai (1956–2008) Phichit. Major star of the 1970s and 1980s, rivalling Sayan. M

1980s

Ad Carabao (1954–) Suphan Buri. Leader of the most successful songs for life band. M
Arisman Phongruangrong (1964–) Ratchaburi. 1980s pop star and red shirt leader. M
Chaloemphon Malakham (1962–) Surin. Biggest male *luk thung molam* star of the 1980s. M
Hongthong Dao Udon (c. 1960–) Udon Thani. *Luk thung molam* singer and red shirt DJ. F
Khwanchai Phetroiet (1952–85) Roi Et. Pioneer of *luk thung Isan* who died early. M
Nong Nut Duangchiwan (1959–) Khon Kaen. Soraphet's first protégé and singing partner. F
Onuma Singsiri (1961–) Nong Khai. Isan singer most famous for "Sao Isan ro rak." F
Phimpha Phonsiri (1969–) Chaiyaphum. Soraphet's main protégé and big star of the 1980s. F

APPENDIX I: WHO'S WHO

Phumphuang Duangjan (1961–92) Chainat. "Queen of *luk thung*," revolutionized its image. F

Somphot Duangsomphong (c. 1960–) *Luk thung molam* singer and Soraphet's protégé. M

Soraphet Phinyo (1951–) Nakhon Ratchasima. Celebrated singer and songwriter. M

Sotsai Rungphothong (1951–) Samut Prakan. Singer, songwriter, and Democrat politician. M

Sumthum Phairimbueng (1949–97) Khon Kaen. Songwriter notable for "Sao Isan ro rak." M

Wichian Khamcharoen [Lop Burirat] (1935–) Lopburi. Singer and songwriter for Phumphuang. M

Yenjit Phonthewi (c. 1960–) Khon Kaen. *Luk thung molam* singer and Sumthum's protégé. F

1990s

Aphaphon Nakhonsawan (1968–) Nakhon Sawan. Comedic singer and actress with Yingyong. F

Asanee Chotikul (1955–) Loei. With brother Wasan (1957–) Most famous Thai rock duo. M

Bird Thongchai McIntyre (1958–) Bangkok. Thailand's King of pop; evergreen and always in fashion. M

Ekachai Sriwichai (1962–) Nakhon Si Thammarat. Southern singer with a gangster image. M

Jintara Phunlap (1971–) Roi Et. Soraphet's protégé who became Isan's biggest star. F

Nik Niranam (c. 1960) Leader of songs for life group Niranam and first husband of Phaijit. M

Noknoi Uraiphon (1957–) Si Sa Ket. *Luk thung molam* singer and leader of Siang Isan. F

Phaijit Aksonnarong (1961–) Buri Ram. Singer in Thai and Chinese married to Wisa Khanthap. F

Phonsak Songsaeng (1960–) Khon Kaen. Veteran *luk thung molam* singer. M

Phimphayom (Iu) Rueangrot (c. 1968) Bangkok. Sweet voiced singer in Thai and Chinese. F

APPENDIX I: WHO'S WHO

Siriphon Amphaiphong (1964–) Udon Thani. Husky voiced *luk thung* and *molam* singer. F

Sunari Ratchasima (1968–) Nakhon Ratchasima. *Luk thung* star. F

Wisa Khantap (c. 1955–) Songs for life singer-songwriter and red-shirt leader. M

Yingyong Yotbua-ngam (1962–) Si Sa Ket. Celebrated singer, songwriter and comedic actor. M

2000s

Chaiya Mitchai (1974–) Ayutthaya. *Like* and TV actor and *luk thung* singer. M

Fon Thanasunthon (1974–) Udon Thani. Beautiful *luk thung* singer and actress. F

Jakrapan (Got) Apkhoraburi (1968–) Nakhon Ratchasima. Grammy *luk thung* singer. M

Jenphop Jopkrabuanwan (1955–) Lopburi. *Luk thung* historian, songwriter for Rung Suriya. M

Joy Sirilak Pongchok (1977–) Bangkok. Actress and *luk thung* singer after *Sao noi cafe*. F

Lanna Commins (1983–) Bangkok. World music singer and daughter of Suntaree Vejanond. F

Luknok Suphaphon (c. 1978–) Kamphaeng Phet. *Luk thung molam* singer of "Khun Lamyai." F

Mangpor Chonticha (1988–) Khon Kaen. Singer with Nopporn and RS. F

Mike Phiramphon (1970–) Udon Thani. Working-class heartthrob with more than twenty albums. M

Monsit Khamsoi (1964–) Mukdahan. *Luk thung* singer who has moved into *lakhon* acting. M

Phi Sadoet (1972–) Khon Kaen. *Luk thung Isan* and country rock singer with Grammy. M

Rung Suriya (1970–) Phitsanulok. "The gentleman of *luk thung*." M

Sala Khunawut (1962–) Ubon Ratchathani. Thailand's most famous living songwriter. M

Sek Loso [Seksan Sukpimai] (1974–) Nakhon Ratchasima. Wild leader of rock group Loso. M

Sompong (Eed) Kunaprathom (1978–) Kalasin. Comedian and leader of Ponglang Sa-on. M

Tai Orathai (1980–) Ubon Ratchathani. *Luk thung* singer, Sala's protégé and former girlfriend. F

Takadaen Chonlada (1983–) Nakhon Ratchasima. Grammy singer and girl next door. F

Wasu Haohan (1970–) Udon Thani. Songs-for-life artist and notable luk thung songwriter. M

2010s

Bai Toei [Suthiwan Thawisin] (1988–) Songkhla. R-Siam singer with raunchy image. F

Chaem Chamram (1976–) Buri Ram. Grammy singer of smooth songs for life blended with pop. M

Ja Nongphani (c. 1991–) Ang Thong. Singer of infamous "Khan hu," now signed to R Siam. F

Khaothip Thidadin Hinon (1989–) Amnat Charoen. Rising Grammy *luk thung morlam* star. F

Kratae (1987–) Lampang. Muay Thai boxer who became a singing star, now with R-Siam. F

Liu Ajariya (1986–) Lamphun. Northern *luk thung* singer, one of the "dancing queens." F

Nim Khanuengphim (1987–) Chiang Rai. Singer through TV show *Academy Fantasia*. F

Phai Phongsathon (1982–) Yasothon. Grammy singer of huge hit "Khon ban diaokan." M

Yingli Sichumphon (1985–) Buri Ram. Grammy singer of 2013 hit "Kho chai thoe laek boe tho." F

Appendix II
Important Dates in Thai Popular Music History

c. 1900　The Royal Anthem "Phleng sansoen phra barami" (Song in Praise of the Royal Majesty) is the first Thai song using homophonic texture to be widely performed throughout the country.

1903　The Gramophone Company's recording engineer Fred Gaisberg tours Southeast Asia and makes the first commercial recordings in Siam.

1903　One of the earliest Thai songs using Western harmony, "Waltz Pluemjit," is written by Prince Nakhon Sawan Woraphinit.

c. 1908　The sung dance-drama genre *lakhon rong* (also known as *lakhon Pridalai* after the theater in which it was performed) appears in the latter part of the reign of King Chulalongkorn.

1917　A royal music school, called Rongrian Phran Luang, is opened; one of the school's new ensembles is the Wong Khrueangsai Farang Luang (Large Western String Ensemble).

1925　Sino-Thai T. Ngekchuan starts recording records on his Kratai (Rabbit) label.

1928–29　A non-royal known as Phranbun (real name Juangjan Jankhana) begins writing songs in a new style called *nuea rong tem* (one note per word, without *uean*) or *nuea chapho* (only lyrics) within the genre of *lakhon rong*.

APPENDIX II: IMPORTANT DATES

1931   Radio broadcast of *Lakhon rong Rosita*, featuring songs written by Phranbun and Phetcharat, and including a new adaptation of "Waltz Pluemjit."

1931   The first Thai sound film, *Long Thang* (*Lost Way*), produced by the iconic Thai film company Srikrung in 1931, is released, featuring a number of specially written songs.

1936   Uea Sunthonsanan (1910–81) assembles a group that includes a number of classical musicians who had lost their royal appointments.

1938   Used by official historians to date the origin of *luk thung*, the first *phleng Thai sakon* with a rural subject, Hem Wechakon's "Chao sao chao rai" (The Vegetable Farmer's Bride), is sung by Khamron Sambunnanon.

1939   Uea Sunthonsanan's group becomes the official band for Phibunsongkhram's Public Relations Department and later becomes known as Suntharaphon, a name that becomes synonymous with the elite popular genre of *phleng luk krung* (city songs).

1944   Phibunsongkhram introduces a suite of official dance songs known as *ramwong*, in which men and women dance in a circle, in order to compete with the popularity of Western dances such as the foxtrot and waltz.

1953   Suraphon Sombatjaroen's first recording "Namta Lao Wiang" (Tears of a Vientiane Girl) is released on T. Ngekchuan's Kratai label.

1959   "Phuyai Li," the most enduring song of the 1960s, is written by Phiphat Boribun and performed by his wife Saksri Sri-akson. The song satirizes local officials in Isan, who were not used to central Thai language and were easily confused by government edicts.

1961   Suraphon Sombatjaroen and Phongsri Woranut become Thailand's biggest musical pairing but split in acrimonious circumstances, never to speak again.

1964   The term *phleng luk thung* (country songs) is coined by Jamnong Rangsikun, the music manager of Channel Four.

1968   The king of *luk thung*, Suraphon Sombatjaroen, is murdered.

APPENDIX II: IMPORTANT DATES

1970 The film *Monrak Luk thung* opens, featuring songs by Surin Phaksiri and Phaibun Butkhan and the singing talents of Buppha Saichon, Phongsri Woranut, Banchop Charoenphon and Phraiwan Lukphet.

1971 Nophadon Duangphon begins a *molam prayuk* (adapted or Westernized) band under the name Phin Prayuk but changes the name to Phet Phin Thong following an audience with the king.

1973 Sayan Sanya and Saksayam Phetchomphu's bands vie for pre-eminence in the luk thung industry.

1975 Caravan launches the *phleng phuea chiwit* (songs for life) protest genre with their first album *Khon kap khwai* (*Man and Buffalo*).

1981 Carabao (the Tagalog word for buffalo) is formed and later becomes the most popular and enduring songs for life group.

1982 Soraphet Phinyo's duet, "Num na khao, sao na kluea" (Rice-Farming Boy, Salt-Farming Girl), performed with Nong Nut Duangchiwan, becomes a huge hit.

1983 Phaibun Damrongchaitham founds Grammy, which goes on to become the dominant Thai music company.

1984 Phumphuang Duangjan (1961–1992) releases *Hang noi, thoi nit* (Move a Little Closer) featuring the disco-influenced compositions of Wichian Khamcharoen (Lop Burirat).

1985 *Luk thung Isan* legend Chaloemphon Malakham records his first album.

1986 The first album of Bird Thongchai McIntyre is launched. Bird goes on to be the most successful singer in Thailand's history, selling more than 20 million albums.

1989 *Luk thung* is officially recognized and celebrated with the "Half Century of *Luk thung*" awards and concerts.

1992 Phumphuang Duangjan, the queen of *luk thung*, dies from a stroke caused by lupus. "Somsri 1992" becomes a bestselling song for singer-songwriter Yingyong Yotbua-ngam.

1993 Rock Khong Khoi from Surin in southern Isan release their landmark *kantruem* album *Siao Woi*.

APPENDIX II: IMPORTANT DATES

1997   Aphaphon Nakhonsawan's "Loek laeo kha" becomes the soundtrack of the Thai experience of the Asian Economic Crisis.

2000   Mike Phiramphon's fifth album for Grammy, *Yachai khonchon* (*Darling of the Poor*) reportedly sells more than one million cassettes.

2001   Luknok Supphaphon has a huge hit with the *luk thung Isan* sound of "Khun Lamyai."

2005   Groundbreaking Isan entertainment group Ponglang Sa-on, led by comedian Sompong "Eed" Kunaprathom, emerges.

2008   Death of 1970s superstar and sex symbol Yodrak Salakchai spurs renewed interest in vintage *luk thung*.

2009   "Khon ban diaokan" (People of the Same Village) becomes a massive hit for Phai Phongsathon.

2014   Yingli Sichumphon's "Kho chai thoe laek boe tho" (Your Heart for My Number) becomes the first *luk thung* song to achieve 100 million hits on YouTube.

Notes

Editor's note: All links to musical examples given in the notes are part of an updated and expanded list available at www.thaimusicinventory.org/silkworm.

Introduction

1. On *enka* see Christine Yano's Tears of Longing (2002), and on *dangdut* see Andrew Weintraub's Dangdut Stories (2010).

Chapter 1

1. Without capitalization, *molam* refers to the musical genre; capitalized it is the title for a practitioner.
2. *Toei* is one of three segments of a traditional *lam klon* performance. According to Miller (2005, 98), "lam toei is metrical (often described as danceable), 'minor'-sounding, and upbeat."
3. Both Benjamin's song and Suraphon's response can be heard at http://youtu.be/KFUNR0Tg4P0.
4. See http://youtu.be/DaSoJLPuSdA.
5. See Ubonrat (1990, 68–69) and Lockard (1998, 191).
6. It is customary for *luk thung* singers to use stage names that indicate where they were born. For example, Chinakon Krailat was born in Krailat district in Sukhothai Province. Suphan Buri Province figures in the names of several singers such as Sonphet Sonsuphan, Waiphot Phetsuphan, Kan Kaeosuphan, Sathika Suphansa, and others.
7. Samai should also be remembered as an early world music artist because he toured Asia from 1970 and Europe from 1971.
8. See Ubonrat (1990, 61), Lockard (1998, 184–85, 191), and Amporn (2006, 24).

9. It was not until the late 1970s that Thai professional historians such as Chatthip Nartsupha and Nidhi Eoseewong became interested in writing about ordinary people and their culture, using "Marxist socio-analysis as a lever to pry the chronicles and archives away from royalist and nationalist myth-making concerns" (Reynolds and Lysa 1983, 96). Several articles were published on *luk thung* between 1978 and 1985—Anake (1978), Phayong (1984), Sujit (1984), and Kobkul (1985)—all more or less classifying it as updated Thai folk music. Arguably the most well known Thai-historian, Nidhi, responded to these articles in 1985, arguing that *luk thung* was like many other forms of popular culture in that it borrowed from numerous sources including Western and Latin American dance music, *phleng Thai sakon*, and Thai folk and classical music. His main thesis was that *luk thung* began in urban areas and had more urban influences than rural. Despite Ubonrat agreeing with Nidhi, the view of *luk thung* as rural music has persisted in the popular media and academia.

Chapter 2

1. In *lukthung molam* the major subdominant chord (IV) is often used. Ethnomusicologist John Garzoli points out that the *thang yao* mode in *molam* employs a natural 6th. This means that popular songs based on *molam* (such as *lam phloen*) often have a major subdominant chord.
2. See http://youtu.be/V1UWy5ER48o.
3. *Thao* composition uses augmentation, diminution, and the doubling of tempo to create new versions of melodies so that the original melody is unrecognizable. See Morton (1976, 182, 185).
4. The Mon are an ancient ethnic group who formed an early civilization in central Thailand and now reside mainly in Myanmar.
5. See http://youtu.be/PI3Su7p_-cE.
6. The *khim* (dulcimer) was introduced to Thailand in the late 1800s by Chinese immigrants living in the Yaowarat district of Bangkok.
7. See http://youtu.be/P5OEx_1Q3to.
8. Phra Lo is the hero of *Lilit Phra Lo*, a sixteenth-century Siamese poem.
9. *Lae* is one of the central Thai folk traditions discussed later in this chapter.
10. See parts one and two at http://bit.do/Vjjp and http://bit.do/Vjjp2.
11. See http://youtu.be/BSQAOL34iyw.
12. See http://youtu.be/g9IK5Lfpcus, which includes footage of the film *Mon rak luk thung*.
13. See http://youtu.be/iDbShCb0R-M.
14. See http://youtu.be/9YTceZw9q5Y.
15. See http://youtu.be/Fb87YxFEXdM.
16. Instruments such as the *khaen*, as well as *phin* (Lao three-stringed guitar),

wot (Isan pan pipes), and *pong lang* (Isan vertical xylophone), are frequent markers of Isan influence in *luk thung*.
17. See http://youtu.be/_fkPyEClWqs.
18. See http://youtu.be/I_Td4cuo3u4.
19. See http://youtu.be/XRZKu3bAb0o.
20. See http://youtu.be/WE-Vc4Z9P1M.
21. See http://youtu.be/vLJasBnGDLo.
22. *Nu luk thung* is one name for the smooth blend of *luk thung* and *phleng phuea chiwit* now being produced by Grammy and RS.
23. See http://youtu.be/uIRBpXvDTrs.
24. See http://youtu.be/gKzqX7v6I-k.
25. See http://youtu.be/ELVyKxpkCCg.
26. See http://youtu.be/5LzErU6XIOo.
27. See http://youtu.be/SSQGDJtnvLo.
28. See http://youtu.be/ap2cdB-dcI8.
29. See http://youtu.be/xqB54ez4XKA.
30. Album name refers to an item or sofa used to welcome guests.
31. See Liu's "Huachai mi ngan khao" (My Heart Has Work to Do) at http://youtu.be/HU41yRX8Rd4.
32. See Christine Yano's *Tears of Longing: Nostalgia and the Nation in Japanese Popular Song* (2002). There are many similarities between *enka* and *luk thung*: both genres recall lost loves and distant homelands and dwell on the subject of loneliness. Both are hybrid genres that have resisted the inflow of American popular music by selective choice of influence and the use of traditional melody. However, *enka* in Japan is very much a backwater genre for older working-class listeners, whereas *luk thung* has become the dominant popular genre in Thailand and now draws a wide-ranging audience.
33. See http://youtu.be/tdZ3F9GX6ho.
34. See http://youtu.be/73HgYEJn-_I.
35. See http://youtu.be/nD_t9gplcJM.
36. See http://youtu.be/aN5rCSdgOQw.
37. See http://youtu.be/yLlpL4rOf9Y.
38. See http://youtu.be/tlyDqvE3IqY.
39. See http://youtu.be/GSCHG6hYJDg.
40. See http://monrakplengthai.blogspot.com/2008/10/blog-post_20.html.
41. See Peter Doolan's post on Sumit at http://monrakplengthai.blogspot.com/2012/08/phleng-thai-tham-nong-india.html.
42. See http://youtu.be/mpe4xxgmaIg.
43. See http://youtu.be/f5D0n_s9loc.
44. See http://youtu.be/5NsMGS5ouks.

Chapter 3

Parts of this chapter appeared in James Mitchell, "Sorapet Pinyoo and the Status of Pleeng Luuk Tung," *Journal of Southeast Asian Studies* 40, no. 2 (2009): 295-321. Reproduced by permission of the *Journal of Southeast Asian Studies*.

1. *Mo* (as in *Molam, Mokhaen*) denotes a skilled practitioner.
2. See http://youtu.be/uIRBpXvDTrs.
3. See, for example, a particularly garish version by Ui from Buddha Bless and Aphaphon Nakhonsawan at http://youtu.be/pdxfFZTOX_4.
4. Some websites and Pattana Kitiarsa date this song to 1982, but that seems unlikely because Phimpha would have only been thirteen years old. I've talked to Soraphet about this and he thinks this is the right year.
5. A girl asks her girlfriend to write a letter for her to a boy, but the boy ends up going out with the girlfriend. Soraphet remembers these albums as being 1987, but I have gone with the date according to the majority of sources.
6. See http://youtu.be/Ar9RBn7QHQ4.
7. See http://youtu.be/xWlK95GVHRg.
8. See Committee (1989, 126) and (1991, 191). Within each fifty, the songs were not assigned a hierarchy.
9. While "disciple" is the usual translation of *luksit*, "protégé" is probably a better fit for the *luk thung* context.
10. Online distribution does allow Thai entertainment companies to more effectively reach Thai diaspora communities. Sites such as ethaicd.com offer a wide range of Thai music, mainly from the dominant companies Grammy and RS Promotion, including Loog Toong (*luk thung*), Music for Life (*phleng phuea chiwit*) and Morlum (*molam*).
11. Politicians in Thailand are required to have a bachelor's degree.

Chapter 4

Parts of this chapter appeared in James Mitchell, "Khon ban diaokan or 'We're from the Same Village': Star/Fan Interaction in Thai Lukthung," *Perfect Beat* 12.1 (2011): 69-89. Reproduced by permission of *Perfect Beat*.

1. See http://youtu.be/CvFpXi3Tvro for a more recent live performance of the song.
2. Coyote dancers perform risqué dance routines and are often employed as entertainment at bars and clubs. The term became popular in the wake of the film *Coyote Ugly* (2000).
3. Tulloch and Jenkins (1995, 23) draw a similar distinction between fans, who claim a social identity, and followers, who do not.
4. Lockard notes that Thai society is "constructed from the top down, with reciprocal, vertical links between the elite and their clients" (1998, 163).

Several factors including age, education, family status, profession, and even skin color contribute to one's place in society.

5. Both Suthep and Chai are National Artists. For a cover by Bai Toei and Ja R-Siam, see http://youtu.be/TOLw2zK7byc.
6. See http://www.thailandqa.com/forum/showthread.php?t=2062.
7. See http://youtu.be/p414CRLAk-s.
8. See http://youtu.be/CKDwsFbq1_c. Yingli's music video already has approximately 150 million views. This song was written by Ubon Ratchathani–born Boi Khemrat.
9. See http://youtu.be/ahkGRFhyxx4.
10. See http://youtu.be/OsZu7jTZpvo.
11. See http://youtu.be/wv-G-kM9pUs.
12. See http://youtu.be/4S8CHCvRzrU?t=1m52s.
13. See http://youtu.be/eDRHZthtExs?t=1m53s.
14. See http://youtu.be/OczoOU8gglU?t=1m49s.
15. See http://youtu.be/K_-K9gYhNaY?t=2m "Thephi ban phrai" is written by *nu luk thung* star Nu Mithoe.
16. Many Isan village names begin with *khok*, which refers to a small, dry hill.
17. See http://youtu.be/DghVcRM4TTo.

Chapter 5

Parts of this chapter appeared in James Mitchell, "Red and Yellow Songs: A Historical Analysis of the Use of Music by the United Front for Democracy against Dictatorship (UDD) and the People's Alliance for Democracy (PAD) in Thailand," *South East Asia Research* 19, no. 3 (2011): 569–606. Passages extracted from *South East Asia Research* copyright 2011 SOAS. Reproduced by permission of IP Publishing Ltd.

1. In 2013 an ill-advised attempt to pass an amnesty bill by Yingluck's Phuea Thai government gave momentum to an umbrella protest group known as the People's Democratic Reform Committee (PDRC), which was led by veteran Democrat Party politician Suthep Thaugsuban and incorporated the yellow shirts. The PDRC's Occupation of Bangkok ran from January 13 to March 2, 2014, using similar organization and tactics to the PAD in 2005, with the aim of replacing the elected government with an unelected "People's Council." Their protests led to the 2014 coup d'etat.
2. Artists in these genres who joined the PAD campaigns between 2005 and 2008 include (Western) classical musicians Nat Yontararak and his wife Wongduean Intharawut, Suthep Wongkamhaeng, Umaphon Buaphueng, and Saken Sutthiwong (*luk krung*), jazz singer Kannika Arisaman, electronica artists The Photo Sticker Machine and Noraset Matkhong or DJ Seed, and alternative rock groups Apartment Khunpa and Phumjit. In the late 1940s

and 1950s, King Bhumibol's affinity for and proficiency in jazz cemented its place as an elite genre associated with royalty. Other popular music genres with appeal restricted to the urban elite were represented by artists such as Suchat Chawangkun and Nata Wiyakan (*phleng wan*, which is slow, sweet pop similar in nature to the older *luk krung*), Rik Wachiraphilan and Lanna Commins (world music), Job Banjop (reggae), and Nathi "Ui" Ekwijit from the rap group Buddha Bless.

3. See http://youtu.be/YUxvaG_guX8.
4. See http://youtu.be/45jhC2yguYE.
5. In 2004 RS Promotion put out *Rock rak chat*, a collection of heavy rock interpretations of *phleng plukchai*, including "Rak kan wai thoet," written by one of Thailand's early rock 'n' rollers Nakhon Thanormsap, also known as Gungadin.
6. During this period of consolidation the most popular red-shirt singers included Muk Methini, "Nut" Phojaman Nilanak (previously famous as Phojaman Phimjan), Wanchana Koetdi, Porm Krongthong, and Rangsi Serichai (*luk thung*); Somchainoi Phumimala, Sathian Noi, and EE-Sompo (*molam*); Phithan Songkamphon, better known as Pae Bangsanan (country rock), and Om Khaphasadi (*kantruem* and country rock). For more detailed ethnographic description of Pae and Om, see Tausig (2013).
7. This song can be heard at http://youtu.be/7fgzeOoQoQs.
8. See, for example, http://www2.manager.co.th/mwebboard/listComment.aspx?QNumber=311267&Mbrowse=9.
9. See http://youtu.be/SQWgOa9YFoI.
10. See http://youtu.be/CoooFTaXHfo.
11. See Siriphon (2004, 119) and Thiraphap (1998, 61).
12. A translation of *Samakhom phithak phon prayot phu khap rot taxi*.
13. See Myers-Moro (1986, 99).
14. See Lockard (1998, 191) and Vater (2003). According to Nga Surachai from Caravan: "When I was young I listened to 'Luk Thung,' but I was looking for something else. We wanted to shout at the government. 'Luk Thung' lyrics did not deal with serious issues" (Vater 2003).
15. Chot adopted the last name Kamachon because it means "proletariat."
16. This song can be heard at http://youtu.be/MIPiAYVEszw.
17. Adison incorrectly remembers the original title as "Suraphon ma laeo" (Suraphon Has Come), which is actually a different Suraphon song.
18. "Songs of Phuphan." Phuphan is a mountain area near Sakon Nakhon in Isan.
19. On the side of the PAD/PDRC Somkiat Phongphaibun, Somsak Kosaisuk, Chaiwat Sinsuwong, Amon Amonrathananon, Pipop Thongchai, Thoetphum Jaidi, Nga Caravan, Thirayut Bunmi, Wirot Tangwanit, and politicians Phondet Pinprathip and Khamnun Sitthisaman were

"Octobrists" involved with the student movement or the CPT insurgency. On the UDD side Octobrists included Weng Tojirakarn (who was initially in the PAD) and his wife Thida Thawornset, Jaran Dittapichai, Suthachai Yimprasert, Adison Phiangket, Wisa Khantap, and Surachai Danatthananusorn, the latter being a leader of splinter group Red Siam. For a full analysis see Kanokrat (2012).

20. See http://youtu.be/2CBqvcqsmMM. See an English translation at http://2bangkok.com/06-squarefacesong.html.
21. In 1998, King Bhumibol adopted a stray dog and, in 2002, wrote a popular book about her, which stressed how respectful and well behaved she was despite coming from a lowly background.
22. See, for example, http://search.japantimes.co.jp/cgi-bin/nn20090518a6.html.
23. See, for example, http://www.telegraph.co.uk/news/worldnews/asia/thailand/6212585/Stateless-boy-allowed-to-leave-Thailand-for-paper-aeroplane-contest.html.
24. See http://www.nationmultimedia.com/2009/10/13/politics/politics_30114293.php.
25. See http://youtu.be/Pdw2sfDheaE and http://www.trust.org/item/20140117102903-gcbzr.
26. See http://youtu.be/_AuUq37ivIo.
27. See http://youtu.be/rrfboNyNddg.
28. See http://wikileaks.org/gifiles/docs/82/826182_tha-thailand-asia-pacific-.html.
29. Channel 3 faced a dilemma when the extremely popular *lakhon Nuea mek 2* (*Above the Clouds*) was perceived to be critical of Thaksin. In a clear sign that power had shifted in Thailand, the corporation chose to offend viewers and royalists rather than Yingluck's Phuea Thai government. On January 4, 2013, the final four episodes of *Nuea mek 2* were canceled because, according to the official press release, they contained "content that was unsuitable and inappropriate for broadcasting."
30. See http://youtu.be/3s96VGDYm6E.
31. See http://youtu.be/obIziXm_zNI.
32. A cheap housing development in Khon Kaen.
33. The first lines of this version are: (M) "My village drinks alcohol, alcohol before food every time." (F) "I like to drink beer, I drink beer before looking for food."
34. Found on an undated VCD purchased at a red shirts' demonstration in Khon Kaen on January 31, 2010.
35. Another humorous response is sometimes "Chan pen suea nam ngoen", literally "I am a dark-blue shirt." However, separately *nam* (water) and *ngoen* (silver) are the color of money, so the meaning is that "I'm someone who is too busy earning a living to worry about politics."

36. See http://www.boringdays.net/joy-pad-beloved/.
37. See http://youtu.be/N3aCFifX-V4.
38. See http://youtu.be/e-w7mgZlYwY.
39. This observation was born out by Facebook comments from the winner of Miss Universe Thailand 2014, television personality Weluree "Fai" Ditsayabut, in which she called red shirts "antimonarchists" who should be executed, and said the country would be cleaner without them. See "Miss Universe Thailand" (2014).
40. See http://youtu.be/MrAnCzUc4jE.
41. See http://youtu.be/yc_KkCDbLXY.
42. See http://www.boringdays.net/wet-firewood/.
43. See http://www.manager.co.th/Entertainment/ViewNews.aspx?NewsID=9530000042247.

Coda

1. I learned this from Athit Khitsiri, the husband of Phuwiang Watthalisak.

References

Amporn Jirattikorn. 2006. "*Lukthung*: Authenticity and Modernity in Thai Country Music." *Asian Music* 37 (1): 24–50.
Anake Nawigamune. 1978. *Phleng nok sathawat*. Bangkok: Muang Boran.
Ash, Lucy. 2009. "Crossing Continents: Thailand's Red-Shirts 23 Apr 09." *Crossing Continents*. BBC Radio 4.
Barmé, Scot. 1993. *Luang Wichit Wathakan and the Creation of a Thai Identity*. Singapore: Institute of Southeast Asian Studies.
"Blacklist Cut Down to 3 Songs." 2003. *The Nation* (Bangkok). Via *Paknam Web Forums*, accessed February 12, 2009. http://www.thailandqa.com/forum/showthread.php?t=2062.
Chaba Mueangjan. 2004. "Jenphop Jopkrabuanwan—Sangsan phuea ngan lukthung." *Watthanatham Thai*: 1–10.
Chuwat Rerksirisuk. 2007. "Can We Fight Evenly—For Once?" *Prachatai* (Bangkok), June 29. http://www.prachatai.com/english/news.php?id=64.
Clewley, John. 1994. "The Many Sounds of Siam." In *World Music: The Rough Guide, Volume 2*, edited by Simon Broughton. London: Rough Guides Ltd.
———. 2000. "Thailand: Songs for Living." In *World Music: The Rough Guide Vol. 2; Latin and North America, Caribbean, India, Asia and Pacific*, edited by Simon Broughton and Mark Ellingham, 241–53. London: Rough Guides.
———. 2007. "Thailand's Quiet Coup: How Music Helped Oust Square Face." *Songlines* 41:42–43.
Collier, Simon, and Ken Haas. 1995. *Tango! The Dance, the Song, the Story*. New York: Thames and Hudson.
Committee for the Office of National Culture. 1989. *Kueng satawat phleng luk thung Thai*. Bangkok: Amarin Printing Group.
———. 1991. *Kueng satawat phleng luk thung Thai, phak 2*. Bangkok: Amarin Printing Group.

REFERENCES

Condie, Bill. 2006. "Thailand's Culture Police Turn an Opera into a Censorship Drama." *The Guardian*, (London) November 26. http://www.guardian.co.uk/music/2006/nov/26/classicalmusicandopera.

Connell, John, and Chris Gibson. 2002. *Sound Tracks: Popular Music, Identity, and Place*. London and New York: Routledge.

De Kosnik, Abigail. 2008. "Participatory Democracy and Hillary Clinton's Marginalized Fandom." *Transformative Works and Cultures* 1: http://journal.transformativeworks.org/index.php/twc/article/view/47.

"Editors Found Guilty of Defamation." 1999. *Bangkok Post*, February 20, 1999.

"Half a Century of Thai Country Music." 1991. *Thai Cultural Newsletter* (June): 4–5.

Haughton, James. 2009. "Building Modern Communities in Capitalist Thailand." In *Tai Lands and Thailand: Community and State in Southeast Asia*, edited by Andrew Walker. Singapore: NUS Press.

Hayes, Michael. 2004. "Capitalism and Cultural Relativity: The Thai Pop Industry, Capitalism and Western Cultural Values." In *Refashioning Pop Music in Asia: Cosmopolitan Flows, Political Tempos and Aesthetic Industries*, edited by Brian Shoesmith, Allen Chun, and Ned Rossiter. Richmond: Curzon.

Hesse-Swain, Catherine. 2006. "Programming Beauty and the Absence of *Na Lao*: Popular Thai TV and Identity Formation among Youth in Northeast Thailand." *GeoJournal* 66 (3): 257–72.

Jaiser, Gerhard. 2012. *Thai Popular Music*. Bangkok: White Lotus Press.

Jory, Patrick. 2003. "Problems in Contemporary Thai Nationalist Historiography." *Kyoto Review of Southeast Asia* 3 (March): http://kyotoreview.org/issue-3-nations-and-stories/problems-in-contemporary-thai-nationalist-historiography/.

Kanokporn Chanasongkram. 2007. "Patrons of the Arts." *Pantip* (web board), accessed July 2, 2009. http://topicstock.pantip.com/chalermkrung/topicstock/2007/10/C5911590/C5911590.html.

Kanokporn Chanasongkram. 2008. "Pride of the Northeast." *Bangkok Post*, October 17. http://www.bangkokpost.com/171008_Realtime/17Oct2008_real020.php.

Kanokrat Lertchoosakul. 2012. "The Rise of the Octobrists: Power and Conflict among Former Left Wing Student Activists in Contemporary Thai Politics." PhD thesis, London School of Economics and Political Science.

Keil, Charles, and Steven Feld. 1994. *Music Grooves: Essays and Dialogues*. Chicago: University of Chicago Press.

Kelley, Shawn. 2009. "Color-Coded Contest for Thailand's North." *Asia Times* (Hong Kong), July 31. http://www.atimes.com/atimes/Southeast_Asia/KG31Ae02.html.

Keyes, Charles F. 1971 (1967). *Isan: Regionalism in Northeastern Thailand*. Ann Arbor, Michigan: University Microfilms International.

Kitchana Lersakvanitchakul. 2010. "Country Cult and Culture." *The Nation* (Bangkok), April 23. http://www.nationmultimedia.com/home/2010/04/23/life/Country-cult-and-culture-30127716.html.

Klausner, William. 2004. "Voices from the Past." *Thailand Monitor*. Bangkok: Thai World Affairs Center.

REFERENCES

Kobkul Putharaporn. 1985. "Country Folk Songs and Thai Society." In *Traditional and Changing Thai World View*, edited by Amara Pongsapich. Bangkok: Chulalongkorn University Research Institute and Southeast Asian Studies Programme.

Kreangsak Suwanpantakul. 2005. "Cracking Up the Egg Emperor." *The Nation* (Bangkok), August 8. http://www.nationmultimedia.com/2005/08/08/art/index.php?news=art_18285418.html.

Lamnao Eamsa-ard. 2006. "Thai Popular Music: The Representation of National Identities and Ideologies within a Culture in Transition." PhD thesis, Edith Cowan University.

"Lao Protests Knock Drama off Thai TV." 2007. *The Nation* (Bangkok), February 14. http://www.newsmekong.org/lao_protests_knock_drama_off_thai_tv.

Lent, John A. 2000. "Dance of Life: Popular Music and Politics in Southeast Asia. (Review)." *Pacific Affairs* 73 (1): 140–41.

"Li-ke song khrueang." 1994. *Anurakthai.com*, accessed December 12, 2010. http://www.anurakthai.com/thaidances/likay/likay2.asp (site discontinued).

Lockard, Craig A. 1998. *Dance of Life: Popular Music and Politics in Southeast Asia*. Honolulu: University of Hawaii Press.

"Luk thung tin top plot rawang." 2010. *Super Banthoeng Online*, March 29. http://www.manager.co.th/Entertainment/ViewNews.aspx?NewsID=9530000042247.

Mae Wanpen. 2009. "'Mae yok' yok radap pen 'faenclub'?" *Ks Ks*: 48–52.

Manuel, Peter Lamarche. 1988. *Popular Musics of the Non-Western World: An Introductory Survey*. New York: Oxford University Press.

Marks, Tom. 1994. *Making Revolution: The Insurgency of the Communist Party of Thailand in Structural Perspective*. Bangkok: White Lotus.

Marre, Jeremy, and Hannah Charlton. 1985. *Beats of the Heart: Popular Music of the World*. New York: Pluto Press.

Martin, Peter J. 1995. *Sounds and Society: Themes in the Sociology of Music*. Manchester: Manchester University Press.

McCargo, Duncan, and Krisadawan Hongladarom. 2004. "Contesting Isan-ness: Discourses of Politics and Identity in Northeast Thailand." *Asian Ethnicity* 5 (2): 219–34.

Miller, Terry E. 1985. *Traditional Music of the Lao: Kaen Playing and Mawlum Singing in Northeast Thailand*. Westport, Connecticut: Greenwood Press.

———. 1998. "Thailand." In *Garland Encyclopaedia of World Music Volume 4: Southeast Asia*, edited by Terry E. Miller and Sean Williams. New York: Garland Publishing.

———. 2005. "From Country Hick to Rural Hip: A New Identity through Music for Northeast Thailand." *Asian Music* 36 (2): 96–106.

"Miss Universe Thailand Sparks Uproar." 2014. *Bangkok Post*, May 20. http://www.bangkokpost.com/news/local/410577/miss-universe-thailand-sparks-uproar.

Mitchell, James. 2009. "Thai Television and *Pleeng Luuk Tung*: The Role of Television in the Isan Cultural Revival." *Perfect Beat* 10 (1): 79–99.

Mitchell, Tony. 2001. "Dick Lee's Transit Lounge: Orientalism and Pan-Asian Pop." *Perfect Beat* 5 (3): 18–45.

Moro, Pamela. 2004. "Constructions of Nation and the Classicisation of Music: Comparative Perspectives from Southeast and South Asia." *Journal of Southeast Asian Studies* 35 (2): 187–211.

Morton, David. 1976. *The Traditional Music of Thailand*. Berkley: University of California Press.

Mulder, Niels. 2000. *Inside Thai Society*. Chiang Mai: Silkworm Books.

The Musical Compositions of His Majesty King Bhumibol Adulyadej. 1996. Bangkok: Chitralada School.

Myers-Moro, Pamela. 1986. "Songs for Life: Leftist Thai Popular Music in the 1970s." *Journal of Popular Culture* 20 (3): 93–114.

———. 1989. "Thai Music and Attitudes towards the Past." *The Journal of American Folklore* 102 (404): 190–94.

———. 1993. *Thai Music and Musicians in Contemporary Bangkok*. Berkeley: University of California at Berkeley.

Nidhi Eoseewong. 1985. "Phleng *luk thung* nai prawatsat watthanatham Thai." *Sinlapa Watthanatham* 6 (6): 94–109.

Nilubol Pornpitagpan. 2002. "Bandit Takes Up the Baton." *Bangkok Post*, February 10.

Nostitz, Nick. 2009. "Saturday Red, Sunday Yellow: The Temperature Rises Again." *New Mandala*, November 16. http://asiapacific.anu.edu.au/newmandala/2009/11/16/saturday-red-sunday-yellow-the-temperature-rises-again/.

Palitano, Mong. 2010. "Thailand's 'Colored' Protesters." UPI Asia, accessed April 10, 2011. http://globalvoicesonline.org/2009/04/12/thailand's-"colored"-protesters/.

Palphol Rodloytuk. 2009. "Evolution of People's TV in Thailand: The PAD Experiment." Asian Media Information and Communication Center (AMIC), accessed March 20. 2010. http://www.amicaltmedia.net/research.php?pid=30 (site discontinued).

Pasuk Phongpaichit and Christopher John Baker. 2014. "Thailand's Turbulent Politics: Peering Ahead." GRIPS Forum, Tokyo, March 27.

Pattana Kitiarsa. 2009a. "*Farang* as Siamese Occidentalism." In *The Ambiguous Allure of the West: Traces of the Colonial in Thailand*, edited by Rachel V. Harrison and Peter A. Jackson, 57–74. Hong Kong: Hong Kong University Press.

———. 2009b. "The Lyrics of Laborious Life: Popular Music and the Reassertion of Migrant Manhood in Northeastern Thailand." *Inter-Asia Cultural Studies* 10 (3): 381–98.

Phayong Mukda. 1984. "Rueangrao kiaokap phleng *luk thung*." In *Chak phleng Thai thueng phleng luk thung*. Bangkok: Sun Sangkit Silp.

Phrakruvinaitorn Manop Palaphan, Songkoon Chantachon, and Pornpen Tanprasert. 2009. "Succession and Development of Lae Melody of Desana Mahajati Sermon in Central Thailand." *The Social Sciences* 4 (5): 483–88.

Pravit Rojanaphuk. 2014. "PDRC Must 'Face Up to Being a Minority.'" *The Nation*

REFERENCES

(Bangkok), January 16. http://www.nationmultimedia.com/politics/PDRC-must-face-up-to-being-a-minority-30224411.html.
Reynolds, Craig J., 2002. *National Identity and Its Defenders: Thailand Today*. Chiang Mai, Thailand: Silkworm Books.
Reynolds, Craig J. and Hong Lysa. 1983. "Marxism in Thai Historical Studies." *The Journal of Asian Studies* 4 (1): 77–104.
Rogers, Martyn. 2009. "Between Fantasy and 'Reality': Tamil Film Star Fan Club Networks and the Political Economy of Film Fandom." *South Asia: Journal of South Asian Studies*, 32 (1): 63–85.
Shohat, Ella and Robert Stam. 1994. *Unthinking Eurocentrism: Multiculturalism and the Media*. New York: Routledge.
Siriphon Kropthong. 2004. *Wiwathanakan phleng luk thung nai sangkhom Thai*. Bangkok: Phanthakit Publishing.
Somchai Phatharathananunth. 2001. "Civil Society in Northeast Thailand: The Struggle of the Small Scale Farmers' Assembly of Isan." PhD thesis, University of Leeds.
Somtow Sucharitkul. 2006. "Why Artistic Freedom Matters." *The Nation* (Bangkok), accessed May 30, 2010. http://www.nationmultimedia.com/2006/11/16/opinion/opinion_30019095.php.
Sujit Wongthet. 1984. "Phleng Thai thueng phleng *luk thung*." In *Chak phleng Thai thueng phleng luk thung*. Bangkok: Sun Sangkit Silp.
Sukanya Jitpleecheep. 1998. "Revived Luk Thung Industry Singing a Happy Tune." *Bangkok Post*, January 7.
Sukanya Sujachaya. 1982. *Phleng patiphak: Bot phleng haeng patikan khong chao ban Thai* [Dialogue songs: Lyrics of responsive songs of rural Thais]. Bangkok: The Office of National Culture, Ministry of Education.
Surin Phaksiri, Phongsak Chantharukkha, Thinakon Thipamat, Sanya Chulaphon, and Tho Suraphappradit. 2004. *Hat daeng phleng doi withithammachat*. Bangkok: Khlet Thai.
Tausig, Ben. 2013. "Bangkok is Ringing." PhD diss., New York University.
Terwiel, Barend Jan. 1980. *Field Marshal Plaek Phibun Songkhram: Thailand's Prime Minister from 1938–44 and from 1948–57*. St. Lucia, Queensland: University of Queensland Press.
Textor, Robert B. 1961. *From Peasant to Pedicab Driver: A Social Study of Northeastern Thai Farmers Who Periodically Migrated to Bangkok and Became Pedicab Drivers*. New Haven: Yale University, Southeast Asia Studies.
Thanapol Eawsakul, ed. 2007. *Ratthaprahan 19 kanya: Ratthaprahan phuea rabob prachathipatai an mi phramahakasat song pen pramuk*. Bangkok: Fa Diaokan.
Thanong Khanthong. 2002. "PM Thaksin to Embrace Suraphol Doctrine?" *The Nation* (Bangkok), September 6.
Thiraphap Lohitakul. 1998. *Pathom bot phleng luk thung lae phleng phuea chiwit nai Mueang Thai (1937–1957)*. Bangkok: Samnak Phim Somsan.
Thompson, John B. 1995. *The Media and Modernity: A Social Theory of the Media*. Cambridge: Polity Press.

REFERENCES

Thongchai Winichakul. 2000. "The Others Within: Travel and Ethno-Spatial Differentiation of Siamese Subjects 1885–1910." In *Civility and Savagery: Social Identity in Tai States*, edited by Andrew Turton. London: Curzon Press.

———. 2008a. "Former Left-Right Alliance against Globalization and America." *Prachatai*, (Bangkok), July 28. http://www.prachatai.com/english/news.php?id=715.

———. 2008b. "Nationalism and the Radical Intelligentsia in Thailand." *Third World Quarterly* 29 (3): 575–91.

Tulloch, John, and Henry Jenkins. 1995. *Science Fiction Audiences: Watching Doctor Who and Star Trek*. London: Routledge.

Ubonrat Siriyuvasak. 1990. "Commercialising the Sound of the People: Pleng Luktoong and the Thai Pop Music Industry." *Popular Music* 9 (1): 61–77.

———. 1998. "Thai Pop Music and Cultural Negotiation in Everyday Politics." In *Trajectories: Inter-Asia Cultural Studies*, edited by Kuan-Hsing Chen. London and New York: Routledge.

———. 2000. "Cultural Control and Globalized Culture." *International Workshop on Local Agency and Local Identity in Television: Comparative Perspectives on Media Content and Reception in Asia*. Universiti Sains Malaysia and University of Wisconsin–Madison.

Vater, Tom. 2003. "Real Rebel Music—Tom Vater Talks to Thailand's Bob Dylan." *Tom Vater* (blog), accessed October 6, 2010. http://www.tomvater.com/thailand/real-rebel-music/.

Veena Thoopkrajae. 2006. "Music for Freedom." The Nation, April 17. http://www.nationmultimedia.com/2006/04/17/entertainment/entertainment_30001860.php.

Waeng Phalangwan. 2002. *Luk thung Isan: Prawatsat Isan tamnan phleng luk thung*. Bangkok: Ruean Panya (RP Books).

Ware, Vicki-Ann. 2006. "Stylistic and Cultural Transformations in Bangkok Fusion Music from 1850 to the Present Day, Leading to the Development of Dontri Thai Prayuk." PhD thesis, School of Music–Conservatorium, Monash University.

Wat Wanlayangkun, ed. 2003. *Sailom blian thit . . . tae duangjit midai blian loei: Phalueck haeng chiwit lae siang phleng patiwat Thai*. Bangkok: The Collective of Thai Revolutionary Songs Project.

———. 2009. "Lak sila klang nam chiao 1." *Khaosot* (Bangkok), November 19. http://www.khaosod.co.th/view_news.php?newsid=TUROb1lYQXhNREk1TVRFMU1nPT0=.

Wise Kwai. 2010. "The Late, Great Apichatpong." *The Nation* (Bangkok), April 20. http://www.nationmultimedia.com/home/2010/04/20/life/The-late-great-Apichatpong-30127420.html.

Wong, Deborah Anne. 2001. *Sounding the Center: History and Aesthetics in Thai Buddhist Performance*. Chicago: University of Chicago Press.

Yano, Christine. 2002. *Tears of Longing: Nostalgia and the Nation in Japanese Popular Song*. Cambridge: Harvard University Asia Center.

Index

Abhisit Vejjajiva, 152–53, 159, 165, 169–70
acculturation, 47, 71, 76, 92
Adison Phiangket, 137–39, 145–46, 156, 161, 177–78,
"Ai na liam," 150–51, 162–63
audience, 18–19, 27, 76, 102, 122, 143, 163
   Isan, 14–16, 26, 74, 105, 108, 125
   luk thung, 99, 111–15, 126–27, 159–60, 177, 193n32
Ayutthaya, 38, 49, 55, 172

Bai Toei, 110, 116, 123, 138, 186, 194n5
Benjamin, 12, 14–20, 22, 29, 48–49, 53–54, 56–57, 60, 64–65, 68, 72–73, 94, 141
Buddhism, 51, 55, 61, 71, 103, 148

Cambodia/Cambodian, 13, 22, 61, 156, 168
Caravan, 136, 145, 149, 169, 196n14
censorship, 13, 21, 31, 69, 122–23, 134–35, 139, 141–44, 147, 173
cha-cha, 2, 13, 16, 29, 46, 63–66, 68–69, 76, 86, 147

Chai Mueangsing, 13, 28, 49, 60, 69, 75, 79, 101, 110, 121, 141, 195n5
China/Chinese, 73–75, 135, 139, 152
   communism, 145–47
   See also Sino-Thai community
Chuchok, 16, 55
comedian, 3, 7, 18, 24, 41–42, 128–30
Communist Party of Thailand (CPT), 137, 145–48, 160, 170, 178, 196n19. *See also under* Isan
community experience of *luk thung*, 106, 111, 114–17, 125–26, 141, 148
company (record), 4, 9, 32, 75, 77, 79–80, 84, 88, 93, 95–99, 110, 113–21, 150, 166
concerts, 1–5, 79, 108–9, 111–21, 127, 138, 158, 167–71
   red shirts, 5, 138, 140, 161, 163, 177
   Half a Century of *Luk Thung*, 37, 41, 149, 189
coup. *See under* military
copyright, 93, 98–99, 105, 150, 166
curse, 90, 151–52, 157

dancers (*luk thung*). *See hang khrueang*

INDEX

dangdut, 5, 110, 191n1
Democrat Party, 137, 154, 156, 163, 169–70, 195n1

enka, 5, 70, 191n1, 193n32
establishment, the, 40, 87, 103, 147, 149, 158–59, 169, 175

fans, 2–4, 15–16, 74, 86, 97, 146, 169, 177, 194n3
   and interaction with stars, 109–23, 126–27
film in Thailand, 9–12, 22, 24–25, 27–28, 30, 32, 42–43, 72, 74, 109, 142, 192n12

GMM Grammy, 120–21, 123, 126, 138, 151, 177, 193n22, 194n10
   and *luk thung Isan*, 59, 73, 87, 169
   and *luk thung* songwriters, 78, 98, 124, 139
   luk thung subsidiary of (Grammy Gold), 42, 190
   Phaibun Damrongchaitham (owner), 150, 189
   and *string*, 32, 135–36

hang khrueang, 28, 130, 160, 164
hegemony, 40, 151, 159
hybrid music, 42, 46, 52, 55, 115, 172, 175, 193n32

India/Indian, 22, 56, 58, 62, 71–72, 92
Indonesia/Indonesian, 5, 62, 110
Isan (region), 5, 7, 20–22, 30–31, 36–37, 74, 100, 126, 143, 167
   insurgency in, 144–49, 165, 168, 177

Japan/Japanese, 5, 22, 70–71, 75, 153, 193n32
Jintara Phunlap, 42, 64, 87–88, 90, 98, 109, 121, 167

kantruem, 61, 63, 159, 196n6
khaen, 12, 16, 21, 24–25, 42, 53, 57–61, 79, 86, 96, 138, 165, 169, 192n16
"Khon ban diaokan," 124–26, 155
Khon Kaen, 4, 21, 33–34, 42–43, 78–80, 88, 93–94, 137–38, 163–65, 197n34
khru-luksit relationship, 25, 87–88, 94–96, 125
khwai, 133, 142–43, 155–57, 168–69, 172–73
King Bhumibol, 136, 145, 167, 195n2, 197n21
King Chulalongkorn, 9–10, 38, 48, 51, 63, 137
King Mongkut, 8, 162, 175, 178
Korea/Korean, 16–17, 22, 71–73
Kratae, 54, 62, 116

lae, 19, 50, 55–56, 61, 135
lakhon (stage drama), 8, 9–10, 11, 47–48. *See also under* television
lam klon, 16, 53–54, 57–59, 191n2
lam phloen, 30, 58–60, 131, 192n1
Lao-Isan identity, 7, 37, 41–43, 86, 92, 107, 131, 177
Laos, 145, 172–73, 176–77
like, 51–52, 121–22, 142
luk krung, 11, 27, 35, 38–39, 48–50, 54, 63–64, 67–68, 122, 134–36, 172, 195n2
luksit. See *khru-luksit* relationship
luk thung Isan (Isan *luk thung*, *luk thung prayuk*, *luk thung molam*), 29–34, 53, 58–61, 69, 73, 78, 87–88, 130, 178
lyrics (*luk thung*), 46, 100–104, 110, 196n14

malai, 56, 110–14, 118, 121, 127, 160, 163
Malaysia, 22, 62, 91, 113
Mangpor Chonticha, 1–4, 42, 67, 70, 115–21

206

INDEX

migration (urban and economic), 21–22, 37, 43, 88–90, 101, 158, 160–61, 163
military, 8, 16, 43, 63, 138, 144, 154–55, 158–59
  coup, 11, 31, 55, 150, 154, 175–76
molam, 32–34, 39–40, 57–61, 72, 76, 90–92, 138–39, 167–69, 172–73, 178, 192n1
  influence on *luk thung*, 15, 121–22
Mon Rak Luk Thung, 22, 27, 72, 140, 192n12
monarchy, 10–11, 35–37, 48, 95, 134, 136–37, 157, 171
Muk Methini, 161–63, 196n6

"Namta mia Sa-u," 58, 87–93, 105
National Artist. See Sinlapin haeng chat
nirat, 22, 160
Nong Nut Duangchiwan, 33, 49, 80–87, 166–67
Nopporn Silver Gold, 1–3, 115–16
Northern *luk thung*, 61–62
"Num na khao sao na kluea," 63, 66, 80–87, 165–67

patron-client relationship, 18, 73, 94, 110, 118–21
PDRC (People's Democratic Reform Committee), 135, 155, 169, 172, 175, 195n1, 196n19
pentatonic scale, 46, 53–55, 57–58, 61, 144
Phaibun Butkhan, 8, 13, 23, 27, 52, 55–56, 68, 99, 133–34, 142, 169–70, 173
Phaijit Aksonnarong, 75, 139–40, 156
Phibunsongkhram, Plaek, 11–13, 35–36, 52, 141–45
Phimpha Phonsiri, 34, 58, 87–93, 105
phin, 24, 42, 59, 86, 130, 192n16
phleng chiwit, 13, 51–52, 140–44, 173, 178
phleng kae, 17–20, 49, 54, 82, 163

phleng phuea chiwit, 32, 40, 61–63, 133, 135, 144–50
phleng phut, 26, 140
phleng plaeng, 86, 140, 142, 146, 152, 155, 161, 165–67, 169–70, 178
phleng plukchai, 100, 135–37, 164, 172, 196n5
phleng talat. See phleng chiwit
phleng Thai doem, 38, 47–51, 71, 75
phleng Thai sakon, 8–11, 35, 38–39, 52, 63–64
Phloen Phromdaen, 26, 28, 50, 139, 140, 169
Phongsri Woranut, 17–20, 23–24, 27–28, 54, 64–66, 75, 139, 145
Phumphuang Duangjan, 33, 69–70, 90, 116, 119, 123, 168
"Phuyai Li," 23–24, 53, 59, 68–69
phuang malai. See malai
play on words, 123, 125, 152
political movements. See Communist Party of Thailand; PDRC; red shirts; yellow shirts
politicians, 37, 99, 101, 105, 141, 151, 194n11, 195n1, 196n19
politics, 4–5, 35, 40, 129, 131–33, 137–49, 157–68, 175–78, 197n35
  sexual, 88–91
pong lang, 42, 86, 130, 192n16
Pong Prida, 21, 29, 58–60, 95–96, 141
popular music, 8, 12–13, 34–42, 95–96, 128, 145, 158, 193n32, 195n2
  Thai, 10, 54, 68, 74, 121, 148
  Western, 40, 46
Preah Vihear (Phra Wihan), 13, 168–69
propaganda, 4, 145–46, 168–71
Public Relations Department, 11, 139

radio, 18, 27, 30, 35, 69, 108, 141–42, 147
  DJ, 31–32, 119
  lakhon, 10, 79–80, 188

radio (*continued*)
    red shirt, 138–39, 163
ramwong, 8, 11–13, 17, 35–36, 60, 65, 69, 79, 146–48
    ostinato, 16, 52–54, 61, 68
record company. *See* company
red shirts (UDD), 131, 137–40, 144, 149, 152–78, 196n6
R-Siam, 110, 116, 120–21, 123, 138

Saksri Sri-akson, 23–24, 53, 59–60, 68–69
Sala Khunawut, 42, 78, 98, 124, 138–39
Samai Onwong, 24, 30, 60, 79
Saneh Komarachun, 13, 51–52, 142–44
Sarit Thanarat, 13, 16, 18, 36, 55, 143
satire, 52, 123, 128, 140–44, 149–56, 159, 164–65, 168
Sayan Sanya, 31, 32, 34, 66, 139, 145, 160
sexual content, 33, 70, 90, 109–10, 122–23, 159
singers. *See individual names*
Sinlapin haeng chat (National Artist), 38, 49, 99, 136, 137, 195n5
Sino-Thai community, 9, 24, 73–74, 75, 135, 150, 168, 172, 192n6
social status of *luk thung*, 34–41, 75, 78, 96, 99, 113, 118, 121, 124, 127, 149, 176
soeng, 2, 46, 60, 63, 65, 107, 130
song (*phleng*) types. *See individual Thai names*
songwriting, 15–16, 24–26, 46, 78, 142, 148–49, 178
    luk thung, 87–95, 100–104, 124–26, 139
    red shirt, 163–67
    yellow shirt, 170–71
Sonthi Limthongkul, 134, 139, 160, 162
Soraphet Phinyo, 33, 49, 58, 66, 72, 77–106, 165–67
Southern *luk thung*, 62, 71, 136

string (Thai pop), 27, 32, 36, 39, 68, 103
Suntharaphon, 11–12, 24, 27, 48–49, 62–63, 65, 73, 168,
Suphan Buri, 14, 26, 33, 118–19, 191n6
Suraphon Sombatjaroen, 13–20, 27, 53–54, 65–66, 68, 70, 157
Surin Phaksiri, 22, 25–27, 29–32, 56, 58, 62–64, 66, 68–72, 76, 78, 94, 105–6

Takadaen Chonlada, 42, 126, 138, 161
taxi driver, 34, 126, 139, 144
television, 2, 22, 26–27, 57, 123, 127–28, 134, 137–38
    lakhon, 43, 105, 115–16, 129–31, 135, 168, 197n29
Teochew, 24, 74, 135
Thai pop. See *string*
Thai social order. *See* establishment, the; patron-client relationship; *khru-luksit* relationship
Thaksin Shinawatra, 131, 134, 136–39, 154–65, 169, 197n29
Thepphon Phetubon, 31–32, 80, 124

Vietnam/Vietnamese, 20, 22, 69, 148, 168
vocal style, 46, 49, 52, 159

wai khru ceremony, 94–85
Wichit Wathakan, 11, 35, 37, 102
wordplay. *See* play on words

yellow shirts (PAD), 133–38, 149, 155, 162, 166–67, 171–72, 195n2, 196n19
Yingli Srichumphon, 42, 123, 168
Yingluck Shinawatra, 149, 155, 165, 172, 175, 195n1, 197n29
Yingyong Yotbua-ngam, 42, 93, 98
Yodrak Salakchai, 32, 69, 112–13, 127, 139, 146

www.ingramcontent.com/pod-product-compliance
Lightning Source LLC
Chambersburg PA
CBHW021141230426
43667CB00005B/211